The FCC Rule Book

By
Richard K. Palm, K1CE

Updated by
Phil Sager, WB4FDT
  Regulatory Information Branch Manager

Production
  Leslie K. Bartoloth, KA1MJP
  Michelle Chrisjohn, WB1ENT
  Deborah J. Sandler

This edition includes all amendments
to Part 97 through July 31, 1986.

American Radio Relay League
Newington, CT USA 06111

Author's note: Special thanks to John Johnston,
W3BE, of the FCC staff, for his assistance with the
editorial production of "Washington Mailbox" and
this book.

FOREWORD

Every U.S. amateur licensee, and anyone actively pursuing a ham ticket, should have handy a copy of the current FCC rules and regulations governing Amateur Radio. This ARRL publication is designed to meet that need in a compact, inexpensive volume.

But *The FCC Rule Book* does even more! Taking its cue from the popular "Washington Mailbox" column in *QST*, it presents explanations of the rules in a style that is easy to read and understand.

You'll learn how FCC rules are made, and how you can have a voice in the process. You'll learn about the Communications Act of 1934, which still governs all telecommunications in the country five decades after its original enactment. You'll discover the international agreements which affect our daily Amateur Radio operation, and why decisions made in far-off places like Geneva, Switzerland, are so important to hams.

In a dynamic society rules and regulations are constantly changing, and Amateur Radio is no exception. This book was as accurate and up-to-date as we could make it when it went to press, but to be sure you have the latest word, you should read *QST* each month. *QST* is one of the many benefits of League membership; if you're not a member, why not join today!

David Sumner, K1ZZ
Executive Vice President
Newington, Connecticut

WHAT'S NEW

The FCC, acting on petitions from ARRL and others concerning the expansion of operating privileges for Novices, has issued a notice of Proposed Rulemaking (NPRM), PR 86-161. **This is probably the most important FCC proposal of the 1980s** and **very closely** follows the Novice Enhancement Petition requests by the ARRL. (For background information, see It Seems to Us, July, 1985 *QST.*)

The following are the specific FCC proposals:

• The 10-meter Novice band would be expanded to 300 kHz from the present 28.1-28.2 MHz to 28.1-28.5 MHz. CW and digital communications (eg RTTY, AMTOR and packet) would be allowed in the 28.1-28.3 MHz sub-band, and *SSB* and CW emissions on 28.3-28.5 MHz at the present power limit of 200 watts.

• The 1.25-meter band, on 220-225 MHz, would be added to Novice privileges, allowing them all authorized emissions with a power of 25 watts. The Commission cautions, however, that there are several petitions for rulemaking pending requesting the use of this band for other services. Until these petitions are resolved, the Commission cannot finalize any rulemakings permitting Novice amateurs on this band.

• A portion of the 23-cm band, 1246-1260 MHz, would be added to Novice privileges, allowing all authorized emissions with a power of 5 watts.

• Novices would *not* be allowed to be a control operator or a licensee of a station that is in repeater, auxilliary or beacon operation. A so-called "alternative" proposal would split the present Technician/General class written Element 3 into two different examinations: A VHF/UHF exam for Technicians called Element 3(A) and an HF exam for the General class called Element 3(B). Currently, if a Novice passes the 50-question Element 3 exam, he or she becomes a Technician and need only pass the 13-WPM code test for the General. Under this alternate proposal a Novice would need to pass a 25-question Element 3(A) (VHF/UHF) exam to receive the Technician class license, and a 25-question Element 3(B) exam and the 13-WPM code test for the General class license.

Another important aspect of the FCC's proposal was their solicitation of comments on the ARRL's request to expand the Novice examination to 30 questions. (The ARRL *does not* want to make the examination more difficult. The League wants to increase the comprehensiveness of the examination in order to accommodate the operational aspects of the additional privileges available to Novice class operators.) The ARRL also requested that Section 97.28 be amended to require that each Novice examination be administered by two volunteer examiners holding General class licenses, or above, rather than the presently required one examiner, in order to maintain the integrity of the Novice examination.

The ARRL hopes the basic elements of this dramatic Novice enhancement proposal will survive and move quickly through the Commission's administrative processes. The sooner we can make Amateur Radio more attractive to newcomers, without compromising the entrance requirements that are so important to maintaining a quality Service, the sooner the future of Amateur Radio will be assured.

Table of Contents

Chapter 1

Introduction

Radio. Webster's popular book defines the term as the "wireless transmission and reception of electrical impulses or signals by means of electric waves," and the "use of these waves for the wireless transmission of electric impulses into which sound is converted."

Its appeal is that when these electrical waves are formed in certain ways, radio becomes a medium for communication unfettered by cumbersome cables and wires. The appeal is so great, in fact, that radio is manifested in just about every nook and cranny in the modern world. A myriad of radio services exists for the needs of individuals, business, government, science and others. This illustrates radio's integral role in modern life in the U.S. and other developed countries today.

Along with the proliferation of radio services within the physical confines of the radio spectrum comes the need for controls. Without such controls, chaos would reign supreme with services colliding with each other. Not surprisingly, controls have developed over the years, and have been implemented at both the international and domestic levels. Why international? Because radio waves know no geographical or political boundaries — they do not stop for customs inspections.

The International Telecommunication Union, a specialized agency of the United Nations, allocates portions of the radio spectrum to the various services vying for their own slice of the pie. It fashions regulations designed to reduce potential interference problems. The process occurs at the international conference table. Member nations' delegates bring to the table their countries' positions. They debate the merits of these positions, taking into consideration changes in technologies since the previous conference and the needs of each administration. They finally arrive at a table of allocations and rules. For example, in 1979, a World Administrative Radio Conference (WARC) was held in Geneva. This conference was the first in 20 years to take a top-to-bottom look at the international Table of Frequency Allocations. As a result, a new Table was generated, and other changes in the Radio Regulations of the ITU were made. The United States, a world leader in the telecommunications arena, was an active participant in the conference. Years of preparation culminated in sweeping changes that will affect the worldwide radio services, until the next general WARC.

The Federal Communications Commission and Congress

With a copy of the international agreements clutched firmly in hand, WARC delegates return home, and their governments implement the accords. In the United States, once the Senate advises and consents to ratification, this task falls upon the Federal Communications Commission (FCC) and the National Telecommunications and Information Administration (NTIA). Once ratification occurs, FCC will amend its rules to bring them into line with the new International Radio Regulations.

What is the Federal Communications Commission? The FCC is the United States Government agency charged with regulating interstate and foreign communication involving radio, television, wire, cable and satellite. The object of FCC regulation is to provide for orderly development and operation of radio services, and to make available a rapid, efficient, nationwide and worldwide telegraph and telephone system.

The FCC promotes the safety of life and property through the use of wire and radio communications. It employs communication facilities in the national defense. The FCC does not function under any other government department. It is a sovereign federal agency created by Congress and, as such, reports directly to Congress.

In the early days of radio regulations, jurisdiction over wire and radio communications at various times was handled by the Department of Commerce, Post Office Department, Interstate Commerce Commission and the Federal Radio Commission. Technological developments and interference problems, however, necessitated coordination of these functions in a single agency. The Communications Act, signed June 19, 1934, created the Federal Communications Commission for that purpose.

Today's Commission allocates bands of frequencies to non-Government communications services and assigns frequencies to individual stations. It licenses and regulates stations and operators, and regulates common carriers in interstate and foreign communications by telegraph, telephone and satellite. The agency promotes safety through the use of radio on land, water and in the air. The FCC encourages more effective and widespread use of radio. One job it does *not* do is regulate Federal Government radio operations; this is done by the NTIA, under delegated authority from the President.

The FCC consists of five Commissioners appointed by the President with the approval of the Senate. No Commissioner can have a financial interest in any Commission-regulated business. Appointments are for seven years, except in filling an unexpired term. One of the Commissioners is designated Chairman by the President. The Chairman's tenure during his or her term of office is at the pleasure of the President.

As with many federal agencies, the Commissioners function as a unit, supervising all FCC activities, with delegations of responsibilities to boards and committees of Commissioners, individual Commissioners and staff units. The Chairman is responsible for the administration of the internal affairs of the Commission.

Policy determinations are made by the Commission as a whole. Commission practices conform to the Communications Act of 1934, as amended, the Administrative Procedure Act and other applicable laws.

Organization and Authority

FCC staff is organized on a functional basis. There are four operating bureaus — Mass Media, Common Carrier, Field Operations and Private Radio — and seven staff offices — Managing Director, Science and Technology, Public Affairs, Plans and Policy, General Counsel, Administrative Law Judges and the Review Board. Its headquarters are in two buildings in Washington, DC.

The FCC field staff is located in field offices throughout the country. It engages, for the most part, in engineering work. This includes monitoring the radio spectrum to see that station operation meets technical requirements, inspecting stations of all types, conducting operator examinations and issuing permits or licenses to those found qualified. It also locates and closes unauthorized transmitters, furnishes radio bearings for aircraft or ships in distress, locates sources of interference and suggests remedial measures. The field staff also performs special engineering work for the other Government agencies, and obtains and analyzes technical data for Commission use.

The FCC cooperates with other agencies. In international and domestic matters, it works with various Government agencies involved with radio and wire communication. It also cooperates with radio-user groups such as the American Radio Relay League.

FCC regulation of radio includes consideration of applications for construction permits and licenses for all classes of non-Government stations, and frequency, power and call-sign assignments. The Commission is involved in authorization of communica-

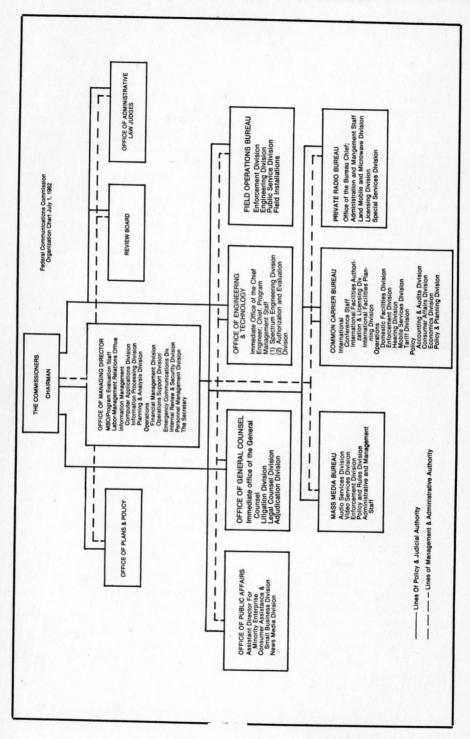

Federal Communications Commission
Organization Chart July 1, 1982

THE COMMISSIONERS
CHAIRMAN

OFFICE OF ADMINISTRATIVE LAW JUDGES

REVIEW BOARD

OFFICE OF PLANS & POLICY

OFFICE OF MANAGING DIRECTOR
MBO/Program Evaluation Staff
Labor-Management Relations Office
Information Management
   Computer Applications Division
   Information Processing Division
   Planning & Analysis Division
Operations
   Financial Management Division
   Operations Support Division
Emergency Communications Div.
Internal Review & Security Division
Personnel Management Division
The Secretary

OFFICE OF ENGINEERING & TECHNOLOGY
Immediate Office of the Chief Engineer; Chief, Program Management Staff
(1) Spectrum Engineering Division
(2) Authorization and Evaluation Division

FIELD OPERATIONS BUREAU
Enforcement Division
Engineering Division
Public Service Division
Field Installations

PRIVATE RADIO BUREAU
Office of the Bureau Chief;
Administration and Mangement Staff
Land Mobile and Microwave Division
Licensing Division
Special Services Division

OFFICE OF GENERAL COUNSEL
Immediate office of the General Counsel
Litigation Division
Legal Counsel Division
Adjudication Division

COMMON CARRIER BUREAU
International
   Conference Staff
   International Facilities Authorization & Licensing Div.
   International Facilities Planning Division
Operations
   Domestic Facilities Division
   Enforcement Division
   Hearing Division
   Mobile Services Division
   Tariff Division
Policy
   Accounting & Audits Division
   Consumer Affairs Division
   Economics Division
   Policy & Planning Division

MASS MEDIA BUREAU
Audio Services Division
Video Services Division
Enforcement Division
Policy and Rules Division
Administrative and Management Staff

OFFICE OF PUBLIC AFFAIRS
Assistant Director For Minority Enterprise
Consumer Assistance & Small Business Division
News Media Division

——— Lines Of Policy & Judicial Authority

– – – Lines of Management & Administrative Authority

Introduction   1-3

tions circuits, modification and renewal of licenses, and inspection of transmitting equipment and regulation of its use. The Commission has enforcement powers and may levy fines in cases of non-compliance of its Rules. In sum, the Federal Communications Commission carries out the Communications Act.

Of course, the FCC has authority over the Amateur Radio Service. But it also concerns itself with a number of other services. These include Aviation (aircraft and ground); Marine (ship and coastal); Public Safety (police, fire, forestry conservation, highway maintenance, local government, special emergency and state guard). FCC holds jurisdiction in Industrial Services including business, forest products, manufacturers, motion pictures, petroleum, power, relay press, special industrial and telephone maintenance. The Land Transportation Services cover railroad, passenger and truck, taxicab and automobile emergency communications. Other services include Personal (CB), Disaster, Experimental and Common Carrier. This latter service covers a wide range of communications including paging, land mobile, microwave relay, broadcast relay, and international radiotelephone and radiotelegraph.

International agreement provides for national identification of a station by the first character or first two characters of its call sign, and for this purpose apportions the alphabet among the nations. The United States uses the first letters K, N and W exclusively, and part of the A series. Call signs are assigned by the Commission on an individual basis.

As we've seen, the FCC is charged with taking care of radio and wire service provisions of treaties and international agreements to which the United States is party. Under Department of State auspices, the Commission participates in related international conferences. It licenses radio and cable circuits from the U.S. to foreign points, and regulates the operating companies. It also licenses radio stations on American planes and ships in international service, and, under international agreements and upon request, inspects the radio equipment of foreign vessels touching U.S. ports. In addition, it is the medium for resolving cases of interference between domestic and foreign radio stations.

The Commission is required to "study new uses for radio, provide for experimental uses of frequencies, and generally encourage the larger and more effective use of radio in the public interest." Cooperation is maintained with Government and commercial research activities. The FCC operates a laboratory at Laurel, Maryland. It also carries out policy studies to provide information on complex questions facing the Commission.

Wire and radio communication facilities used to aid the national defense form one of the basic requirements of the Communications Act. The President has delegated certain of these functions to the FCC. Among other things, the Commission supervises the Emergency Broadcast System to notify and instruct the public in the event of enemy attack.

Private Radio Bureau

Where does Amateur Radio fit into the Commission's scheme of things? Amateur Radio is administered by the Commission's Private Radio Bureau. Formerly called the Safety and Special Radio Services, the Private Radio Services are used mostly for the two-way communications of individuals, organized groups, businesses and non-federal government agencies. These services are designated "private" because they are used for private purposes, unlike broadcasting, which serves a public audience, or common-carrier services, which provide a communications service for hire.

There are at least 34 Private Radio Services. For regulatory purposes, the FCC divides them into eight categories, each governed by a separate part of the rules.

- Stations on Land in the Maritime Services (Part 81)
- Stations on Shipboard in the Maritime Services (Part 83)
- Aviation Services (Part 87)

- Private Land Mobile Radio Services (Part 90)
- Private Operational-Fixed Microwave Service (Part 94)
- Personal Radio Services (Part 95)
- Amateur Radio Service (Part 97)
- Disaster Communications Service (Part 99)

These services provide communications for safety and other purposes in land, sea and air transportation; in law enforcement and fire prevention; in commerce and agriculture; in education and science; in civil and medical emergency; and in personal travel and recreation.

How Amateur Radio Fits In

The Amateur Radio Service is for individuals who are interested in the technical side of radio and are able to provide emergency communications in disasters, all for the general benefit of the public. It is called "amateur" because it is strictly non-commercial; no business may be transmitted on amateur frequencies. The Amateur Radio Service is a voluntary, disciplined communications service guided by five traditional objectives:

1) to provide emergency or public service communications when normal communications are disrupted;
2) to advance the state of the art;
3) to improve individual skills in radio operation;
4) to provide a reserve pool of qualified radio operators and technicians; and
5) to promote international goodwill.

Anyone, regardless of age, can qualify for an Amateur Radio license by passing the FCC examinations for one of the five progressive levels of achievement: Novice, Technician, General, Advanced and Amateur Extra. Exams include tests of applicants' understanding of the technical and practical aspects of the Amateur Radio Service as well as tests of their skills in Morse code telegraphy. The higher the class, the more difficult the exams and the greater the privileges of the license.

Amateur Radio began with a few experimenters in the early 1900s, and has since grown to over 400,000 licensed operators in the U.S. Both the operators and the Service, as regulated in Part 97 of the FCC Rules, represent principles of radio communications that have endured and advanced since the days of the radio pioneers.

Today, the service flourishes. At WARC-79, Amateur Radio was granted a number of new frequency bands. Such action clearly points out the significance attached to the amateur service by the international telecommunication community. In the United States, FCC attaches the same importance to the Service, as evidenced by the amount of spectrum space it is allocated.

Unregulation

There are many Commission-watchers representing the interests of the various radio services whose operations are profoundly affected by the agency's actions. The ARRL is one of them. The National Cable Television Association and the National Association of Broadcasters are others who represent their respective industries. These Commission-watchers have noted, with varying degrees of concern, the FCC's trend toward deregulation. During the past few Administrations, and including the present one, the mandate has been handed down to Government agencies that the people should have less intrusion into their lives by the Federal Government. Under the FCC Chairman appointed by President Reagan, Mark Fowler, deregulation has accelerated.

Informed sources say that one of Fowler's first acts was to change the name of the Commission's softball team from the Regulators to the Unregulators!

The American Radio Relay League has, for the most part, supported the Commission's deregulatory actions, as the amateur service has demonstrated its ability to keep its own shop over the years. In recent times, we have seen the Commission ax logging requirements, simplify station ID, permit ASCII, AMTOR and other digital codes, and commit many other sections of Part 97 to oblivion.

However, the League opposed a 1979 Commission proposal to rewrite the amateur service rules (Part 97) into so-called "plain language." Although the League supports the concept of deregulation, simplification and clarification of rules, "plain language" was not the appropriate vehicle for accomplishing these objectives. In representing its recommendations for the retention of existing Part 97, ARRL said:

> The present rules for the Amateur Radio Service (Part 97) were adopted over a period of many years, usually by rulemaking proceedings and always by appropriate reports and orders which have built up a large body of legislative history. Interpretations and applications of the present rules are reported in the official *Reports of the Federal Communications Commission* and in the recognized service of *Pike & Fischer Radio Regulations,* and are summarized in digests of those services by rule number and title . . . A wholesale rewriting of the rules such as proposed by the instant NPRM will require extensive cross-referencing and will severely limit the usefulness of past orders and decisions and the summaries in the digest.

FCC subsequently withdrew its proposal.

It is likely that amateurs will see further actions as the FCC unregulators continue on their course of whittling away needless regulations. In August 1981, two members of the Commission's Office of Plans and Policy presented to the Commission a paper designed to stimulate discussion and critical comment on issues involving FCC policy. Working Paper No. 6 generally calls for much greater flexibility in the regulation of personal radio, including radio amateurs. Although the authors claim the opinions are their own, and do not necessarily reflect policies or views of the FCC, it's clear that their ideas are consistent with the recent trends within the Commission. At pages 18-19, for example, the authors offer the following on the technical state of Amateur Radio:

> Most observers would agree that the service is adequately meeting the public service and international goals. In contrast, many would also agree that the goals of expanding technical skills and manpower and advancing the radio art have fallen on hard times in recent years . . . If there is criticism of amateurs for not being technically more advanced, it could be misdirected. Perhaps one should place some responsibility on the regulations, not the licensees.

The authors then point out their belief that a number of regulations seem inconsistent with the goals of the amateur service: "They probably no longer serve any useful purpose either because of technological advances or because they were in the first place overly pessimistic predictions of troubles that might arise." The authors suggest that some rules collectively may place serious constraints on goal achievement within the service, and that they are "symptomatic of the numerous petty federal regulations so unpopular these days among the American body politic." The report calls for systematic analysis of technical areas in the service and how to increase technical competency among its licensees. "In summary," the authors conclude, "among the rules we think should be eliminated or greatly liberalized are the following: (a) restrictions on third-party traffic; (b) restrictions against automatic control and repeaters on HF, which appear to prevent not only conventional two-channel repeaters but also such (spectrum-efficient) techniques as HF packet switching and automatic "electronic mailboxes"; (c) requirements for separate control operators on repeaters; (d) identification requirements that hamper the use of advanced technologies; and (e) nonauthorization of novel technologies like spread-spectrum modulation."

To a degree, these means are being achieved as this is being written. And, thanks to the Goldwater Bill signed into law in 1982 (P.L. 97-259), the Commission's deregulatory efforts will reach new pinnacles in the future.

On the Horizon

September 14, 1982, was a red-letter day for Amateur Radio, as President Reagan signed into law a measure that has opened the door to sweeping changes in the amateur service. The law amends the Communications Act of 1934 in several critical areas:

1) FCC has the authority to regulate the susceptibility of electronic equipment to radio-frequency interference, authority that is needed to stem the flow of electronic devices that cannot function normally in the presence of RF energy. This provision is a significant victory for amateurs weary of their long-standing battle with such devices in the households of uninformed neighbors having TVI troubles.

2) The Amateur Service is exempted from the "secrecy of communications" provisions of Section 705 of the Communications Act, thus clearing the way for a more active role on the part of amateurs in policing their own bands.

3) FCC is authorized to use volunteers in monitoring for rules violations. Volunteers will be able to issue advisory notices to apparent violators to convey information to Commission personnel, but will not be authorized to take enforcement actions themselves. This is the basis for the ARRL Volunteer Monitoring Program (VOLMON).

4) FCC is authorized to use volunteers in preparing and administering amateur exams, a necessary response to the effects of budget cuts on the Commission's ability to prepare and supervise exams. The Volunteer Examiner Program (VEP) is now active and Volunteer Examiners are administering exams in places the FCC rarely, if ever, had time to visit. The ARRL/VEC administered more exams in 1985 than the FCC handled in its last 12 months of Field Office testing.

5) The term of amateur station licenses is 10 years, increased from 5 to reduce the administrative burden on the Commission and its licensees.

The new law is a milestone in Amateur Radio. It is seen as the catalyst for a new, dynamic service, with amateurs playing a more integral role in processes that affect them. It is an enabling law in every sense of the word. As ARRL Executive Vice President David Sumner noted in a recent *QST* editorial, "Where protecting the future of Amateur Radio is concerned, it boils down to this: If we, the amateur community, won't do it, no one will."

The purpose of this book is to present the current rules in a manner that lends depth and understanding. A keen appreciation of the rules will offer amateurs increased levels of enjoyment in their avocation. The rules have evolved over a long time, and will continue to evolve along the lines suggested in this chapter. The rules are dynamic because the amateur service is dynamic — constantly changing to meet and create new technologies to better serve the public and society.

Chapter 2

A Journey Through Part 97

The purpose of this book is to present not only the rules governing Amateur Radio, but to describe them so all licensed amateurs will know their responsibilities. With a firm grasp of the rules, one is able to more fully appreciate Amateur Radio, and its benefits to the licensee and to the public. Public service, after all, is what we are all about!

With this in mind, let's take a brief look at what lies ahead in our journey through Part 97. We'll start with the all-important purpose of Amateur Radio.

Why Is There Amateur Radio?

The basic purposes of Amateur Radio are found in Section 97.1, the very beginning of the amateur rules.

Recognition and enhancement of the value of the amateur service to the public as a voluntary noncommercial communication service, particularly with respect to providing emergency communications.

Probably the best-known aspect of Amateur Radio in the public eye is its ability to provide life-saving emergency communications when normal means of contact are down. In hurricanes, earthquakes, tornadoes, airplane crashes, missing person cases, and other accidents and disasters affecting the civil population, Amateur Radio is often the first contact with the outside world available to an affected area. Red Cross and civil preparedness agencies often rely heavily on the services of volunteer radio amateurs. One of the more noteworthy aspects of our service is its noncommercial nature. In fact, amateurs are prohibited from receiving any form of payment for operating their stations. This means that hams, whether they are assisting a search-and-rescue operation in the high Sierras, relaying health-and-welfare messages from a disaster-stricken Caribbean island or providing communications assistance at the Boston Marathon, make available their services free of charge. We operate our stations for the benefit of the public, and for our own personal enjoyment. The Amateur Radio Service is strictly *non*-business!

Continuation and extension of the amateur's unique ability to enhance international goodwill.

Hams are unique — they can travel to the far reaches of the earth and talk with other amateurs in foreign countries simply by walking down a flight of stairs to their ham shacks. H. G. Wells had his time machine — hams have their space machines! In this day and age when international peace and coexistence are so important, amateurs represent their respective countries as ambassadors of goodwill. Amateur-to-amateur communications often transcend the cultural boundaries between societies. Amateur Radio is a teacher in Lincoln, Nebraska, trading stories with a London boarding school headmaster; a tropical fish enthusiast learning about different species in the Amazon River from a missionary stationed in Brazil; it is a means of making friends everywhere.

Continuation and extension of the amateur's proven ability to contribute to the advancement of the radio art.

For 80 years hams have carried on a tradition of learning by doing, and since the beginning have remained at the very forefront of technology. Through experimenting and building, hams have pioneered advances such as the techniques for single sideband, and are currently engaged in state-of-the-art designs in packet radio and spread-spectrum techniques. Amateurs were among the first to bounce signals off the moon to extend signal range. And hams' practical experience has led to numerous technical refinements and cost reductions beneficial to the commercial radio industry.

Encouragement and improvement of the Amateur Radio Service through rules which provide for advancing skills in both the communication and technical phases of the art.

It is the Commission's obligation to see that the Rules allow room for amateurs to move in new directions so they can live up to their potential for advancing technical and communications skills. The Amateur Service is constantly changing to meet new challenges, and dynamic Rules are needed to provide for this. And, as we will see in a few pages, amateurs themselves may play an important role in the rulemaking process. Stay tuned!

Expansion of the existing reservoir within the Amateur Radio Service of trained operators, technicians and electronic experts.

Self-training, intercommunication and technical investigation are the names of the game for the Amateur Radio Service — the more amateurs proficient in communications techniques, the greater the national resource to the public.

The bases and purposes found in the very first section of the Commission's Rules place a large responsibility on the shoulders of the amateur community. It is the Commission's responsibility to ensure that amateurs are able to operate their stations properly without interfering with other radio services. To this end, the FCC examines *all* amateurs; an applicant must pass exams in theory, regulations and Morse code before a license will be issued authorizing operation in the Amateur Radio Service.

With discussion of the *basis and purpose* behind us for the moment, we'll continue our journey through Part 97. The rules are divided into nine subparts, plus appendices. The subparts are:

Subpart A — General
Subpart B — Amateur Operator and Station Licenses
Subpart C — Technical Standards
Subpart D — Operating Requirements and Procedures
Subpart E — Prohibited Practices and Administrative Sanctions
Subpart F — Radio Amateur Civil Emergency Service (RACES)
Subpart G — Operation of Amateur Radio Stations in the United States by Aliens Pursuant to Reciprocal Agreements
Subpart H — Amateur-Satellite Service (ASAT)
Subpart I — Volunteer-Examiner Coordinators

The appendices, while not specific rules, contain information necessary to amateurs to maintain compliance with the rules found in the various subparts. More on these appendices later. Let's look at each subpart.

SUBPART A — GENERAL

Subpart A contains the basis and purpose of Amateur Radio (discussed above) and a series of definitions. These descriptions or definitions of key terms serve to nail down the rules that follow in the other subparts. They carry the weight of law. Key definitions include:

Amateur Radio Service. A radio communication service of self-training, intercommunication, and technical investigation carried on by Amateur Radio operators.
Amateur Radio communication. Non-commercial radio communication by

Amateur Radio stations for personal, not business, interest. Business communica tions and Amateur Radio don't mix!

Amateur Radio operator means a person holding a license to operate an Amateur Radio station issued by the Federal Communications Commission.

Amateur Radio license. The ticket issued by the Federal Communications Commission is made up of a station license, and in the case of the primary station also includes an operator license.

Amateur Radio station. A station licensed in the Amateur Radio Service with equipment at a particular location used for Amateur Radio communication.

Amateur Radio operation. Amateur Radio communication by Amateur Radio operators from Amateur Radio stations . . .

In addition to these general key terms, a number of others are defined in the Rules for clear understanding and interpretation. These other terms will be defined as the various topics arise throughout this book.

SUBPART B — AMATEUR OPERATOR AND STATION LICENSES

This subpart lists in part the different classes of Amateur Radio licenses; the privileges of each; how to apply for, modify or renew a license; how to conduct a Novice exam; antenna height limitations and how call signs are assigned. It lays the groundwork for licensing involving both stations and operators.

SUBPART C — TECHNICAL STANDARDS

Technical Standards. Granted, the name can impart a certain amount of anxiety in the non-technically oriented, but there is nothing in this subpart that is beyond the comprehension of any amateur. To avoid chaos in the amateur bands, it is necessary to define certain standards such as types of transmissions authorized on certain frequencies, maximum power and "clean" transmissions.

At one time, amateurs were required to provide specific means of monitoring the emitted signal. But the Commission deleted the rule, saying it was unnecessary, but that amateurs are simply held responsible for maintaining their signals within certain standards, regardless of the measurement techniques used. This is an example of the Commission's continuing philosophy of unregulation in the services it administers.

Digital transmission is becoming popular in amateur activities. Hams are using special binary codes for such purposes as radio teleprinter (RTTY) communication; control of amateur stations, models and other objects; transfer of computer programs or direct computer-to-computer communications; and communications in various types of data networks (including so-called "packet switching" systems).

SUBPART D — OPERATING REQUIREMENTS AND PROCEDURES

As its title states, Subpart D talks about how to operate a station properly and legally. It describes control operator requirements — a fundamental set of rules that provides for proper operation of an amateur station, and designates specific responsibilities of the control operator and the station licensee. Availability of the station and operator licenses is covered in this subpart. Station identification requirements are included. Emergency operations are provided. Special provisions for remote control of model crafts, and for mobile stations aboard ships and aircraft, are included. Other rules explain station operation away from home, such as in foreign countries and international waters, or airspace. Subpart D rules prescribe proper operation of repeaters, auxiliary stations and stations operated by remote control. Points of communications and one-way communications are also covered.

Subpart D is a very important section of the Rules and every amateur should have a thorough knowledge of its contents.

SUBPART E — PROHIBITED PRACTICES AND ADMINISTRATIVE SANCTIONS

Subpart E contains the no-no's of Amateur Radio. With a forbidding title indeed, subpart E tells you what you cannot do, and what the FCC can do to you if you're caught doing what you cannot do!

Fifteen "thous shall nots" are covered. Being paid for your amateur work is NOT permitted. Broadcasting is out-of-bounds. Automatically retransmitting other radio services' signals is forbidden. Routine business communications are illegal. Other sections prohibit music, transmission for illegal purposes, ciphers, obscenities, false signals, malicious interference, failure to ID, intentional damage to amateur equipment, and cheating on exams.

Subpart E provides the procedures for replying to official FCC mail. Some amateurs have had their licenses revoked for failure to reply to an FCC notice!

SUBPART F — RADIO AMATEUR CIVIL EMERGENCY SERVICE (RACES)

The Radio Amateur Civil Emergency Service, as part of the Amateur Radio Service, provides radio communications for civil defense purposes *only,* during periods of local, regional or national civil emergencies.

Emergency communications are a major part of the radio amateur's purposes — it says so smack in the middle of Section 97.1, The Basis and Purpose of Amateur Radio. Government agencies are realizing the potential service that hams who are familiar with emergency communications techniques can provide. In fact, it is FEMA, the Federal Emergency Management Administration, that feeds and cares for the RACES service!

SUBPART G — OPERATION OF AMATEUR RADIO STATIONS IN THE UNITED STATES BY ALIENS PURSUANT TO RECIPROCAL AGREEMENTS

This portion of Part 97 provides rules and procedures that allow foreign amateurs to operate their stations in the United States. By special agreement between the U.S. and a number of countries, aliens may obtain reciprocal operating permits to operate in this country. And U.S. hams may get permission to operate their stations in other countries. Subpart G is devoted to the restrictions placed on the alien operator in this country: frequencies, emissions, ID requirements and so forth. It's the smallest of all the subparts.

SUBPART H — THE AMATEUR-SATELLITE SERVICE (ASAT)

Satellites are unique in that many travel virtually over every country on earth, and coordination is required to prevent interference and chaos.

The Amateur Satellite Service rules were created to help the Commission meet its international obligations by requiring amateurs to inform the FCC staff of certain detailed information about planned space, in-space and post-space operation of their stations. The rules are not limited to space satellite operation, however. They also cover earth and telecommand operation, and specify frequencies and other restrictions on such operation.

The ASAT rules represent the newest of all the subparts. We will be taking a further look at this space-age technology from the rules standpoint in pages to come.

SUBPART I — VOLUNTEER-EXAMINER COORDINATORS

The rules in this subpart are designed to provide for Volunteer-Examiner Coordinators to (what else!) coordinate the efforts of field Volunteer Examiners. These VEs, as you will learn in the pages to come, are now the folks who will be giving Technician and higher class exams.

THE APPENDICES

As we pointed out earlier, Part 97 is appended with information necessary to carry out amateur operation within the Rules. Examples include information on how to calculate height above average terrain (HAAT) and effective radiated power (ERP) for repeater station licensees so they can meet the station records and power requirements of the Rules. The various emissions are defined in the appendices. Pertinent sections of the ITU Radio Regulations are reproduced. Other information is provided to assist amateurs in understanding the rules they must abide by.

In the chapters that follow, we will examine each of the subparts in considerable detail. FCC-approved interpretations will be provided to assist the reader in determining the legality of practical everyday amateur activities. We'll be taking a look at so-called "gray areas" within the Rules. A good understanding of the Rules is an ideal way to increase the pleasure and meaningfulness of Amateur Radio.

International and Domestic Laws

The International Radio Regulations of the ITU affect all radio amateurs. The U.S. has a responsibility to make rules that are consistent with these international agreements. The Communications Act of 1934, as amended, is the chief tool by which the U.S. carries out its obligations to the world's telecommunications community. Let's take a closer look at the IRR and the Communications Act.

The Radio Regulations of the ITU define the Amateur Service and Amateur stations as follows:

Amateur Service — A radiocommunication service for the purpose of self-training, intercommunication and technical investigations carried on by amateurs, that is, by duly authorized persons interested in radio technique solely with a personal aim and without pecuniary interest.

Amateur station — A station in the Amateur Service.

Amateur-Satellite Service — A radiocommunication service using space stations on earth satellites for the same purposes as those of the Amateur Service.

In considering international and domestic rulemaking proceedings, it's important to have at least a basic knowledge of the other major categories of radio services that affect, directly or indirectly, our Amateur Service. The IRR offers the following definitions of key services:

Radiocommunication Service: A service involving the transmission, emission and/or reception of *radio waves* for specific *telecommunication purposes.*

Fixed Service: A radiocommunication service between specified fixed points.

Fixed-Satellite Service: A radiocommunication service between earth stations at specified fixed points when one or more satellites are used.

Mobile Service: A radiocommunication service between mobile and land stations, or between mobile stations.

Land Mobile Service: A mobile service between base stations and land mobile stations, or between land mobile stations.

Maritime Mobile Service: A mobile service between coast stations and ship stations, or between ship stations.

Aeronautical Mobile Service: A mobile service between aeronautical stations and aircraft stations, or between aircraft stations.

Broadcasting Service: A radiocommunication service in which the transmissions are intended for direct reception by the general public.

Radiodetermination Service: A radiocommunication service for the purpose of radiodetermination.

Radionavigation Service: A radiodetermination service for the purpose of radionavigation. Loran systems, for example. Exists for the purpose of safe operation of planes and ships.

Radiolocation Service: A radiodetermination service for the purpose of radiolocation of objects: RADAR is used for tracking movement of ships and planes, for example.

Safety Service: Any radiocommunication service used permanently for the safeguarding of human life and property.

Other important international rules are found in Article 32 of the IRR:

International Radio Regulations — Amateur Stations

Article 32: Amateur Service and Amateur-Satellite Service

Section I. Amateur Service

§1. Radiocommunications between amateur stations of different countries shall be forbidden if the administration of one of the countries concerned has notified that it objects to such radiocommunications.

§2.(1) When transmissions between amateur stations of different countries are permitted, they shall be made in plain language and shall be limited to messages of a technical nature relating to tests and to remarks of a personal character for which, by reason of their unimportance, recourse to the public telecommunications service is not justified.

(2) It is absolutely forbidden for amateur stations to be used for transmitting international communications on behalf of third parties.

(3) The preceding provisions may be modified by special arrangements between the administrations of the countries concerned.

§3.(1) Any person seeking a license to operate the apparatus of an amateur station shall prove that he is able to send correctly by hand and to receive correctly by ear, texts in Morse code

Section II. Amateur-Satellite Service

§6. The provisions of Section I of this Article shall apply equally, as appropriate, to the amateur-satellite service.

§7. Space stations in the amateur-satellite service operating in bands shared with other services shall be fitted with appropriate devices for controlling emissions in the event that harmful interference is reported in accordance with

signals. The administrations concerned may, however, waive this requirement in the case of stations making use exclusively of frequencies above 30 MHz.

(2) Administrations shall take such measures as they judge necessary to verify the operational and technical qualifications of any person wishing to operate the apparatus of an amateur station.

§4. The maximum power of amateur stations shall be fixed by the administrations concerned, having regard to the technical qualifications of the operators and to the conditions under which these stations are to operate.

§5.(1) All the general rules of the Convention and of these Regulations shall apply to amateur stations. In particular, the emitted frequency shall be as stable and as free from spurious emissions as the state of technical development for such stations permits.

(2) During the course of their transmissions, amateur stations shall transmit their call sign at short intervals.

the procedure laid down in Article 22. Administrations authorizing such space stations shall inform the IFRB and shall ensure that sufficient earth command stations are established before launch to guarantee that any harmful interference that might be reported can be terminated by the authorizing administration (see No. 2612).

The Communications Act of 1934

The complete text of the Communications Act of 1934 would occupy many pages. The only parts given are those most applicable to Amateur Radio station licensing and regulations in this country (with which every amateur should be familiar). Note particularly Sections 324, 325 and 705 and the penalties outlined in Sections 501 and 502.

Be it enacted by the Senate and House of Representatives of the United States of America in Congress assembled,

Section 1. For the purpose of regulating interstate and foreign commerce in communication by wire and radio so as to make available, so far as possible, to all the people of the United States, a rapid, efficient, nationwide and worldwide wire and radio communication service with adequate facilities at reasonable charges, for the purpose of the national defense, for the purpose of promoting safety of life and property through the use of wire and radio communication, and for the purpose of securing a more effective execution of this policy by centralizing authority heretofore granted by law to several agencies and by granting additional authority with respect to interstate and foreign commerce in wire and radio communication there is hereby created a commission to be known as the "Federal Communications Commission," which shall be constituted as hereinafter provided, and which shall execute and enforce the provisions of this Act.

Section 2.(a) The provisions of the Act shall apply to all interstate and foreign communication by wire or radio and all interstate and foreign transmission of energy by radio, which originates and/or is received within the United States, and to all the licensing and regulating of all radio stations as hereinafter provided; but it shall not apply to persons engaged in wire or radio communication or transmission in the Canal Zone, or to wire or radio communication or transmission wholly within the Canal Zone . . .

Section 4.(a) The Federal Communications Commission (in this Act referred to as the "Commission") shall be composed of seven commissioners appointed by the President, by and with the advice and consent of the Senate, one of whom the President shall designate as chairman.

Section 4.(f)

(4)(A) The Commission, for purposes of preparing any examination for an amateur station operator license, may accept and employ the voluntary and uncompensated services of any individual who holds an amateur station operator license of a higher class than the class license for which the examination is being prepared. In the case of examinations for the highest class of amateur station operator license, the Commission may accept and employ such services of any individual who holds such class of license.

(B) The Commission, for purposes of administering any examination for an amateur station operator license, may accept and employ the voluntary and uncompensated services of any individual who holds an amateur station operator license of a higher class than the class license for which the examination is being conducted. In the case of examinations for the highest class of amateur station operator license, the Commission may accept and employ such services of any individual who holds such class of license. Any person who owns a significant interest in, or is an employee of, any company or other entity which is engaged in the manufacture or distribution of equipment used in connection with Amateur Radio transmissions, or in the preparation or distribution of any publication used in preparation for obtaining amateur station operator licenses, shall not be eligible to render any service under this subparagraph.

(C)(i) The Commission, for purposes of monitoring violations of any provision of this Act (and of any regulation prescribed by the Commission under this Act) relating to the Amateur Radio Service, may —

(I) recruit and train any individual licensed by the Commission to operate an amateur station; and

(II) accept and employ the voluntary and uncompensated services of such individual.

(ii) The Commission, for purposes of recruiting and training individuals under clause (i) and for purposes of screening, annotating, and summarizing violation reports referred under clause (i), may accept and employ the voluntary and uncompensated services of any amateur station operator organization.

(iii) The functions of individuals recruited and trained under this subparagraph shall be limited to —

(I) the detection of improper Amateur Radio transmissions;

(II) the conveyance to Commission personnel of information which is essential to the enforcement of this Act (or regulations prescribed by the Commission under this Act) relating to the Amateur Radio Service; and

(III) issuing advisory notices, under the general direction of the Commission, to persons who apparently have violated any provision of this Act (or regulations prescribed by the Commission under this Act) relating to the Amateur Radio Service.

Nothing in this clause shall be construed to grant individuals recruited and trained under this subparagraph any authority to issue sanctions to violators or to take any enforcement action other than any action which the Commission may prescribe by rule.

(J) With respect to the acceptance of voluntary uncompensated services for the preparation, processing, or administration of examinations for amateur station operator licenses pursuant to subparagraph (A) or (B) of this paragraph, individuals, or organizations which provide or coordinate such authorized volunteer services may recover from examinees reimbursement for out-of-pocket costs. The total amount of allowable cost reimbursement per examinee shall not exceed $4, adjusted annually every January 1 for changes in the Department of Labor Consumer Price Index. Such individuals and organizations shall maintain records of out-of-pocket expenditures and shall certify annually to the Commission that all costs for which reimbursement was obtained were necessarily and prudently incurred.

Section 301. It is the purpose of this Act, among other things, to maintain the controls of the United States over all the channels of interstate and foreign radio transmission; and to provide for the use of such channels, but not the ownership thereof, by persons for limited periods of time, under licenses granted by Federal authority, and no such license shall be construed to create any right, beyond the terms, conditions and periods of the license. No person shall use or operate any apparatus for the transmission of energy or communications or signals by radio . . . except under and in accordance with this Act and with a license in that behalf granted under the provisions of this Act.

Section 302. (a) The Commission may . . . make reasonable regulations (1) governing the interference potential of devices which in their operation are capable of emitting radio frequency energy . . . in sufficient degree to cause harmful interference to radio communications and (2) establishing minimum performance standards for home electronic equipment and systems to reduce their susceptibility to interference from radio frequency energy. Such regulations shall be applicable to the manufacture, import, sale, offer for sale, or shipment of such devices and home electronic equipment and systems, and to the use of such devices. (b) No person shall manufacture, import, sell, offer for sale, or ship devices or home electronic equipment and systems, or use devices which fail to comply with regulations promulgated pursuant to this section . . .

Section 303. Except as otherwise provided in this Act, the Commission from time to time, as public convenience, interest or necessity requires, shall —

a) Classify radio stations

b) Prescribe the nature of the service to be rendered

c) Assign bands of frequencies . . .

d) Determine the location of stations . . .

e) Regulate the kind of apparatus to be used with respect to its external effects and the purity and sharpness of the emissions from each station and from the apparatus therein.

f) Make such regulations not inconsistent with law as it may deem necessary to prevent interference between stations and to carry out the provisions of this Act . . .

g) Study new uses for radio, provide for experimental uses of frequencies, and generally encourage the larger and more effective use of radio in the public interest . . .

j) Have authority to make general rules and regulations requiring stations to keep such records . . . as it may deem desirable . . .

l) 1) Have authority to prescribe the qualifications of station operators . . . and to issue licenses to persons who are found to be qualified by the Commission and who otherwise are legally eligible for employment in the United States . . . 2) Notwithstanding paragraph (1) of this subsection, an individual to whom a radio station is licensed under the provisions of this Act may be issued an operator's license to operate that station. 3) In addition to amateur operator licenses which the Commission may issue to aliens pursuant to paragraph (2) of this subsection, and notwithstanding Section 301 of this Act and paragraph (1) of this subsection, the Commission may issue authorizations, under such conditions and terms as it may prescribe, to permit an alien licensed by his government as an Amateur Radio operator to operate his Amateur Radio station licensed by his government in the United States, its possessions, and the Commonwealth of Puerto Rico provided there is in effect a bilateral agreement between the United States and the alien's government for such operation on a reciprocal basis by United States Amateur Radio operators. Other provisions of this Act and of the Administrative Procedure Act shall not be applicable to any request or application for or modification, suspension or cancellation of any such authorization.

m) 1) Have authority to suspend the license of any operator upon proof sufficient to satisfy the Commission that the licensee — (A) has violated or caused, aided, or abetted the violation of, any provision of any Act, treaty or convention binding on the United States, which the Commission is authorized to administer, or any regulation made by the Commission under any such Act, treaty or convention; or (B) has failed to carry out a lawful order of the master or person lawfully in charge of the ship or aircraft on which he is employed; or (C) has willfully damaged or permitted radio apparatus or installations to be damaged; or (D) has transmitted superfluous radio communications or signals or communications containing profane or obscene words, language or meaning, or has knowingly transmitted — (1) false or deceptive signals or communications; or (2) a call signal or letter which has not been assigned by proper authority to the station he is operating; or (E) has willfully or maliciously interfered with any other radio communications or signals; or (F) has obtained or attempted to obtain, or has assisted another to obtain or attempted to obtain, an operator's license by fraudulent means.

2) No order of suspension of any operator's license shall take effect until fifteen days' notice in writing thereof, stating the cause for the proposed suspension has been given to the operator licensee who may make written application to the Commission at any time within said fifteen days for a hearing upon such order . . .

n) Have authority to inspect all radio installations . . .

o) Have authority to designate call letters of all stations.

p) Have authority to cause to be published such call letters.

q) Have authority to require the painting and/or illumination of radio towers if and when in its judgment such towers constitute, or there is a reasonable possibility that they may constitute, a menace to air navigation.

r) Make rules and regulations . . . to carry out the provisions of this Act, or any international radio or wire communications treaty or convention . . .

Section 308. (b) All applications for station licenses, or modifications or renewals thereof, shall set forth such facts as the Commission by regulation may prescribe as to the citizenship, character, and financial, technical, and other qualifications of the applicant to operate the station; the ownership and location of the proposed station and of the stations, if any, with which it is proposed to communicate; the frequencies and the power desired to be used; the hours of the day or other periods of time during which it is proposed to operate the station; the purposes for which the station is to be used; and such other information as it may require. The Commission, at any time after the filing of such original application and during the term of any such licenses, may require from an applicant or licensee further written statements of fact to enable it to determine whether such original application should be granted or denied or such license revoked. Such application and/or such statement of fact shall be signed by the applicant and/or licensee.

Section 310. (a) The station license required under this Act shall not be granted to or held by any foreign government or the representative thereof. (b) No broadcast or common carrier or aeronautical . . . radio station license shall be granted to or held by (1) an alien . . . (c) In addition to amateur station licenses which the Commission may issue to aliens pursuant to this Act, the Commission may issue authorizations, under such conditions and terms as it may prescribe, to permit an alien licensed by his government as an Amateur Radio operator to operate his Amateur Radio station licensed by his government in the United States, its possessions, and the Commonwealth of Puerto Rico provided there is in effect a bilateral agreement between the United States and the alien's government for such operation on a reciprocal basis by United States Amateur Radio operators. Other provisions of this Act and of the Administrative Procedure Act shall not be applicable to any request or application for or modification, suspension or cancellation of any such authorization.

Section 312.(a) The Commission may revoke any station license or construction permit —

(1) for false statements knowingly made either in the application or in any statement of fact which may be required pursuant to section 308;

(2) because of conditions coming to the attention of the Commission which would warrant it in refusing to grant a license or permit on an original application;

(3) for willful or repeated failure to operate substantially as set forth in the license;

(4) for willful or repeated violation of, or willful or repeated failure to observe any provision of this Act or any rule or regulation of the Commission authorized by this Act or by a treaty ratified by the United States;

(5) for violation of or failure to observe any final cease and desist order issued by the Commission under this section;

(6) for violation of section 1304, 1343, or 1464 of title 18 of the United States Code; or

(7) for willful or repeated failure to allow reasonable access to or to permit purchase of reasonable amounts of time for the use of a broadcasting station by a legally qualified candidate for Federal elective office on behalf of his candidacy.

(b) Where any person (1) has failed to operate substantially as set forth in a license, (2) has violated or failed to observe any of the provisions of this Act, or section 1304, 1343, or 1464 of title 18 of the United States Code, or (3) has violated or failed to observe any rule or regulation of the Commission authorized by this Act or by a treaty ratified by the United States, the Commission may order such person to cease and desist from such action.

(c) Before revoking a license or permit pursuant to subsection (a), or issuing a cease and desist order pursuant to subsection (b), the Commission shall serve upon the licensee, permittee, or person involved an order to show cause why an order of revocation or a cease and desist order should not be issued. Any such order to show cause shall contain a statement of the matters with respect to which the Commission is inquiring and shall call upon said licensee, permittee, or person to appear before the Commission at a time and place stated in the order, but in no event less than thirty days after the receipt of such order, and give evidence upon the matter specified therein; except that where safety of life or property is involved, the Commission may provide in the order for a shorter period. If after hearing, or a waiver thereof, the Commission determines that an order of revocation or a cease and desist order should issue, it shall issue such order, which shall include a statement of the findings of the Commission and the grounds and reasons therefor and specify the effective date of the order, and shall cause the same to be served on said licensee, permittee, or person.

(d) In any case where a hearing is conducted pursuant to the provisions of this section, both the burden of proceeding with the introduction of evidence and the burden of proof shall be upon the Commission.

(e) The provisions of section 9(b) of the Administrative Procedure Act which apply with respect to the institution of any proceeding for the revocation of a license or permit shall apply also with the respect to the institution, under this section, of any proceeding for the issuance of a cease and desist order.

(f) For the purposes of this section:

(1) The term "willful," when used with reference to the commission or omission of any act, means the conscious and deliberate commission or omission of such act, irrespective of any intent to violate any provision of this Act or any rule or regulation of the Commission authorized by this Act or by a treaty ratified by the United States.

(2) The term "repeated," when used with reference to the commission or omission of any act, means the commission or omission of such act more than once or, if such commission or omission is continuous, for more than one day.

Section 318. The actual operation of all transmitting apparatus in any radio station for which a station license is required by this Act shall be carried on only by a person holding an operator's license issued hereunder. No person shall operate any such apparatus in such station except under and in accordance with an operator's license issued to him by the Commission . . .

Section 321 . . . (b) All radio stations, including Government stations and stations on board foreign vessels when within the territorial waters of the United States, shall give absolute priority to radio communications or signals relating to ships in distress.

Section 324. In all circumstances, except in case of radio communications, or signals relating to vessels in distress, all radio stations, including those owned and operated by the United States, shall use the minimum amount of power necessary to carry out the communication desired.

Section 325. (a) No person within the jurisdiction of the United States shall knowingly utter or transmit, or cause to be uttered or transmitted, any false or fraudulent signal of distress, or communication relating thereto, nor shall any broadcasting station rebroadcast the program or any part thereof of another broadcasting station without the express authority of the originating station.

Section 501. Any person who willfully and knowingly does or causes or suffers to be done any act, matter or thing, in this Act prohibited or declared to be unlawful, or who willfully or knowingly omits or fails to do any act, matter or thing in this Act required to be done, or willfully or knowingly causes or suffers such omission or failure, shall, upon conviction thereof, be punished for such offense, for which no penalty (other than a forfeiture) is provided by this Act, by a fine of not more than $10,000 or by imprisonment for a term not exceeding one year, or both . . .

Section 502. Any person who willfully or knowingly violates any rule, regulation, restriction or condition made or imposed by any international radio or wire communications treaty or convention, or regulations annexed thereto, to which the United States is or may hereafter become a party, shall, in addition to any other penalties provided by law, be punished, upon conviction thereof, by a fine of not more than $500 for each and every day during which such offense occurs . . .

Section 503 . . . (b) Any person who is determined by the Commission, in accordance with paragraph (3) or (4) of this subsection, to have — (A) willfully or repeatedly failed to comply substantially with the terms and conditions of any license, permit, certificate, or other instrument or authorization issued by the Commission; (B) willfully or repeatedly failed to comply with any of the provisions of this Act or of any rule, regulation, or order shall be liable to the United States for a forfeiture penalty . . .

(2) The amount of any forfeiture penalty determined under this subsection shall not exceed $2000 for each violation. Each day of a continued violation shall constitute a separate offense . . .

Section 606. . . (c) Upon proclamation by the President that there exists war or a threat of war or a state of public peril or disaster or other national emergency, or in order to preserve the neutrality of the United States, the President... may suspend or amend, for such time as he may see fit, the rules and regulations applicable to any or all stations...within the jurisdiction of the United States as prescribed by the Commission, and may cause the closing of any station for radio communication...and the removal therefrom of its apparatus and equipment, or he may authorize the use or control of any such station...and/or its apparatus and equipment by any department of the Government under such regulations as he may prescribe, upon just compensation to the owners...

Section 705 . . . No person receiving or assisting in receiving, or transmitting or assisting in transmitting, any interstate or foreign communication by wire or radio shall divulge or publish the existence, contents, substance, purport, effect or meaning thereof, . . . to any person other than the addressee, his agent or attorney . . . or in response to a subpoena issued by a court of competent jurisdiction, or on demand or other lawful authority . . . and no person not being entitled thereto shall receive or assist in receiving any interstate or foreign communication by wire or radio and use the same or any information therein contained for his own benefit or for the benefit of another not entitled thereto . . . This section shall not apply to the receiving, divulging, publishing or utilizing the contents of any radio communication, which is transmitted by any station for the use of the general public, which relates to ships, aircraft, vehicles or persons in distress or which is transmitted by an amateur radio station or by a citizens band radio operator . . .

Where Do the Rules Come From?

Most amateurs know that the Federal Communications Commission is the Government agency charged by Congress with the task of regulating the telecommunication services in the U.S. And, most are familiar with its rules. Less familiar, however, is the process by which the Commission makes these rules. Are they simply handed down to us, period? Do we simply drift along with the regulatory current? The answer is a resounding no; amateurs, and any interested parties, have a right, thanks to Congress, to participate in the rulemaking procedure. We can have a profound effect on what rules should be added, dropped or modified. With Amateur Radio the dynamic service it is, it's important that we promote awareness of the Commission's processes as an important step away from stagnation.

This discussion was prepared as a plain-language guide to the amateur rulemaking process by the late ARRL General Counsel Bob Booth, W3PS.

The Administrative Procedure Act

The population growth and the social and technological advances in the United States, particularly since World War I, brought about ever-increasing demands for government services. Examples include the development and growth of aviation, radio communication, and medical services and produces. Recognizing that it had neither the facilities, time nor expertise to administer and regulate such diverse fields and activities, the Congress of the United States established an ever-increasing number of administrative agencies. Certain duties, power and enforcement tools were delegated to each agency.

It was not long before the rules, regulations and policies of the agencies acquired the force and effect of laws just as though enacted by Congress. Persons affected by the rules and the Courts expressed ever-increasing concern over the manner by which the rules were adopted, amended and enforced. Finally, in 1946, Congress enacted the Administrative Procedure Act setting forth the procedures to be followed by all administrative agencies in adopting and amending their rules. The Act also sets forth the procedures to be followed in adjudicatory hearings.

Insofar as rulemaking is concerned, the essential provisions of the Act are (1) public notice of the proposal and (2) the right of interested parties to comment. Certain rules, primarily those relating to agency organization and internal operation, are not subject to the notice and comment procedure. Prior notice need not be given if the agency for good cause finds that notice and comments are impractical, unnecessary or contrary to the public interest. Rules may be adopted, amended or repealed by an agency on its own initiative, or may be requested by an interested person by the filing of a petition for rulemaking.

The Federal Communications Commission, the successor of the Federal Radio Commission of 1927, was established by the Communications Act of 1934 and is one of the many administrative agencies subject to the Administrative Procedure Act.

Petitions for Rulemaking

FCC rules concerning rulemaking procedures are relatively simple and straightforward. Any interested person may petition for the adoption, amendment or repeal of a rule or regulation. The petition should be addressed to the Secretary, Federal Communications Commission, Washington, DC 20554, and typed on 8- × 10-inch, or 8-1/2- × 11-inch paper, preferably double spaced. The petition should set forth the text or substance of the proposed rule, the rule sought to be amended (or repealed), together with all facts, views, arguments and data deemed to support the action requested. The petition should indicate how the interests of the petitioner will be affected. These requirements as to size of paper and number of copies have not been rigidly enforced, particularly in Amateur Radio matters. Many hand-written requests for new rules and amendments of existing rules in the Amateur service have been accepted by the Commission, even when no copies were filed. The sidebar at the top of the page shows the proper caption for a petition and comments.

If preliminary review of a petition concludes that it meets the minimum requirements outlined above, or that a waiver of the requirements is warranted, the Commission will issue a "Public Notice" entitled "Petitions for Rulemaking Filed" giving the file number (RM-), the name of the petitioner, the date of filing and a brief summary of the proposal. Such notices are not printed in the *Federal Register,* but those relating to Amateur Radio are often summarized in amateur journals and magazines. Some petitions that plainly do not warrant Commission consideration are not given RM-file numbers and are acted on by the bureau chief under delegated authority. Any interested person may file a statement in support of or in opposition to a petition for rulemaking not later than 30 days from issuance of the "Public Notice."

Notices of Proposed Rulemaking

Rulemaking involving Amateur Radio matters usually falls under the jurisdiction of the Private Radio Bureau. Occasionally, however, jurisdiction may be with another bureau. Petitions for Rulemaking are referred to the appropriate bureau or office. Petitions involving amateur matters are processed by the Personal Radio Branch, Rules Division, Private Radio Bureau. If a petition has merit, a draft Notice of Proposed Rulemaking may be submitted by the bureau chief to the Commissioners for their consideration. If it is adopted, a docket number will be assigned, and the notice will be released to the public for comments. Depending on the Commission's workload, its priorities and the amount of interest shown by concerned parties, several months or even years may elapse between the filing of a petition and the issuance of a Notice of Proposed Rulemaking or a denial.

A "Notice of Proposed Rulemaking" sets forth either the terms or substance of a proposed rule or a description of the subjects and issues involved, and the dates for filing comments and replies to comments. The notice must be published in the *Federal Register* and must afford interested persons an opportunity to participate in the proceeding through "submission of written data, views, or arguments" (Sec. 1.411; 1.413). Comments should contain the caption or heading contained on the notice and should be on the same sized paper as required for petitions. The original and five copies must be filed. The notice also will afford interested persons an opportunity to submit comments in reply to the original comments. Again, the original and five copies must be filed. Those wishing each Commissioner to have a personal copy of comments or reply comments should file six additional copies, making an original and 11 copies in all. No other comments may be filed without specific permission of the Commission. Comments not filed by the deadline may not be considered. Under the Administrative Procedures Act and FCC Rules, a person who has missed a comment deadline may prepare comments anyway, and then prepare a second document titled "Motion for Leave to Submit Late-Filed Comments." If the Motion shows good cause as to the lateness of the filing, and if the matter is not too far along on the FCC staff work schedule, the petition may be accepted.

As mentioned earlier, the Commission also may propose adoption, amendment or repeal of a rule by issuance of a Notice of Proposed Rulemaking even though a petition has not been received.

Occasionally, a Notice of Inquiry may be issued or combined with a Notice of Proposed Rulemaking. A Notice of Inquiry will set forth the Commission's concern over a particular matter and solicit comments and suggestions as to whether adoption, amendment or repeal of a rule may be desirable. The same notice and comment procedures are followed with notices of inquiry as with notices of proposed rulemaking.

As mentioned earlier, the Commission also may propose adoption, amendment or repeal of a rule by issuance of a Notice of Proposed Rulemaking even though a petition has not been received.

The Report and Order

These comments and replies to a notice are reviewed by the office that prepared the notice. In amateur matters, the responsible office is usually the Personal Radio Branch of the Private Radio Bureau's Rules Division. A draft Report and Order will be prepared by that branch and submitted to the chief of the Private Radio Bureau. A draft Report and Order must be approved at each level within the Bureau, and then coordinated with each other interested bureau or office before being presented to the Commissioners for their consideration and approval. Revision of the Report and Order may take place at any stage. Finally, the matter will be considered by the FCC Commissioners at a meeting usually open to the public. The Commissioners usually request discussion by staff members most familiar with the subject at hand. The Commission may adopt the Report and Order with its rule amendments, may order revisions in the document, or may terminate the NPRM without amending any rules.

Contrary to widespread belief, the rule finally adopted need not be identical to the proposal. In numerous appeals, the United States Courts of Appeals have held that there need be only some relationship between the proposal and the rule finally adopted. The Commission, however, must incorporate in the rules adopted a concise general statement of their basis and purpose.

Petitions for Reconsideration

Section 405 of the Communications Act of 1934, as amended, affords any "person aggrieved or whose interests are adversely affected" by an order (a new or amended rule) the right to petition the Commission for reconsideration. The petitioner shall state with particularity the respects in which the petitioner believes the action taken by the Commission should be changed. A Petition for Reconsideration *must be filed within 30 days* of the date of public notice of the final Commission action (Sec. 1.429). For documents in notice and comment rulemaking proceedings that date is the date of publication in the *Federal Register*.

A Petition for Reconsideration usually is referred to the same Bureau that prepared the original Report and Order. From a practical standpoint it is virtually impossible to obtain favorable action on a Petition for Reconsideration if no new facts are presented. Occasionally, however, if the petitioner shows good cause, the Commission may grant the Petition for Reconsideration and modify the earlier order.

The physical requirements for petitions and comments are the same for Petitions for Reconsideration. Additionally, it must not exceed 25 double-spaced typewritten pages. Oppositions to Petitions for Reconsideration must not exceed this length as well. Replies to oppositions are limited to 10 double-spaced typewritten pages (Sec. 1.429). An original and 11 copies must be filed.

The effective date of a new or amended rule is not automatically postponed by the filing of a Petition for Reconsideration. If a stay of the effective date of the rule amendment is desired, the petitioner must specifically request it and must show good cause why the rule should not go into effect.

Court Appeals

Court review may be sought under Section 402(a) of the Communications Act. The Court may either affirm the action of the Commission, reverse it or remand it to the Commission for further consideration. A Court would set aside a rule-making action of the Commission if the Commission exceeded the authority delegated to it by Congress, or if there was some prejudicial error. The Court traditionally has followed the policy of not substituting its judgment for that of the Commission because of the Commission's expertise in the field of radio communications.

If the Court remands a rule-making matter back to the Commission, usually it will be handled by the same Bureau that handled it originally.

Other Courses of Action

It is clear from this discussion that Petitions for Reconsideration and appeals to the Courts are not guaranteed to bring about changes in rules adopted by rule-making. Thus, the most practical course is to file a new petition for rulemaking after experience has been gained with the new or amended rules and it can be demonstrated that the rule, as amended, is not in the best interest of the amateur community.

Afterword
International And Domestic Regulation — The Early Days

Amateur Radio legislation and regulation was virtually nonexistent in the early days of the art. In 1909, hundreds of high-powered amateur stations outnumbered the Navy and commercial stations. The ham was the king of the bands. Interference and bedlam reigned. The Roberts Bill of 1909, a trust measure sponsored by the U.S. Navy, was one of the first attempts to alleviate this situation. The measure was killed by the Marconi Company, which argued that the interference existed because of the commercial operators' antiquated, obsolete equipment not incorporating state-of-the-art tuners. The Marconi Company, along with the amateurs, were the only operators who used such tuners.

The Roberts Bill marked the beginning of a turbulent legislative period. The Marconi Company remained a powerful ally. Amateur Radio grew to be a major issue during this day and was the subject of much editorial treatment in the journals. However, a lesson learned by the lawmakers was that the amateur community, some 4000 devotees utterly dedicated to their art, could not be snuffed out by an Act of Congress. Other tacks were taken.

The Burke Wireless Bill, and the Depew Wireless Bill, both introduced in 1910, provided for registration of different classes of stations, and declared illegal any outside interference to these stations. The amateur, of course, was not mentioned as a registered station. Both bills were discarded, however, but not until amateurs had registered bitter opposition.

In 1911, the Navy had at it again with the introduction of the Alexander Bill, seemingly designed to see the abolition of Amateur Radio. The Junior Wireless Club (the forerunner of the Radio Club of America), actively opposed the measure. Along with the Wireless Association of Pennsylvania, it worked to defeat the bill, and the Senate version — the Smith Bill, S. 5630. 1912 saw the defeat of 13 pieces of legislation dealing with radio! But, Amateur Radio was to see regulation in a short time.

The provisions of the Berlin Convention of 1906 were ratified in this country in April 1912, in time for U.S. delegates returning from a subsequent London conference to arm lawmakers with detailed regulations for the governing of the new industry and art. The lawmakers in turn sought to base new rules on these international provisions. They took the remnants of the Alexander Bill and pasted it up along the lines of the London treaty. The new rules reigned for 15 years.

The government, still smarting from its losses of prior legislative attempts to abolish Amateur Radio, had a new ploy. Regulation Fifteenth specified that private (amateur) stations were limited to wavelengths of less than 200 meters. The body of scientific thought at the time held that radio waves became more effective and useful as a direct ratio to their length. The feeling was that amateurs would be dissolved by relegating them to the "useless" spectrum 200 meters and below. Just how useless this spectrum actually is can be found today in the worldwide communications systems using but a few watts of power.

In addition to Regulation Fifteenth, the new radio law provided for government licensing granted by the Secretary of Commerce. Willful and malicious interference and false signals were made punishable. Frequency designations were prescribed. A distress signal was established. Provisions were made for enforcement of the treaty and for the protection of government services.

For the radio amateur, however, the message was clear: the Radio Act of 1912, for all intents and purposes of the government, was designed to spell the end of Amateur Radio.

Following the broadcasting boom of the early '20s, the law quickly became obsolete. Several attempts at enactment of an adequate federal regulatory measure failed. Gentlemen's agreements functioned well until the Zenith decision. In it, the U.S. Attorney General said the federal government had no legal control over radio except that expressly authorized in the 1912 Act, which made no reference to broadcasting or high-frequency allocations. Bedlam reigned supreme once again, this time the results of broadcasting stations jumping frequencies and increasing powers. The amateurs, consistent with their tradition of self-discipline, adhered to their assignments and did not follow the example of the broadcasters who claimed wholesale privileges at the expense of others.

In the Radio Act of 1927, the word "amateur" was used for the first time in any statute. This law created the Federal Radio Commission, and gave it the authority to: classify radio stations, prescribe the nature of the service to be rendered by each class, assign frequencies and allot power to the various classes of stations, determine their location, regulate their apparatus, make regulations either for the prevention of interference or to carry out provisions of the Act, and require logs or records of transmission. The Commission's power to license stations was to be exercised only under a prescribed standard of public interest, convenience or necessity. Secrecy of correspondence was imposed, "provided that this . . . shall not apply to the receiving, divulging, publishing, or utilizing the contents of any radio communication broadcasted or transmitted by amateurs . . . for the use of the general public . . ." With the enactment of this law, the Radio Act of 1912 was repealed. Violation of the new Act and its regulations was made criminal. The Secretary of Commerce was given authority to prescribe the qualifications of and to discipline station operators, to inspect stations, and to assign call letters.

Months after the approval of the Radio Act of 1927, more than 70 nations sent delegates to the International Radiotelegraph Conference of 1927. Just as with domestic radio law, international treaties had become antiquated, and new international control was needed to keep up with the pace of the radio art. Threats to Amateur Radio persisted. European nations' radio communication systems were government monopolies, and the amateurs represented unnecessary competition, posing a potential revenue loss. Amateurs also posed a threat to nations' security, it was felt. Additionally, there were many demands for spectrum from many different commercial services all vying for a limited number of frequencies. Participating nations made many adverse recommendations.

This was the situation faced by ARRL and the International Amateur Radio Union prior to the conference. The League battled on two fronts: On the domestic scene, ARRL worked on developing a favorable American position, and was successful. The American delegation would attempt to secure adoption internationally of the privileges afforded amateurs in the United States. On the international front, ARRL Secretary K. B. Warner and Canadian General Manager A. H. Keith Russell spoke before the entire British delegation and representatives of other groups, and won favorable consideration of American demands.

Following eight weeks of deliberations at the Conference, the world had a new International Radiotelegraph Convention; Amateur Radio was, for the first time, included in them. The frequency table finally adopted was as follows:

1715 to 2000 kHz	14,000 to 14,400 kHz
3500 to 4000 kHz	28,000 to 30,000 kHz
7000 to 7300 kHz	56,000 to 60.000 kHz

This constituted a total of 7485 kHz, as opposed to the former American segments of 12,000 kHz. To the American amateur, therefore, the treaty provisions represented a loss of approximately 37.5 percent of spectrum. Of course, for other nations, the reverse was true: foreign amateurs had greatly increased allocations.

The new agreement went into effect on January 1, 1929; it was to be on the books for only five years. A new treaty, the International Telecommunications Convention, replaced it. It had been decided upon by the Madrid conference concluded in December 1932. It was at this conference that Amateur Radio truly became recognized as a definite phenomenon of the radio art, to be preserved and protected. The amateur delegation had again been represented by ARRL and the IARU.

The Communications Act of 1934

The internal status of American amateurs was not modified appreciably but the body of whose authority they operated was modified upon the passage of the Communications Act of 1934. This Act created the Federal Communications Commission, replacing the Federal Radio Commission. To it was delegated authority formerly exercised by the radio commission in radio matters and by the Interstate Commerce Commission in wire telegraph and wire telephone matters.

Amateur interest in the new Act was principally academic. The definitions applying to Amateur Radio, the structure for licensing and regulating — all remained substantially unchanged. Similarly, the FCC perpetuated the amateur regulations of the FRC, together with the personnel actively administering amateur matters.

With the use of higher frequencies by amateurs, the abolition of spark transmitters and the gradual improvement in selectivity of broadcast receivers, the problem of amateur interference with the broadcast service lessened greatly after the summer of 1926. It is a legal cliche, however, that public reaction to annoyances is such that there is a considerable lapse of time before a legislative remedy comes about. So it has been with local attempts at regulation of Amateur Radio. During the period from 1926 to 1929 there was a scattered effort in various state legislatures and municipal councils for the enactment of legislation to protect broadcast listeners from amateur and other interference. In some instances legislation having this intention was passed, such as laws providing direct local control of radio transmission, those prescribing local taxes, restricting the hours of transmission, or dealing with the location of transmitting equipment. For six months, ARRL waged a battle in two states — first in Portland, Oregon, where the offending ordinance was revised before a test case could be consummated, and later in Wilmore, Kentucky — against the constitutionality of such ordinances.

The case of *Whitehurst v. Grimes,* wherein the U.S. District Court for the Eastern District of Kentucky held that a local ordinance imposing a privilege tax upon transmitters was void, came as a result of a suit instituted by amateur operator 9ALM, who was the sole intended victim of the ordinance, and prosecuted by Paul M. Segal, general counsel of the League. This opinion, denying municipalities the right to regulate or restrict amateur operation, has since become highly useful as a precedent in discouraging other similar attempts.

The widespread adoption of broadcast receivers installed in automobiles, beginning in 1933, introduced a new element of conflict in connection with municipal police radio service. Persons with receivers installed in automobiles would pick up police transmissions and hasten to the scene of a crime or disturbance, impeding the functioning of the police authority. In consequence, a number of state legislatures and municipal councils have passed laws declaring the installation and/or use of receivers in automobiles capable of picking up police transmissions to be illegal. Through the efforts of the ARRL, the principle that licensed amateur mobile equipment is a matter for federal regulation and not subject to local control has become generally recognized, and possessors of a federal license ordinarily experience no difficulty in securing a special local permit for the installation and operation of their equipment. Other than this undoubtedly justifiable precaution, state or municipal regulation of Amateur Radio has never been successfully imposed.

Nationally and internationally the status of Amateur Radio is secure. True, there are threats; there are other radio interests greedy for amateur territory, or jealous of amateur achievement; there may even arise a tendency on the part of the government to cater to these interests to amateur disadvantage. But the tangible strength of the amateur, politically and scientifically, is such that for the present, and for many years to come, it will require only skillful, watchful warding on the part of its duly constituted representatives to guard and maintain the amateur art.

It has been said that legislation has always been the arch enemy of Amateur Radio. It is true that legislation has limited privileges, restricted territory, imposed technical and operating requirements. But legislation has also preserved Amateur Radio, protecting it both from itself and its enemies. In 1912, had the art run wild, lacking all semblance of control, the inexorable pressure of government and commercial competition might well have meant extinction as surely as it was believed that banishment to 200 meters and down meant extinction. After the war, without the precedent of legislation and the effective aid of the legislators themselves in the Halls of Congress, the throttling hand of Navy control could well have consigned the amateur to oblivion. In 1927, had not the nations of the world been forced to sign a treaty recognizing and establishing Amateur Radio, the art which was already slowly expiring in many lands, particularly in Europe, would shortly have been made to breathe its last under the crushing boot-heel of state monopoly.

Not only has legislation meant the preservation of Amateur Radio, if in modified form; to its stringencies the amateur owes the propelling force for many of his accomplishments. Necessity is the mother of invention. Had not the amateurs been banished to 200 meters they would never have made that wavelength work as they did, nor would they have explored and developed the shortwaves; some other group, driven by their own burning necessity, would probably have given that invaluable discovery to the world. Had not the Washington convention, and subsequent growth, so compressed the amateur in his limited frequency assignments, the remarkable advances in transmission and reception methods developed by amateurs — leading all the radio world — would not have been necessitated, and these great achievements would doubtless not have been made under amateur auspices. Not only have amateurs benefited from these developments and discoveries but the citizens of all the world have seen time grow longer, distances shorter, entertainment more thrilling, business more rapid, life more satisfying — all because of Amateur Radio and the restrictions, under legislation, that progress has enforced upon it. — *Clinton DeSoto, 200 Meters and Down, ARRL, 1936*

Chapter 3

Licensing, Exams — and the Gettysburg Address

The Commission is required to make sure that folks have the smarts to operate an amateur station properly. The equipment is capable of worldwide transmission — persons *must* be qualified so that interference is avoided. FCC licensing is the manner in which the government ensures that Amateur Radio operators hold the necessary skills to carry out their operations.

Which all brings us to our old friend, Part 97. And Subpart B is the section devoted to spelling out the requirements for obtaining an Amateur Radio license.

First, let's take a look at some key definitions:

Definitions

Operator license: When a basic amateur license is issued, it contains two "licenses" (see Page 2-3): the operator license and the station license. The operator license gives the individual the FCC's permission to operate an amateur station, and has the operator's license class and privileges.

Station license: The second part, the station license, is the ticket that allows an Amateur Radio station to operate. Every station must have one. The call sign is always a part of the station license; call signs are issued to stations, not to operators! Some RACES, club and military recreation groups have station call signs issued for stations established before 1978. (These are discussed later.)

Primary station: The principal amateur station at a specific land location shown on the station license.

Eligibility

Just who is eligible to hold an Amateur Radio license? The following rule says it all: *Anyone except a representative of a foreign government is eligible for an amateur operator license.*

If your name happens to be James Bond, 007, of Her Majesty's Secret Service — forget it; don't bother applying for a U.S. amateur ticket. But if you're simply a U.S. or foreign citizen — go for it!

Eligibility for an amateur station license is a bit more involved because there are a few different kinds of station licenses. Basically, a station license will be issued only to a licensed amateur operator, and in most cases the operator and station licenses are issued on the same slip of paper. The FCC issues your station a primary station license, which is required before any Amateur Radio gear may be operated at that station. And every operator must have only *one* primary station license.

In special cases, other types of station licenses exist: (1) a *club station* license authorizes operation at a bona fide Amateur Radio organization or society, (2) a *military recreation station* license allows for a station at a land location provided for the recreational use of amateur operators under military auspices of the Armed Forces of the U.S., and (3) a *RACES station* license allows for civil defense work.

It's important to point out that the Commission no longer issues new club, military recreation or RACES station licenses, but FCC will renew and modify existing ones. This recent move was consistent with the Commission's ongoing philosophy of unregulation — the government's "hands-off" regulatory policy. In the past, FCC has abolished special station licenses for repeaters, auxiliary stations and secondary stations.

License Classes, Privileges and Exams

There are five classes of amateur operator licenses, each carrying its own special requirements and privileges. Each class of license will be issued only to persons who have passed the associated exam elements. Since operating privileges increase with each class, the degree of difficulty of the class exams increase in the same way. The following table sets forth the requirements and privileges of each class:

License Terms

Amateur operator and station licenses are normally good for 10 years from the

---

Amateur Operator Licenses*

Class	Code Test	Written Examination	Privileges
Novice	5 wpm (Element 1A)	Elementary theory and regulations (Element 2)	Telegraphy in 3700-3750, 7100-7150, 21,100-21,200 and 28,100-28,200 kHz; 200 watts PEP output max.
Technician	5 wpm (Element 1A)	Elementary theory and regulations; general-level theory and regulations. (Elements 2 and 3)	All amateur privileges above 50.0 MHz plus Novice privileges.
General	13 wpm (Element 1B)	Elementary theory and regulations; general theory and regulations. (Elements 2 and 3)	All amateur privileges except those reserved for Advanced and Extra Class; see Section 97.7(a) and (b)
Advanced	13 wpm (Element 1B)	General theory and regulations, plus intermediate theory. (Elements 2, 3 and 4A)	All amateur privileges except those reserved to Extra Class; see Section 97.7(a).
Amateur Extra Class	20 wpm (Element 1C)	General theory and regulations, intermediate theory, plus special exam on advanced techniques. (Elements 2, 3, 4A and 4B)	All amateur privileges

*A licensed radio amateur will be required to pass only those elements that are not included in the examination for the amateur license currently held.

---

issuing date on a new, modified or renewed license. Two year grace periods allow for reinstatement of expired licenses. If your license was issued before January 1, 1984, you have a five-year grace period. After two years, however, you will be issued a new call.

Novice Exams

New procedures for giving Novice class exams were adopted in mid-1983. Under the old program, an applicant for a Novice class ticket was required to pass a code test given by a volunteer examiner. The examiner then sent the applicant's completed Form 610 to Gettysburg FCC and requested a Novice written test. Gettysburg would mail out the written portion, which would then be administered and returned to Gettysburg by the volunteer Novice examiner. The applicant had to wait several weeks before learning the results. This was a tedious process for the applicant and the examiner, and posed a significant paperwork burden for the FCC Licensing Division staff.

Under the new program, the tests are no longer issued by Gettysburg. Instead, the volunteer examiner will devise his or her own written exam based on a Commission-approved pool of publicly released questions (available from ARRL Hq. or any FCC Field Office). Thus, the intermediary step of obtaining the test papers from Gettysburg is eliminated.

Why publish the question pool? A person taking the Novice test must answer 20 questions about Amateur Radio rules, theory and practice. These are drawn from the pool of 200 questions, which are all based on the FCC Element 2 Novice study guide. Publishing the question pool certainly does not give the test away. The Federal Aviation Administration has used this procedure for testing pilots with excellent results. A 200-item pool of questions is sufficiently large; memorization is no shortcut!

How is the test to be given? The code test should be administered prior to the written exam. The code test will be administered as before; the new changes affect only the written portion of the test. The 5-wpm Novice code test may be 5 minutes of a conversation followed by 10 questions, 7 of which must be answered correctly to pass. Or, the examiner may ask for one minute of solid copy out of 5 minutes of plain text. The question pool for the written exam has been subdivided by the FCC into 20 blocks of 10 questions each. An applicant must answer one question, selected by the examiner, from each of the 20 blocks. Fifteen or more correct answers are needed to pass the test.

Upon passing both the code and written tests administered by the Novice examiner, the applicant fills out an FCC Form 610. Then, the examiner completes Section II-A on the back, indicating that both the code and written elements were passed. FCC's November 1985 deletion of Section 97.26(h) of the Rules means that applicants for all license classes no longer must wait 30 days before retesting a failed exam element. The Commission revised PR Bulletin 1035A (Element 2 Examination Questions) to ensure that Novice applicants could not immediately retest the same examination(s) just failed. FCC instructs volunteer examiners giving Novice examinations not to use the same questions or the same telegraphy test when retesting an applicant.

The completed application is sent to the FCC in Gettysburg. The Novice examination papers must be retained for one year by the examiner. Since the FCC Licensing staff does not need to handle test papers or grade tests, the process of issuing a license proceeds much more quickly.

What happened to the multiple-choice answers?

The FCC has issued only the questions in PR Bulletin 1035-A, including this note of explanation: "The examiners may use their discretion as to the form of the examination. It may be a single-answer test, a multiple choice or essay type." This opens several possibilities for the examiner. The test may be conducted entirely on an oral "interview" basis, with the examiner asking the questions and the applicant responding. Alternatively, the test may be conducted in written form with fill-in-the-blank or short essay questions.

Novice examiners are also free to construct true/false and multiple-choice versions of the test in the field. This approach may be preferred by some people, particularly for large test sessions. For those of you who find the new Novice examination process a bit confusing, the ARRL will be issuing a *multiple choice* version of the question pool along with complete instructions to examiners and applicants. The League's version of the FCC Novice exam is available from ARRL Headquarters; ask for the "ARRL Novice Test." There is no charge for the test, but an s.a.s.e. is welcome. It's suggested that·such requests be limited to a maximum of five copies; if more are needed, the tests may be photocopied.

Who may give the Novice test?

Commission Rules list the qualifications for persons who administer a Novice class test. *Each Novice examiner must*

1) hold a current General, Advanced or Extra Class operator license issued by the Commission;

2) be at least 18 years of age;

3) not be related to the applicant;

4) never have had an Amateur Radio station license or Amateur Radio operator's license suspended or revoked;

5) not own a significant interest in or be an employee of any company or other entity engaged in the manufacture or distribution of equipment used in connection with Amateur Radio transmissions, or in the preparation or distribution of any publication used in preparing for obtaining amateur station operator licenses.

Technician and Higher Class Exams

Welcome to the Volunteer Examiner Program! The job that used to be the FCC's now lies with the amateur community itself. Let's take a look at the new examination procedures.

Amateur Radio licensees acting as FCC-accredited Volunteer Examiners (VEs) administer exams at specified locations and times following public announcement. Examples of locations are public halls, schools, conventions and hamfests, club meetings and flea markets. The VEs are present and observe candidates throughout the entire exam process, and are responsible for its proper conduct and supervision. Each candidate must present the examiners with a completed Form 610 on or before the registration deadline if pre-registration is required. Otherwise, applicants will pass along the completed Form 610 to the examiners at the exam session prior to the beginning of the exam. If registration deadlines are imposed, they will be determined by the Volunteer Examiner Coordinator issuing the exam papers to the VEs. Candidates are required by FCC to bring thorough identification documents, including their original (nonphotocopy) license documents.

The candidate must comply with the instructions given by the examiners. The examiners must immediately terminate the exam if the candidate should deviate from the instructions. At the end of the exam, the candidate must turn the test papers over to the examiner.

Candidates with physical disabilities who require special exam procedures must attach a statement to the Form 610. The statement, which will be kept by the VEC, must include a physician's certification indicating the nature of the disability, and the names of the persons taking and transcribing the applicant's dictation of test questions and answers, if such a procedure is necessary.

There is no longer a waiting period before reexamination after failing an exam element. FCC requires, however, that VECs not use the same set of exam questions in successive exam sessions to insure that "re-test" doesn't mean "remembering." Most VECs have informed the League that they will not normally retest a candidate on the same day.

The 13-wpm code test [Element 1(B)] and the 20-wpm code test (Element 1(C)] must be prepared by the examiners or be obtained by the examiners from the VEC. The person preparing these tests must hold an Amateur Extra Class license. The test must prove the applicant's ability to receive the code at the prescribed speeds. The sending test, although still in the rules, is no longer *required* by the FCC. In the case of applicants with physical disabilities, the code test may be administered based on his or her methods of transcribing code; for example, by the use of such devices as loud-speaker transducers for deaf persons. The applicant is responsible for knowing, and may be tested on, the 26 letters of the alphabet, the numerals 0-9, the period, comma and question mark, and procedural signals $\overline{AR}$, $\overline{SK}$, $\overline{BT}$ and $\overline{DN}$.

The formula for creating written tests [Elements 3, 4(A) and 4(B)] will be determined by the FCC. The VEC selects questions for each test from the appropriate pool of questions approved by the Commission. The VEC must keep exam designs in confidence. For copies of the question pools released by the FCC for any exam class, send an s.a.s.e. to ARRL Hq. or any FCC Field Office. The FCC welcomes question suggestions from amateurs. Extra Class hams may submit questions for any exam element. Advanced class licensees may submit questions only for the Technician/General and Novice class exams. Tech/General licensees may also submit questions for the Novice class exams.

Each exam for Technician and higher is administered by a team of three accredited Volunteer Examiners. These examiners must hold Extra Class licenses, unless they are giving the 5-wpm code test and/or the Tech/General Element 3 written test, in which case they may be Extra or Advanced class hams. Novice tests, as in the past, may be administered by one radio amateur who holds a General, Advanced or Extra Class ticket.

Upon completion of the exam, the examiners immediately grade the test papers. Applicants who fail will be notified of their percentage score, and their Form 610s will be returned. The test papers will be forwarded to the VEC for filing. When the applicant passes an exam element, the examiners issue a certificate stating this. This certificate is required for already-licensed applicants operating with newly acquired privileges of a class higher than that of their permanent license. It serves the same purpose as the FCC's former interim permit concept, under which the applicant could operate with new privileges prior to receiving the permanent ticket from Gettysburg. The certificate also carries with it a one-year credit for those code elements passed when taking subsequent exams.

When the candidate passes all of the exam elements for a higher class license, the examiners must certify the following information on the candidate's application form: (1) examiners' names and call signs; (2) examiners' qualifications to give the test; and (3) examiners' signed statements that the applicant has passed the required exam elements. Within 10 days of the exam, the examiners must send the test papers and application of a successful candidate to the VEC, who processes the data before sending it on to the FCC Licensing Office in Gettysburg.

The FCC may reexamine any applicant who obtained an operator license through the volunteer examination process. In fact, FCC reserves the right to give exams itself but will *not* routinely offer test opportunities at Field Offices. These checks and balances will promote integrity and flexibility in the exam process.

As before, applicants pass a written examination if they answer at least 74 percent of the questions correctly. Applicants pass a code test if they prove their ability to receive correctly by ear texts in Morse code at the prescribed speed. Each five characters count as one word; each punctuation mark and numeral count as two characters. The FCC Rules still specify one minute of perfect copy as the criterion for passing the code test, but the FCC also accepts the recent practice of correctly answering 7 of 10 questions based on the 5-minute code test transmission.

Volunteer Examiners

To be accredited by the VEC as a Volunteer Examiner, you must be 18 years old and not related to the candidate. You cannot hold a significant interest in, or be an employee of, any company or other entity that manufactures equipment or publishes study materials of interest to radio amateurs. However, employees who can show that they do not normally communicate with that part of an entity engaged in such manufacture or publishing is eligible to be a VE. VEs may not accept any money for their services. If your license has ever been suspended or revoked, the FCC will not accept your services as a VE.

Finding an Exam Opportunity

To determine when and where an exam will be given, contact your VEC, local club or repeater group. The ARRL/VEC offers information on test activity "all over." Chances are they'll steer you in the right direction. One of the major benefits of the Volunteer Examiner Program is enhanced exam opportunity, an answer to the very limited exam sessions given in the past by FCC.

Volunteer Examiner Coordinators

The VECs are umbrella organizations that serve as interfaces between the Commission and the field Volunteer Examiners. They coordinate the efforts of VEs, print and distribute exam papers to VEs based on monthly test designs provided by FCC, and forward successful applicants' Form 610s to the Commission licensing division.

Volunteer Examiner Coordinators (VECs) have entered into an agreement with the FCC, and have met certain qualifications. A VEC must be organized at least partially for the purpose of furthering Amateur Radio, and be at least regional in scope. It must be able to serve at least one of the FCC's call sign districts, and agree to coordinate test sessions for all classes of license exams (except, of course, Novice). The VECs agree that candidates eligible to take the tests will be registered without regard to race, sex, religion, national origin or membership (or lack thereof) in any Amateur Radio organization.

VECs must not have a conflict of interest. An entity (organization or company) that manufactures or distributes ham gear, or prepares ham radio license study materials may be a VEC only upon showing the Commission that preventive measures have been taken to eliminate any possible conflict of interest.

VECs coordinate the dates and times for scheduling exams set by the local VE teams throughout areas that are regulated by the FCC. A VEC may coordinate scheduling of testing opportunities at other places — U.S. military bases around the world, for example.

It's the VEC's job to accredit a broad range of hams to be Volunteer Examiners, regardless of race, sex, religion or national origin. A VEC may not refuse to accredit a volunteer on the basis of membership (or lack thereof) in an Amateur Radio organization. However, a VEC must *not* accredit a volunteer to be an examiner if (1) he or she does not meet the VE qualifications (see above); (2) the FCC refuses to accept the services of the volunteer; (3) the VEC refuses to accept the services of the volunteer; (4) the VEC determines that the volunteer is not competent to perform the function of a VE; and (5) the VEC determines that questions of the volunteer's integrity or honesty could compromise the exam.

It is the VEC's job to assemble, print and distribute written exams to VEs that are designed according to the FCC's formula. At the completion of each exam, the VEC collects the candidates' application forms, answer sheets and test results from the VEs. Then, the VEC records the date and place of the test, the names of the VEs and their qualifications, the names of the candidates, test results and any related information. It screens applications for completeness and authenticity, and forwards them within 10 days to the FCC's Gettysburg licensing unit. The VEC has available exam records upon FCC request.

VECs are expected to evaluate the clarity and accuracy of exam questions on the basis of experience in the field, and to bring to the attention of the FCC any ambiguous or inaccurate questions.

The FCC has established temporary identifier codes for each class of license. This code will be a slant (/) followed by a two-letter group: KT for Technician class, AG for General class, AA for Advanced class, and AE for Amateur Extra Class. The ID code must be shown on the certificate issued to an applicant on successful completion of the exam. It must be added as a suffix to the licensee's call sign when the licensee operates under temporary authority granted to hams who have passed the requirements for a higher class of license.

Examination Credit

Credit for exam elements will be given only in very narrow circumstances. First, someone already holding a license will be required to pass only those elements of the higher-class exam that are not included in the test for the amateur license already held. Code-credit certificates will be given to amateurs who successfully complete the code element, but who fail the associated written element for a given license class exam. This means that an applicant who passes the Extra Class code (20 wpm) but fails the Extra written portion, need take only the written exam again. Code credit certificates are valid for one year.

Applicants are given code credit if within the past five years they held a commercial radiotelegraph operator license or permit issued by the FCC. Other than these cases, no other examination credit will be granted, although the FCC is *considering* a rules change to permit credit for written elements to be granted in the future.

Protection For FCC Monitoring Stations

If you're planning a fixed or portable station operation near an FCC Monitor-

---

Table 1

FCC Monitoring Stations

Allegan Monitoring Station — P.O. Box 89, Allegan, MI 49010 Phone: 616-673-3055

Anchorage Monitoring Station — P.O. Box 2955, Anchorage, AK 99510 Phone: 907-243-2153

Belfast Monitoring Station — P.O. Box 470, Belfast, ME 04915 Phone: 207-338-4088

Douglas Monitoring Station — P.O. Box 6, Douglas, AZ 85607 Phone: 602-364-3414

Ferndale Monitoring Station — P.O. Box 1125, Ferndale, WA 98248 Phone: 206-354-4892

Fort Lauderdale Monitoring Station — P.O. Box 16027, Fort Lauderdale, FL 33318 Phone: 305-473-9845, 305-472-5511 (recorded information)

Grand Island Monitoring Station — P.O. Box 1588, Grand Island, NE 68801 Phone: 308-382-4296

Kingsville Monitoring Station — P.O. Box 632, Kingsville, TX 78363 Phone: 512-592-2531

Laurel Monitoring Station — P.O. Box 250, Columbia, MD 21045 Phone: 301-725-3474

Livermore Monitoring Station — P. O. Box 311, Livermore, CA 94550 Phone: 415-447-3614

Powder Springs Monitoring Station — P.O. Box 85, Powder Springs, GA 30073 Phone: 404-943-5420

Sabana Seca Monitoring Station — P.O. Box FCC, Sabana Seca, PR 00749 Phone: 809-784-3772

Waipahu Monitoring Station — P. O. Box 1035, Waipahu, HI 96797 Phone: 808-677-3954

---

ing Station (see Table 1 for location and addresses), you should consult with the Field Operations Bureau of the FCC, Washington, D.C. 20554 (tel. 202-632-6980) for possible need to protect the FCC stations from harmful interference.

The Commission may add a clause to the station license for special protection. If you consult with the Commission before filing an application for a station license, chances are you will avoid FCC objections. A word to the wise who are putting together a fixed station within a mile of a monitoring station!

FCC Modifications

The Federal Communications Commission reserves the right to modify your license at any time if it determines that such action is in the public interest, convenience and necessity. At the same time, however, FCC must issue an order for the licensee to show cause why his or her license should not be modified. If the licensee fails to explain adequately why the license should not be modified, or fails to take an active interest in the proceeding, the amateur's license may be changed temporarily or permanently.

Forms, forms, forms

Amateurs and other persons must use Form 610 for renewal of their primary station and operator licenses, modifications such as change of address or call sign, reinstatement of licenses that have expired within the two-year grace period and requests for new Novice licenses. Only the June 1984 and later editions of FCC Form 610 may be used. Applying on earlier editions of the form will delay issuance of your license: Your application will be returned without action and you will be required to refile on a current form.

Club, military recreation and RACES station license renewal or modification applications must be made on FCC Form 610-B (see page 3-13). Alien applications for reciprocal operating permission in the U.S. must be made on FCC Form 610-A. The volunteer examiner team (VET) report at the top of page one is filled out by the VET at the time of the examination. (More on this later.) Applicants should go right to Section I.

Complete **Section I** if you're applying either for a new or upgraded license, or renewal, reinstatement or modification of your present license.

Item 1 — First, attach a photocopy (or the original) of your license and/or interim permit. If you've lost the license or permit (or it was destroyed), simply explain the circumstances in a note attached to the form.

Item 2—This item specifies the purpose of the application: new license, renewal, reinstatement, call sign change (see page 3-13), name change, address change or station location change. Simply check the appropriate box and any corresponding blanks provided to the right of the item. For example, if you're applying for a reinstatement of your license which expired less than two years ago, you would check box 2B and follow the corresponding arrows to fill in the applicable boxes EXPIRATION DATE and LICENSE CLASS.

Important note concerning call signs: Licensees who do not already hold a call sign reflecting their license class may request a call-sign change. All call signs are selected by the Commission, and requests by amateurs for specific call signs will not be honored. If you already hold a call sign reflecting your license class, you are not eligible for a call-sign change unless you are changing your mailing address to a new call-sign district. All amateurs have the option of keeping their present call signs under all circumstances, even if moving to another call-sign district or upgrading to a higher-class license. The Commission will not change your call sign unless you request it and are eligible for a change. Once the change is made, however, your previous call sign cannot be reinstated. Details of the call-sign assignment system can be found on page 3-13.

Item 3—List your call sign if you hold one.

Item 4—Give your operator class and, if applicable, your operator class listed on your interim permit.

Item 5—Enter your name and any suffix such as Jr. or III. Remember that your name must agree with your signature in Item 16.

Item 6—Give your birthdate in the form 12-25-53.

Item 7—Give your current mailing address. Remember that the address must be in the U.S. or its territories. A postal box, RFD number or General Delivery is sufficient. Keep in mind that you will be responsible for all FCC mail sent to that address.

Item 8—Give your current station location (it may be different than that of your mailing address in Item 7). The station location address must be a specific geographical location, *not* a box number. This address must also be within the U.S., American Samoa, Baker Island, Canton Island, Enderbury Island, Guam, Howland Island, Jarvis Island, Johnston Island, Kingman Reef, Kure Island, Midway Island, Navassa Island, Wake Island and Wilkes Island. Any other location is not within FCC jurisdiction.

Item 9—Most amateurs will check "no" to this major action question. A "major action" is defined in the rules as (a) a new antenna or structure, or an increase in height of an existing structure by more than 10%, which results in a final height of over 300 feet, (b) facilities which are to be located in an officially designated wilderness area, wildlife preserve area or a nationally recognized scenic and recreational area, or facilities which will affect sites significant in American History and (c) construction which involves extensive changes in surface features. If the answer to Item 9 is "yes," you must submit the required Environmental Impact Narrative Statement (EINS) along with your application.

Items 10, 11 and 12—If you have any other Amateur Radio application on file with the Commission that has not been acted upon (a renewal, for example), answer "yes." Enter the purpose of the other application in Item 11 and the date it was filed in Item 12.

Item 13—If you've failed an amateur exam within the last 30 days, answer "yes" and give the class of license exam in Item 14 and the date of the exam in Item 15. If the answer to Item 13 is "no" simply disregard items 14 and 15.

Item 16—Sign the application certifying that your statements are true, complete and correct to the best of your knowledge. Date the application in Item 17.

Section II-A is completed by the volunteer examiner who passed a Novice applicant. The information provided by the VE helps the FCC determine if he/she meets the VE requirements. The VE must send the completed form to Gettysburg within 10 days of the successful exam.

Section II-B deals with Technician, General, Advanced and Extra class exams. This section is filled out by all three volunteer examiners (VEs) who will be administering the upgrade test to the applicant. All the VEs must put in the information that qualifies them to be VEs in the first place. It's a way the FCC can keep tabs on who's giving exams.

The applicant should fill out Section I prior to the examination date. If advance registration is required, the applicant should make sure the form is in the hands of the VE team before the registration cut-off date. If advance registration is not required, the applicant can simply bring the completed form to the test site. The VE Team will take it from there.

Before the test, the VET fills out the VET report for each applicant, checking the appropriate boxes, giving exam credit wherever it's due. The team gives the code exams first—5, 13 and 20 WPM in order. The tests are graded as they are completed. Then, the written tests are given and graded, and the VET fills in the appropriate boxes on the Form 610. If the applicant fails to upgrade, the application is returned.

If he or she passes, the VET enters the name of the VEC in item F of the VET report. The place and date of the examination must be entered as well. For more on VEC-sponsored exams, see September and October 1984, and July 1985, *QST*.

All applications except registrations for VEC-sponsored exams should be sent to FCC, Gettysburg, PA 17325. While there are no fees for filing applications for license renewal and modification, you may have to pay up to $4.29 to take a VEC-sponsored examination. The Form 610, 610-A and 610-B are available from FCC offices or ARRL Headquarters, 225 Main St., Newington, CT 06111.

If you have not received a response from the FCC concerning your application within 90 days, write to the Gettysburg FCC office. Include in your letter a photocopy of your application, or the following information: name and address, birthdate, present call sign and class of license, date of application, volunteer examiner's name (if Novice exam), Field Office location (if FCC-supervised exam), or VEC (if VEC-supervised exam).

Renewals/Modifications

What is the meaning of life? How does man fit into the scheme of things? How do I renew my license? — a weighty question, indeed.

To renew your license, follow these simple commandments:

1) Complete Form 610, being careful not to miss any applicable boxes or blanks that apply. Only the June 1984 and later editions of FCC Form 610 may be used.

2) Attach a photocopy (or the original) of your license to Form 610.

3) Mail your application to FCC, Gettysburg, PA 17325.

It's a good idea to retain copies of everything. Make a note of the day you mailed the application. If you file before the expiration date of your license, you may continue to operate your station beyond expiration while waiting for your new ticket. Failure to check all appropriate boxes and fill in all applicable blanks will cause your application to be returned.

Q. But my license has already expired. Can I still renew it?

A. Affirmative—under a *period of grace*. If you have a license good for a five-year term, its grace period, should you fail to renew, is five years. After two years of the grace period has elapsed, you will lose your call sign and will be assigned a new one. (Note that the new 10-year-term licenses, which have been issued since January 1984, have a 2-year grace period.) To renew an amateur license, use FCC Form 610, which is available from FCC or ARRL HQ. There is *no* fee for renewing an amateur license

Note that if you apply for renewal under the grace period (that is, after your license has expired), you must not operate until your new license arrives.

Q. I believe that my license was destroyed accidentally. How do I get a new one?

A. A formal application is not necessary. Simply mail a letter explaining the situation to FCC in Gettysburg. They'll provide you with a duplicate license. If the original license is later found, it or the duplicate should be returned to the Commission's Gettysburg office with a brief letter of explanation.

Q. I've recently moved. How do I notify the FCC?

A. You must file a Form 610 with the Gettysburg office. Note: When applying for modifications such as change of address, the Commission will automatically renew your license along with the modification.

Antenna Structures

Most amateurs probably will not come up against antenna restrictions specified in Part 97 unless they plan to erect an antenna in excess of 200 feet in height, or live near an airport. Many amateurs *are* faced with city ordinances, and/or covenants which limit the location and height of antennas, however. Let's take a look at these restrictions and how they may affect everything from a random wire to that "Big Gun" antenna installation.

Q. *My city has an ordinance which clearly prohibits amateur radio antenna installations. Are there any federal rulings which preempt such ordinances?*

A. Yes, there is an FCC declaratory ruling which announced a *limited* preemption policy. It's called PRB-1. In its *Memorandum Opinion and Order* in PRB-1, the Commission declared, in part, that "state and local regulations that operate to preclude amateur communications in their communities are in direct conflict with federal objectives and must be preempted." We offer its full text in the Appendix, page 164.

Q. *Does this mean that I can ignore the "no antenna" clause in my apartment lease?*

A. No. The Commission exercises no federal preemption over restrictive covenants and *private* contractual agreements such as your lease. Also, the decision does not cover restrictions found in homeowners' association agreements and deed restrictions. (*Memorandum Opinion and Order* in Docket PRB-1)

Q. *My antenna would exceed the height limitation specified in my city ordinance. Am I protected by federal preemption?*

A. It depends. The Commission stated that it would not specify any particular height limitation below which local governments could not regulate. (*Memorandum Opinion and Order* in Docket PRB-1) It noted, however, that: " . . . Local regulations which involve placement, screening, or height of antennas based on health, safety, or aesthetic considerations must be crafted to accommodate reasonably amateur communications, and to represent the minimum practicable regulation to accomplish the local authority's legitimate purpose." The line between legitimate amateur communication goals and the local authority's interests should be determined at the local level.

Q. *In filling out my Form 610, I noticed that Item 9 of Section I asks if a Commission grant of the proposed communication facility would constitute a "major action." What is meant by "major action"?*

A. According to Section 1.1305 of the Commission's rules, a major action is defined, among other things, as: (a) Antenna towers or supporting structures which exceed 300 feet in height; (b) facilities which are located in officially designated wilderness areas, or in areas whose designation as wilderness areas is pending consideration, wildlife preserves, or a nationally recognized scenic or recreational area, or facilities which will affect sites significant in American history; (c) construction which involves extensive changes in surface features.

Q. *What must I do if my antenna installation constitutes a major action?*

A. You must submit an environmental impact narrative statement along with your application Form 610. This statement must include all of the information in Section 1.1311, including: a description of the antenna design and the surrounding environment including power lines and access roads; local use of the surrounding area; zoning classification; rationale for selection of the site; a statement as to whether the construction of the communications facility has been a source of local controversy; and a discussion of steps you took or could take to minimize the adverse environmental impact of the proposed communications facility.

Q. *I live near an airport. What regulations must I keep in mind when erecting my antenna?*

1) Refer to Fig. 1. If you live near an airport that has a long runway (3200 feet in length or more) and is listed in either the *Airport Directory* or the current *Airman's Information Manual,* or is operated by a Federal military agency, you must

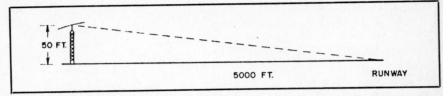

Fig. 1—If you live near an airport runway *more than* 3200 feet long, you must notify the FAA and FCC if your antenna will exceed heights limited by a slope of 100 to 1.

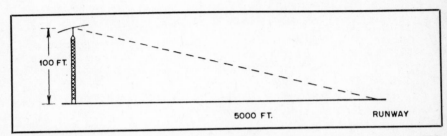

Fig. 2—Where airport runways are *less than* 3200 feet long, you must notify the FAA and FCC if your antenna will exceed heights limited by slope of 50 to 1.

file FAA Form 7460-1 (available at FAA regional offices) and FCC Form 854 (available from your nearest FCC Field Office) with the Commission if your antenna construction will exceed heights limited by an imaginary surface extending outward and upward at a slope of 100 to 1. For example, your tower, 5000 feet away from the nearest runway, must not exceed 50 feet in height if you wish to avoid notifying FCC. A convenient equation for calculating these height limitations is

$$\frac{\text{distance from nearest runway in feet}}{\text{slope}} = \text{antenna height limitation}$$

Using our example,

$$\frac{5000}{100} = 50 \text{ feet}$$

2) Refer to Fig. 2. If you live near an airport with its longest runway *under* 3200 feet in length (excluding heliports and seaplane bases without specified boundaries), then the limiting slope is a figure ot 50 to 1. Using our equation, if you live 5000 feet away from the nearest runway, you may install an antenna up to 100 feet in height without notifying FCC on Form 854 or FAA on Form 7460-1.

3) Refer to Fig. 3. If you live near a heliport listed in the *Airport Directory* or operated by a Federal military agency, you're limited to an antenna height limitation slope of 25 to 1. This means that if your antenna will be constructed 5000 feet away from the nearest take-off and landing area of the heliport, your tower must not exceed 200 feet unless you submit the Form 854 application.

Q. The phrase "near an airport" is very vague. Can you be more specific?

A. Yes — actually what you are concerned with is the distance from the nearest point of the nearest runway of each airport or heliport. In case 1 where the longest runway is longer than 3200 feet, you're affected by these restrictions if you live within 20,000

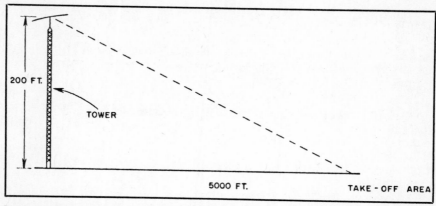

Fig. 3—If there is a heliport near your antenna location, you must notify the FAA and FCC if your antenna will exceed heights limited by a slope of 25 to 1.

feet of the nearest runway. In case 2, where the longest runway is less than 3200 feet long, you're concerned with the additional antenna restrictions if you live within 10,000 feet. And finally, in case 3, you're again affected if you live within 5000 feet of the nearest take-off and landing area of a heliport.

Q. *But what if my tower will be shielded by trees in my backyard?*

A. You may wish to apply for an exemption. If your antenna will be shielded by existing structures such as buildings, trees or hills—so that air traffic would not be adversely affected—file FCC Form 854 requesting exemptions with the Antenna Survey Branch, FCC, Washington DC 20554.

Q. *Are there any other cases in which special application is not required?*

A. Yes — special application is not necessary for antennas of 20 feet or less, except one that would increase the height of another antenna structure.

Further details as to whether an aeronautical study and/or obstruction marking and lighting are required may be obtained from Part 17 of the Commission's rules, "Construction, Marking, and Lighting of Antenna Structures."

Club Stations

A few years ago, the Commission decided that certain special station licenses were luxuries we could not afford. Provisions for issuance of *new* RACES, repeater, auxiliary, military-recreation, special event, secondary and club station tickets were felled under the FCC's deregulatory blade. These various types of special operation are still permitted, of course, but under the auspices of your primary license. FCC *will,* however, continue to modify and renew *existing* club, RACES, and military-recreation station licenses.

Q. *Our club holds a club station license. How do we go about changing our mailing address on record with the FCC?*

A. Take your life into your hands and complete a *Form 610-B.* This form is entitled *Application For Amateur Club Or Military Recreation Station License,* and is one of three in the series of 610 forms.

To change your mailing address for the club or to make any other modification, the station trustee sends the completed Form 610-B to FCC, Gettysburg, PA 17325. FCC will, in turn, modify the license and send it back to the trustee in about a month. The modified club station ticket will bear the same expiration date as the trustee's primary station license. In all cases, the club call sign is retained.

Q. How do we go about renewing the club license?

A. Simply have the station trustee complete the form 610-B, and send it to Gettysburg along with his or her own Form 610 for renewal of the primary station license (remember, the two tickets run for the same duration).

Q. Who is responsible for the proper operation of our club station?

A. The station trustee, together with the control operator, is responsible for the station's operation. The control operator may operate the station up to the privileges of his or her own operator license only. If the privileges in use exceed those of the station trustee's, however, then the station i-d must consist of the club station's call sign followed by the home station call of the control op: WA1JUY/WB1CWD, for example.

Q. How come I got my renewed primary license back three weeks before the renewed club ticket?

A. The trustee will receive his or her renewed primary license two to three weeks before the renewed club ticket is returned because the FCC's primary licensing system is automated and therefore beats the time required for the manual club ticket processing.

Q. Our new club, the Newington Amateur Radio and Vibraphone Society, wants to set up a station at our club headquarters. Since no club station licenses are being issued, what are we supposed to do for station authorization?

A. Designate a responsible member of your group as a station caretaker. Since no club station license is involved, there is no need to inform FCC of your actions. The club station uses the caretaker's own primary station license for authorization and call sign for ID purposes. The caretaker is operating his or her own station in portable operation (at a fixed location, the club hq., away from the station location shown on the caretaker's home ticket). As always, the station licensee (the caretaker) and the duty control operator are responsible for the proper operation of the station.

Call Signs — What the Well-Dressed Ham Will Be Wearing This Year

What's the latest in call-sign fashions from the FCC's spring collection? Let's review the entire amateur institution of call signs.

Q. What is the FCC's call-sign policy?

A. All amateurs not holding calls that reflect their license class are eligible for new calls. (Refer to the Table: Group A calls are assigned to Amateur Extra Class licensees; Group B calls go to Advanced class ops; Group C calls to Technicians and Generals; and Group D calls are issued to Novice class operators.) In addition, amateurs are eligible for new call signs, (1) when upgrading license class, and (2) when moving to a new call-sign district.

Q. Can I keep my present call?

A. Yes — a call sign will not be changed unless the licensee specifically requests, and is eligible for, a call-sign change. Licensees always have the option of keeping their present calls when they renew, upgrade, change station location, change mailing address or change name.

Q. How do I apply for a call-sign change?

A. To request a change, an eligible licensee must place a mark in Item 2E on the latest Form 610 (don't use the old form dated August 1980; the Commission will process only applications made on the current form dated June 1984 or later). Important note: If you do *not* want a new call sign, *do not* check box 2E!

Q. I'm moving to a new call area and want a new call sign. What group will it be issued from?

A. You will receive a call sign from the group that corresponds to your license class and new call area. If you presently hold a "preferred" call under the old rules, you may lose this preferred status should you choose a new call. (A hypothetical situation: An old-timer, Eliot, W1MJ, moves to Stratocaster, Nebraska and applies for a change in mailing address and call sign. Since he is a General class licensee, the Commission will issue him a General class call, Group C 1 × 3 format, such as NØAOK, *not* another 1 × 2 call.)

Q. Is it possible to receive a secondary station call sign?

A. No. Secondary licenses will not be issued, renewed or modified. A holder of a secondary station license may request that his or her secondary station call sign become the primary station call (this request may be made up to two years following the expiration date of the secondary license).

Q. How many call signs are available for distribution?

A. For the contiguous 48 states, there are approximately 100,000 calls in Group A. Groups B and C have roughly 500,000 call signs each. Group D has a whopping 7.2 million. There are enough to last a while. Phase I started with blocks containing never-before-issued call signs, in most instances, to prevent the assignment of a call already assigned to another station. No schedule has been established for recovering formerly assigned call signs now unassigned. Present policy calls for the assignment of call signs from the next lower group when the existing group's call-sign supply is depleted. For example, once the block number 92 is depleted in Group A, Extra Class licensees will be issued calls from block 93, which is Group B.

Q. How does the Commission decide which call sign to issue?

A. Calls are issued sequentially and systematically. Once the calls in a certain block

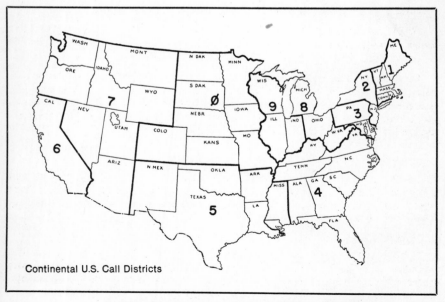

Continental U.S. Call Districts

(see the Table) are assigned, the next block is opened for use by the Commission. Group A (Amateur Extra Class call signs) is divided into 92 blocks. Blocks 1, 2 and 3 are the K-, N- and W-prefixed "1 × 2" calls. Blocks 4 through 13 contain AA- through AK-prefixed "2 × 1" call signs such as AJ1R. Block 83 contains the AA- prefixed "2 × 2" call signs — AA6DX, for example. In Group B, the Commission began issuing call signs from block 2 (except in the first call area where block 1 calls were first used). An example of a Group B call sign is KB6FR. Group C calls were first issued from block 2 — N1AFQ, for example. And last, but not least, Group D call signs were first issued from block 1. An example of a Group D call is KA0HJD.

United States Radio Districts

District No. 1, 1600 Customhouse, India & State Sts., Boston, MA 02109. The states of *Connecticut, Maine, Massachusetts, New Hampshire, Rhode Island* and *Vermont.*

District No. 2, 201 Varick St., corner of Houston St., New York, NY 10014. In the state of *New York,* the counties of Albany, Bronx, Columbia, Delaware, Dutchess, Greene, Kings, Nassau, New York, Orange, Putnam, Queens, Rensselaer, Richmond, Rockland, Schenectady, Suffolk, Sullivan, Ulster and Westchester; in the state of *New Jersey,* the counties of Bergen, Essex, Hudson, Hunterdon, Mercer, Middlesex, Monmouth, Morris, Passaic, Somerset, Sussex, Union and Warren.

District No. 3, One Oxford Valley Office Building, Room 404, 2300 E. Lincoln

Group A Call Signs

Block no.	Contiguous USA
*1	K#$$
*2	N#$$
*3	W#$$
4-13	AA#$-AK#$
14-36	KA#$-KZ#$
37-59	NA#$-NZ#$
60-82	WA#$-WZ#$
83-92	AA#$$-AK#$$
93	Group B

The following prefixes will *not* be assigned to stations in the contiguous 48 states: AH KH NH NL AL KL WL KP NP WP AP WH. Pacific-area stations will be assigned AH#$ KH#$ NH#$ WH#$, then Group B. Alaska-area stations will get WL7$ AL7$ KL7$ NL7$, then Group B. Atlantic-area stations will be assigned KP#$ NP#$ WP#$, then Group B.

Group B Call Signs

Block no.	Contiguous USA
1[1]	KA1$$
2-23	KB#$$-KZ#$$
24-46	NA#$$-NZ#$$
47-69	WA#$$-WZ#$$
70	Group C

[1]KA prefixes will be assigned only to persons living in the first call district. Other KAs are assigned to U.S. personnel living in Japan. The following prefixes will *not* be assigned to stations in the contiguous 48 states: KH KL KP NH NL NP WH WL WP. Pacific-area stations will be assigned calls in the format, AH#$$, Alaska-area stations, AL7$$, and Atlantic-area stations, KP#$$. Once these blocks are used up, assignments will be made from Group C call signs.

Group C Call Signs

Block no.	Contiguous USA
*1	K#$$$
2	N#$$$
*3	W#$$$
4	Group D

Pacific-area stations will be assigned KH#$$ NH#$$ WH#$$, in that order; Alaska-area stations KL7$$ NL7$$ WL7$$; Atlantic-area stations NP#$$ WP#$$. After these are depleted, Group D will be used.

*Call signs using these prefixes are not currently being issued.

Group D Call Signs

Block no.	Contiguous USA
1-23[1]	KA#$$$-KZ#$$$
24-41	WA#$$$-WZ#$$$

[1]Except KC4AAA-AAF and KC4USA-USZ.
The following call sign formats will *not* be assigned to stations in the contiguous 48 states:
KH#$$$ KL#$$$ KP#$$$ WC#$$$WH#$$$ WK#$$$ WL#$$$ WM#$$$ WP#$$$ WR#$$$ WT#$$$. Pacific-area stations will be assigned KH#$$$ WH#$$$; Alaska-area stations KL7$$$ WL7$$$; Atlantic-area stations KP#$$$ WP#$$$.

Hwy., Langhorne, PA 19047. In the state of *Pennsylvania,* all counties; in the state of *New Jersey,* the counties of Atlantic, Burlington, Camden, Cape May, Cumberland, Gloucester, Ocean and Salem; and the county of Newcastle in the state of *Delaware.*

District No. 4, 1017 Federal Building, 31 Hopkins Plaza, Baltimore, MD 21201. The state of *Maryland;* the counties of Kent and Sussex in the state of *Delaware;* the state of *West Virginia;* in *Virginia,* the counties of Arlington, Fairfax, Loudoun and Prince Williams.

District No. 5, Military Circle, 870 North Military Highway, Norfolk, VA 23502. The state of *Virginia* (except the part lying in District 4); and the state of *North Carolina,* all counties.

District No. 6, 1365 Peachtree St., N.E., Room 440, Atlanta, GA 30309. The states of *Georgia, South Carolina* and *Tennessee,* and the state of *Alabama* except that part lying in District 7.

District No. 7, 8675 NW 53 St., Miami, FL 33101. The state of *Florida* and in the state of *Alabama,* Baldwin and Mobile Counties.

District 7T, ADP Building, Suite 601, 1211 North Westshore Blvd., Tampa, FL 33607. Specialized office with no designated administrative area.

District No. 8, 800 West Commerce, Room 505, New Orleans LA 70123. The states of *Arkansas, Louisiana* and *Mississippi.*

District No. 9, Suite 900, 1225 North Loop West Houston, TX 77008. In the state of *Texas,* the counties of Angelina, Aransas, Atascosa, Austin, Bandera, Bastrop, Bee, Bexar, Blanco, Brazoria, Brazos, Brooks, Burleson, Caldwell, Calhoun, Cameron, Chambers, Colorado, Comal, DeWitt, Dimmit, Duval, Edwards, Fayette, Fort Bend, Frio, Galveston, Gillespie, Goliad, Gonzales, Grimes, Guadalupe,Hardon, Harris, Hays, Hidalgo, Jackson, Jasper, Jefferson, Jim Hogg, Jim Wells, Karnes, Kendall, Kenedy, Kerr, Kinney, Kleberg, LaSalle, Lavaca, Lee, Liberty, Live Oak, Madison, Matagorda, Maverick, McMullen, Medina, Montgomery, Nacagdoches, Newton, Nueces, Orange, Polk, Real, Refugio, Sabine, San Augustine, San Jacinto, San Patricio, Starr, Travis, Trinity, Tyler, Uvalde, Val Verde, Victoria, Walker, Waller, Washington, Webb, Wharton, Willacy, Williamson, Wilson, Zaputa and Zavala.

District No. 10, 9330 LBJ Freeway, Suite 1170, Dallas, TX 75243. The state of *Texas* except that part lying in District 9 and the state of *Oklahoma.*

District No. 11, Suite 501, 3711 Long Beach Blvd., Long Beach, CA 90807. The state of *Arizona;* in the state of *Nevada,* the county of Clark; in the state of *California,* the counties of Imperial, Inyo, Kern, Los Angeles, Orange, Riverside, San Bernardino, San Diego, San Luis Obispo, Santa Barbara and Ventura.

District 11SD, 7840 El Cajon Blvd., La Mesa, CA 92041. Specialized office with no designated administrative area.

District No. 12, 323A Customhouse, 555 Battery St., San Francisco, CA 94111. The state of *California* except that part lying in District 11; the state of *Nevada* except the county of Clark, and the state of *Utah.*

District No. 13, 1782 Federal Office Bldg., 1220 S.W. 3d Ave., Portland, OR 97204. The state of *Oregon;* the state of *Idaho* except that part lying in District 14; in the state of *Washington,* the counties of Clark, Cowlitz, Klickitat, Skamania and Wahkiakum.

District No. 14, One Newport, Suite 414, 3605 132nd Ave. SE, Bellevue, WA 98006. The state of *Montana;* the state of *Washington* except that part lying in District 13; in the state of *Idaho,* the counties of Benewah, Bonner, Boundary, Clearwater, Idaho, Kootenai, Latah, Lewis, Nez Perce and Shoshone.

District No. 15, 12477 W. Cedar Dr., Lakewood, CO 80228. The states of *Colorado, New Mexico, North Dakota, South Dakota* and *Wyoming.*

District No. 16, 316 North Roberts St., St. Paul, MN 55101. The state of *Minnesota,* the state of *Michigan,* the counties of Alger, Baraga, Chippewa, Delta, Dickinson, Gogebic, Houghton, Iron, Keweenaw, Luce, Mackinac, Marquette, Menominee, Ontonagon and Schoolcraft and Wisconsin, except for the part lying in District 18.

District No. 17, Room 320 Brywood Office Tower, 8800 E. 63rd Street, Kansas City, MO 64133. The states of *Iowa, Kansas, Missouri* and *Nebraska.*

District No. 18, Park Ridge Office Park, Room 306, 1550 Northwest Hwy., Park Ridge, IL 60068. The states of *Illinois* and *Indiana;* in the state of *Wisconsin,* the counties of Brown, Calumet, Columbia, Crawford, Dane, Dodge, Door, Fond du Lac, Grant, Green, Iowa, Jefferson, Kenosha, Keewanee, Lafayette, Manitowoc, Marinette, Milwaukee, Oconto, Outagamie, Ozaukee, Racine, Richland, Rock, Sauk, Sheboygan, Walworth, Washington, Waukehsa and Winnebago; the state of *Kentucky* except the part lying in District 19.

District No. 19, 1054 New Federal Bldg., 231 W. Lafayette St., Detroit, MI 48226. The state of *Ohio;* the state of *Michigan* except that part lying in District 16; in the state of *Kentucky,* the counties of Bath, Bell, Boone, Bourbon, Boyd, Bracken, Breathitt, Campbell, Carter, Clare, Clay, Elliott, Estill, Fayette, Fleming, Floyd, Franklin, Gallatin, Garrad, Grant, Greenup, Harlan, Harrison, Jackson, Jessamine, Johnson, Kenton, Knott, Knox, Laurel, Lawrence, Lee, Leslie, Letcher, Lewis, Lincoln, Madison, Magoffin, Martin, Mason, McCreary, Menifee, Montgomery, Morgan, Nicholas, Owen, Owsley, Pendleton, Perry, Pike, Powell, Pulaski, Robertson, Rockcastle, Rowan, Scott, Wayne, Whitley, Wolfe and Woodford.

District No. 20, 1307 Fed. Bldg., 111 W. Huron St., Buffalo, NY 14202. The state of *New York* except that part lying in District 2.

District No. 21, Waipio Access Road, Next to the Ted Makalena Golf Course, P.O. Box 1030, Waipahu HI 96797. The state of *Hawaii* and outlying Pacific possessions.

District No. 22, 747 Federal Bldg., Hato Rey, PR 00918, *Puerto Rico* and the *Virgin Islands.*

District No. 23, 6721 West Raspberry Rd., Anchorage AK 99502. The state of *Alaska.*

Chapter 4

A Safari Through the Technical Standards Jungle

The word *standard* means consistency and order — and this is what the Technical Standards section of the Rules is all about. The Commission has made these standards a basic framework so all the different kinds of operation in ham radio can live together peacefully.

The Ham Bands

Amateurs may operate in certain sections of the radio spectrum from 1800 kHz and up. With the international frequency agreements in hand, the Commission subdivides these allocations into various subbands based on types of operation, and the class of license held by the control operator. These segments are always subject to change. The Amateur Service is dynamic — as changes occur, rules must change to allow growth.

160 Meters

This popular amateur band extends from 1800 to 2000 kHz, with the Amateur Radio Service having secondary status from 1900 to 2000 kHz. We must not cause interference to radiolocation, and must accept interference from radiolocation, in that portion of the band. Worldwide, the band is allocated on the scheme found in Table 1 (page 4-19). This chart reflects the changes made at WARC-79. The 160-meter band has traditionally been known as the "gentleman's band" or "top band." Accordingly, a voluntary band plan has developed over time to provide coordination of the various operating activities:

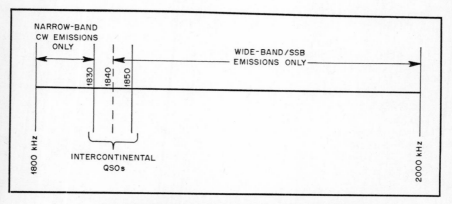

As of June 17, 1985, amateurs are authorized to use CW, RTTY, phone, FAX and slow-scan television on 160. In the Report and Order authorizing these new privileges, the FCC declined to mandate a band plan for 160. The Commission chose instead to support the formation of a voluntary band plan by the amateur community. As this book is published, the band plan is not yet finalized. Details will be reported in *QST* and the *ARRL Letter* as they develop.

The 160-meter band is the lowest-frequency amateur allocation. Its history can be traced to the earliest experiments at "200 meters and down." As are all amateur bands, it is put to a variety of uses: local and regional ragchewing, DXing and some net operation. The band is available equally to General, Advanced and Extra Class licensees.

One feature of operation on the band is the use of "DX windows," which permit weak signals from other continents to be heard. Narrow segments of the band are avoided by North American stations so their neighbors can hear DX stations without local interference. Were it not for the voluntary cooperation of all operators on the band in keeping these segments clear, DXing would be difficult and frustrating at best. Take a look at the band plans, fire up your rig, and enjoy the fine 160-meter band!

80 Meters

The 80-meter band extends from 3500 to 4000 kHz. It is often chosen as a good band for regional ragchewing, DXing and net/roundtable operating. It affords CW privileges throughout. RTTY (frequency- or carrier-shift keying) is authorized on the non-phone portion only, 3500 to 3750 kHz. Television and facsimile are authorized on the voice segment at 3750 to 4000 kHz.

Internationally, the band is divided according to the chart in Table 1, from IRR, Geneva, 1982 (see end of this chapter).

The *Novice* operating segment is 3700 to 3750 kHz. Morse code is the only emission allowed for use by *Novices* and *Technicians* in this segment. (Technicians have all Novice privileges.) *General* class licensees are allowed to operate from 3525 to 3750. Their phone band extends from 3850 to 4000 kHz. *Advanced* class operators have additional phone space at 3775 to 4000 kHz, along with the CW segment 3525 to 3750 kHz. *Extras* have access to the entire band. (Note: U.S. stations licensed in the Pacific outside of Region 2 do *not* have access to the 3900- to 4000-kHz segment.)

The considerate operator recognizes 3610 to 3630 kHz as the RTTY activity area, and 3845 kHz for SSTV (slow-scan television) activity.

40 Meters

This amateur band extends from 7000 to 7300 kHz. CW emissions are allowed throughout the band. RTTY, (frequency-shift keying) is allowed on the "non-voice" frequencies, 7000 to 7150 kHz. The phone segment occurs at 7150 to 7300 kHz. Television and facsimile are also permitted at the phone segment 7150 to 7300 kHz. Stations in Hawaii and Alaska may operate phone on 7075-7100 kHz. (Note: U.S. stations in the Pacific outside of Region 2 do *not* have access to 7100 to 7300 kHz. These stations may, however, operate phone at 7075-7100 kHz. Novices: CW only at 7050-7075.)

The *Novice* subband on 40 meters occurs at 7100-7150 kHz—Morse code only (ditto for *Technicians*). *General* class licensees are allowed operation on 7025-7150 kHz, and 7225-7300 kHz. *Advanced* class operators have privileges at 7025-7300 kHz; *Extras* the entire band 7000-7300 kHz. Worldwide, the band is allocated on the basis shown in Table 1. Broadcasting is the primary service outside of Region 2, at 7100-7300 kHz. The range 7090-7100 kHz is generally recognized as the RTTY zone. Slow-scan TV centers around 7171 kHz.

US Amateur Subband Allocations, 1.8 to 148 MHz

Power Limits: All US amateurs are limited to 200 watts PEP output in the Novice segments and in the 30-meter band. On all other segments, 1500 watts PEP output is permitted. In addition, there are ERP limitations for stations in repeater operation. (See 97.67, FCC rules.) At all times the power level should be kept down to that necessary to maintain communications.

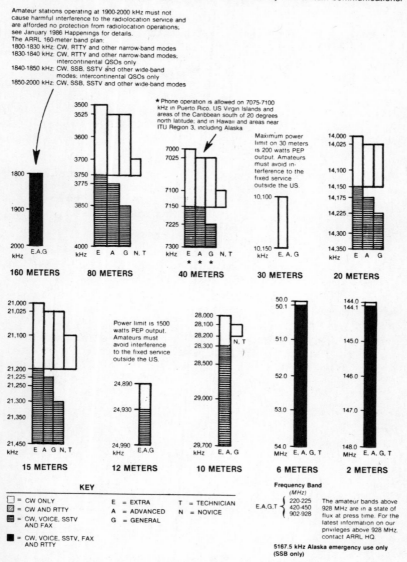

Amateur stations operating at 1900-2000 kHz must not cause harmful interference to the radiolocation service and are afforded no protection from radiolocation operations; see January 1986 Happenings for details.
The ARRL 160-meter band plan:
1800-1830 kHz: CW, RTTY and other narrow-band modes
1830-1840 kHz: CW, RTTY and other narrow-band modes; intercontinental QSOs only
1840-1850 kHz: CW, SSB, SSTV and other wide-band modes; intercontinental QSOs only
1850-2000 kHz: CW, SSB, SSTV and other wide-band modes

★ Phone operation is allowed on 7075-7100 kHz in Puerto Rico, US Virgin Islands and areas of the Caribbean south of 20 degrees north latitude; and in Hawaii and areas near ITU Region 3, including Alaska

Maximum power limit on 30 meters is 200 watts PEP output. Amateurs must avoid interference to the fixed service outside the US.

Power limit is 1500 watts PEP output. Amateurs must avoid interference to the fixed service outside the US.

160 METERS
80 METERS
40 METERS
30 METERS
20 METERS

15 METERS
12 METERS
10 METERS
6 METERS
2 METERS

KEY

☐ = CW ONLY
▨ = CW AND RTTY
▤ = CW, VOICE, SSTV AND FAX
■ = CW, VOICE, SSTV, FAX AND RTTY

E = EXTRA
A = ADVANCED
G = GENERAL
T = TECHNICIAN
N = NOVICE

Frequency Band
(MHz)

E,A,G,T { 220-225
420-450
902-928

The amateur bands above 928 MHz are in a state of flux at press time. For the latest information on our privileges above 928 MHz, contact ARRL HQ.

5167.5 kHz Alaska emergency use only (SSB only)

Operators with Technician class licenses and above may operate on all amateur bands above 50 MHz.

30 Meters

U.S. amateurs holding General, Advanced and Extra Class licenses may use up to 200 watts PEP output and CW and RTTY emissions in the band 10.100-10.150 MHz. Voice modes are not permitted. Amateur stations must avoid interfering with stations in the Fixed Service outside the U.S.

20 Meters

A premier DX band, 20 meters is worldwide amateur exclusive (see Table 1). CW is permitted throughout the band, with the voice segment appearing at 14,150-14,350 kHz. TV and facsimile are permitted on this voice segment also. RTTY is permitted on the non-voice segment 14,000-14,150 kHz.

No *Novice* or *Technician* privileges are afforded at 20 meters. The *General* class segments of the band occur at 14,025-14,150 and 14,225-14,350 kHz. *Advanced* class licensees have access to 14,025-14,150 kHz, and 14,175-14,350 kHz. *Extras* have the entire band 14,000-14-350 kHz. RTTY activity is found between 14.07 and 14.10 MHz; SSTV is at 14.23 MHz.

15 Meters

Another popular DX band, 15 meters is also worldwide amateur exclusive, and runs from 21,000 to 21,450 kHz. (See Table 1.) CW is permitted throughout the band, with the phone segment appearing at 21,200-21,450 kHz. Television and facsimile are permitted on this voice segment only. RTTY (frequency-shift keying) is permitted on the non-voice segment only: 21,000-21,200 kHz.

The *Novice/Technician* subband occurs at 21,100-21,200 kHz, Morse code only. *General* class operators are allowed to use the 21,025-21,200 kHz, and 21,300-21,450 kHz segments. *Advanced* class licensees have 21,025-21,200 kHz, and 21,225-21,450 kHz. *Extras,* the entire band: 21,000-21,450 kHz.

RTTY activity occurs at 21.09-21.10 MHz. SSTV happens at 21.34 MHz.

12 Meters

The 12-meter band (24.890 to 24.990 MHz) was made available for use by U.S. amateurs at 0001 UTC on June 22, 1985. Maximum power permitted is 1500 watts PEP output. CW and RTTY are authorized from 24.890 to 24.930 MHz. CW, phone, FAX, SSTV and narrow-band FM are authorized from 24.930 to 24.990. While the amateur allocation is primary in the U.S., amateurs must avoid interfering with the Fixed Service outside the U.S.

10 Meters

Ten meters (28,000-29,700 kHz) is worldwide amateur exclusive (see Table 1). CW emissions are allowed throughout the band, but like most other bands, CW predominates at the lower portions. The voice segment at 28.3-29.7 MHz also carries television and facsimile privileges. RTTY, (frequency-shift keying) is permitted on the non-voice segment 28.00-28.3 MHz.

The *Novice* (and *Technician*) subband is 28.10-28.20 MHz. *Generals, Advanced* and *Extra* Class licensees have access to the band in its entirety.

RTTY activity generally occurs between 28.09 and 28.10 MHz. SSTV activity centers around 28.68 MHz.

Satellite downlinks exist between 29.30 and 29.50 MHz (downlink refers to satellite transmitting frequencies to earth). *Repeater* operation is allowed from 29.50 to 29.70 MHz, with inputs appearing from 29.52 to 29.58 MHz, and repeater outputs from 29.62 to 29.68 MHz. Fm simplex operation occurs at 29.60 MHz.

According to the ARRL-approved band plan, repeater frequency pairs in MHz (input/output) are:

29.520/29.620   29.560/29.660
29.540/29.640   29.580/29.680

6 Meters

Six meters is the lowest VHF band available to amateurs. In Region 2, it is amateur exclusive (see Table 1 for international allocation, Geneva, 1982). The entire band is available for use by *Technicians, Generals, Advanced* and *Extra* Class licensees. No *Novice* privileges exist on this band.

CW is permitted throughout the band, and there is a CW *exclusive* subband from 50.0 to 50.1 MHz. RTTY (frequency-shift keying) is permitted above the CW segment, as are all the remaining emissions with the exception of Pulse, and unmodulated carriers (unmodulated carriers are permitted from 51 to 54 MHz).

Activities in the 6-meter band are depicted in the following band plan that, while not carrying the weight of law, has developed over time among 6-meter operators:

50.000-50.100	CW and beacons as follows:
50.060-50.080	Automatically controlled beacons
50.100-50.600	SSB and AM as follows:
50.110	SSB DX calling frequency
50.200	SSB domestic calling frequency (Note: Suggest QSY up for local and down for long-distance QSOs)
50.400	AM calling frequency
50.600-51.000	Experimental and Special Modes as follows:
50.700	RTTY Calling Frequency
50.800-50.980	Radio Control (R/C), 10 channels with 20-kHz spacing.
51.000-51.100	Pacific DX window
51.100-52.000	FM Simplex
52.000-52.050	Pacific DX window
52.000-54.000	FM repeater and simplex

Six meters is a popular band, especially for newcomers to the amateur VHF region. Operators enjoy working the various propagation types and modes from home and from hilltops, where spectacular distance communications can be had when conditions are right.

2 Meters

The most popular amateur VHF band is 2 meters, where much FM repeater activity occurs. The band extends from 144 to 148 MHz, and has a CW-only segment from 144.00 to 144.10 MHz. CW is also allowed or the entire band. All of the remaining emissions are permitted (except Pulse) above 144.1 MHz. The following band plan explains typical operation on the 2-meter band:

144-148 MHz

The following band plan has been proposed by the ARRL VHF-UHF Advisory Committee.

144.00-144.05	EME (CW)
144.05-144.06	Propagation beacons
144.06-144.10	General CW and weak signals
144.10-144.20	EME and weak-signal SSB
144.200	National calling frequency
144.20-144.30	General SSB operation
144.30-144.50	New OSCAR subband
144.50-144.60	Linear translator inputs
144.60-144.90	FM repeater inputs
144.90-145.10	Weak signal and fm simplex
145.10-145.20	Linear translator outputs
145.20-145.50	FM repeater outputs
145.50-145.80	Miscellaneous and experimental modes
145.80-146.00	OSCAR subband
146.01-147.37	Repeater inputs
146.40-146.58	Simplex
146.61-146.97	Repeater outputs
147.00-147.39	Repeater outputs
147.42-147.57	Simplex
147.60-147.99	Repeater inputs

Repeater frequency pairs (input/output):

144.61/145.21	144.87/145.47	146.40 or 147.60/147.00*
144.63/145.23	144.89/145.49	146.43 or 147.63/147.03*
144.65/145.25	146.01/146.61	146.46 or 147.66/147.06*
144.67/145.27	146.04/146.64	147.69/147.09
144.69/145.29	146.07/146.67	147.72/147.12
144.71/145.31	146.10/146.70	147.75/147.15
144.73/145.33	146.13/146.73	147.78/147.18
144.75/145.35	146.16/146.76	147.81/147.21
144.77/145.37	146.19/146.79	147.84/147.24
144.79/145.39	146.22/146.82	147.87/147.27
144.81/145.41	146.25/146.85	147.90/147.30
144.83/145.43	146.28/146.88	147.93/147.33
144.85/145.45	146.31/146.91	147.96/147.36
	146.34/146.94	147.99/147.39
*local option	146.37/146.97	

Internationally, the band is located as shown in Table 1, page 4-21.

There are thousands of 2-meter repeaters across the country. Two-meter FM communications remains one of the most popular activities in ham radio today.

The 220-225 MHz Band

Gaining in popularity with both repeater users and other VHF operators, the 220-MHz band affords all emission privileges with the exception of Pulse. The band is available for use by all licensees except *Novice*. It is, however, shared with other services, and thus not exclusively an amateur band. See Table 1, page 4-22, for the international allocation scheme for this band. More and more 220-MHz repeaters are popping up as a result of overcrowding on the 2-meter band. The following band plan has been approved by the ARRL to coordinate activities on this popular band:

220.00-220.05	EME (Earth-Moon-Earth)
220.05-220.06	Propagation beacons
220.06-220.10	Weak signal CW
220.10	Calling Frequency
220.10-220.50	General weak signal, rag chewing and experimental communications

220.50-221.90	Experimental and control links
221.90-222.00	Weak-signal guard band
222.00-222.05	EME
222.05-222.06	Propagation beacons
222.06-222.10	Weak-signal CW
222.10	Calling frequency
222.10-222.30	General operation CW or SSB, etc
222.34-223.38	Repeater inputs
223.34-223.90	Simplex and repeater outputs (local option)
223.94-224.98	Repeater outputs

Simplex frequencies:

223.42	223.52	223.62	223.72	223.82
223.44	223.54	223.64	223.74	223.84
223.46	223.56	223.66	223.76	223.86
223.48	223.58	223.68	223.78	223.88
223.50*	223.60	223.70	223.80	223.90

* National simplex frequency

Repeater frequency pairs (input/output):

222.32/223.92	222.54/224.14	222.76/224.36	222.98/224.58	223.20/224.80
222.34/223.94	222.56/224.16	222.78/224.38	223.00/224.60	223.22/224.82
222.36/223.96	222.58/224.18	222.80/224.40	223.02/224.62	223.24/224.84
222.38/223.98	222.60/224.20	222.82/224.42	223.04/224.64	223.26/224.86
222.40/224.00	222.62/224.22	222.84/224.44	223.06/224.66	223.28/224.88
222.42/224.02	222.64/224.24	222.86/224.46	223.08/224.68	223.30/224.90
222.44/224.04	222.66/224.26	222.88/224.48	223.10/224.70	223.32/224.92
222.46/224.06	222.68/224.28	222.90/224.50	223.12/224.72	223.34/224.94
222.48/224.08	222.70/224.30	222.92/224.52	223.14/224.74	223.36/224.96
222.50/224.10	222.72/224.32	222.94/224.54	223.16/224.76	223.38/224.98
222.52/224.12	222.74/224.34	222.96/224.56	223.18/224.78	

The 420-450 MHz Band

This popular UHF band carries all emission privileges except Pulse and is available to all licensees except *Novices*. The band is shared by amateurs with Government Radio location services (RADAR); amateurs must not interfere with these priority Government stations. As part of WARC-79 proceedings, the 420-430 MHz portion of the band was removed from the Amateur Radio Service north of Line A (see figure).

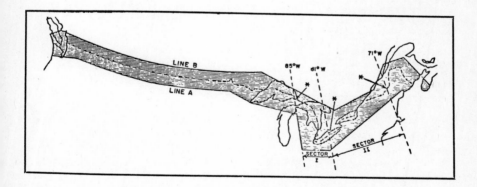

In a later action, FCC allocated portions of the band 421-430 MHz to the Land Mobile Service within 50-mile radii centered on Buffalo, Detroit and Cleveland. Amateur stations south of Line A in the vicinities of these cities may continue to operate in the 421-430 MHz spectrum as long as they do not cause interference to land mobile or government radiolocation users. Additionally, 50-watt PEP output power limitations apply to certain amateurs operating within circles of designated military installations in the U.S. (See the discussion in the power limits section of this chapter). Internationally the band is divided according to Table 1, page 4-22.

The following band plan explains typical operation on the 450-MHz band:

420.00-426.00	ATV repeater or simplex with 421.25-MHz video carrier control links and experimental
426.00-432.00	ATV simplex with 427.250-MHz video carrier frequency
432.00-432.070	EME (Earth-Moon-Earth)
432.07-432.08	Propagation beacons
432.08-432.10	Weak-signal CW
432.100	70-cm calling frequency
432.10-433.00	Mixed-mode and weak-signal work
433.00-435.00	Auxiliary/repeater links
435.00-438.00	Satellite only (internationally)
438.00-444.00	ATV repeater input with 439.250-MHz video carrier frequency and repeater links
442.00-445.00	Repeater inputs and outputs (local option)
445.00-447.00	Shared by auxiliary and control links, repeaters and simplex (local option); (446.0: national simplex frequency)
447.00-450.00	Repeater inputs and outputs

Repeater frequency pairs (input/output is local option):

442.000/447.000	442.600/447.600	443.200/448.200	443.800/448.800	444.400/449.400
442.025/447.025	442.625/447.625	443.225/448.225	443.825/448.825	444.425/449.425
442.050/447.050	442.650/447.650	443.250/448.250	443.850/448.850	444.450/449.450
442.075/447.075	442.675/447.675	443.275/448.275	443.875/448.875	444.475/449.475
442.100/447.100	442.700/447.700	443.300/448.300	443.900/448.900	444.500/449.500
442.125/447.125	442.725/447.725	443.325/448.325	443.925/448.925	444.525/449.525
442.150/447.150	442.750/447.750	443.350/448.350	443.950/448.950	444.550/449.550
442.175/447.175	442.775/447.775	443.375/448.375	443.975/448.975	444.575/449.575
442.200/447.200	442.800/447.800	443.400/448.400	444.000/449.000	444.600/449.600
442.225/447.225	442.825/447.825	443.425/448.425	444.025/449.025	444.625/449.625
442.250/447.250	442.850/447.850	443.450/448.450	444.050/449.050	444.650/449.650
442.275/447.275	442.875/447.875	443.475/448.475	444.075/449.075	444.675/449.675
442.300/447.300	442.900/447.900	443.500/448.500	444.100/449.100	444.700/449.700
442.325/447.325	442.925/447.925	443.525/448.525	444.125/449.125	444.725/449.725
442.350/447.350	442.950/447.950	443.550/448.550	444.150/449.150	444.750/449.750
442.375/447.375	442.975/447.975	443.575/448.575	444.175/449.175	444.775/449.775
442.400/447.400	443.000/448.000	443.600/448.600	444.200/449.200	444.800/449.800
442.425/447.425	443.025/448.025	443.625/448.625	444.225/449.225	444.825/449.825
442.450/447.450	443.050/448.050	443.650/448.650	444.250/449.250	444.850/449.850
442.475/447.475	443.075/448.075	443.675/448.675	444.275/449.275	444.875/449.875
442.500/447.500	443.100/448.100	443.700/448.700	444.300/449.300	444.900/449.900
442.525/447.525	443.125/448.125	443.725/448.725	444.325/449.325	444.925/449.925
442.550/447.550	443.150/448.150	443.750/448.750	444.350/449.350	444.950/449.950
442.575/447.575	443.175/448.175	443.775/448.775	444.375/449.375	444.975/449.975

The 902-928 MHz Band

U.S. amateurs are authorized the use of the 902-928 band as of 0001 UTC September 28, 1985. The following interim band plan was adopted by the ARRL Board of Directors in October 1984:

Segment	Use
902-904 MHz	Narrow-bandwidth, weak-signal communications
902.0-902.8	SSTV, FAX, ACSB, experimental
902.8-903.0	Reserved for EME, CW expansion
903.0-903.05	EME exclusive
903.07-903.08	CW beacons
903.1	CW, SSB calling frequency
903.4-903.6	Crossband Linear Translator inputs
903.6-903.8	Crossband Linear Translator outputs
903.8-904.0	Experimental beacons exclusive

904-906	Digital Communications
906-907	Narrow-bandwidth FM-simplex services, 25-kHz channels
906.50	National simplex frequency
907-910	FM repeater inputs, paired with 919-922 MHz; 119 pairs every 25 kHz, e.g. 907.025, 050, 075, etc. 908-920 MHz uncoordinated pair.
910-916	ATV
916-918	Digital communications
918-919	Narrow-bandwidth, FM control links and remote bases
919-922	FM repeater outputs, paired with 907-910 MHz
922-928	Wide-bandwidth experimental, simplex ATV, Spread Spectrum

Canadian amateurs note: The amateur service will continue to have secondary status in the band 902-928 MHz throughout Canada.

Before operation in this band, Canadian amateurs licensees are required to ocnsult with their DOC District Office to ensure interference will not be caused to other services operating in the area as per Section 45 of the General Radio Refulations Part 11, given in TRC 25.
Government of Canada shipborne radiolocation service is permitted within 150 km of the East and West Coasts, Arctic Ocian, Hudson Bay, James Bay and up the St. Lawrence River as far as Rimourski on pre-coordinated channels in the 902-928 MHz band.

The 1240-1300 MHz Band

Again, all emission privileges (except Pulse) are allowed on this band, and are available to all licensees except Novices. The band, as are virtually all amateur bands between 220 MHz and 24.250 GHz (24.00-24.05 GHz is an exception) is allocated to amateurs on a secondary, non-interference basis, to the primary Government Radilocation services. The following band plan was adopted by the ARRL Board of Directors meeting in January 1985.

Segment	Use
1240-1246	ATV #1
1246-1248	Narrow-bandwidth FM point-to-point links and digital, duplex with 1258-1260
1248-1252	Digital Communications
1252-1258	ATV # 2
1258-1260	Narrow-bandwidth FM point-to-point links and digital, duplexed with 1246-1252
1260-1270	Satellite uplinks, reference WARC '79
1260-1270	Wide-bandwidth experimental, simplex ATV
1270-1276	Repeater inputs, FM and linear, paired with 1282-1288, 239 pairs every 25 kHz, e.g. 1270.025, .050, .075, etc. 1271.0-1283.0 uncoordinated test pair
1276-1282	ATV #3
1282-1288	Repeater outputs, paired with 1270-1276
1288-1294	Wide-bandwidth experimental, simplex ATV
1294-1295	Narrow-bandwidth FM simplex services, 25-kHz channels
1294.5	National FM simplex calling frequency
1295-1297	Narrow bandwidth weak-signal communications (no FM)
1295.0-1295.8	SSTV, FAX, ACSB, experimental
1295.8-1296.0	Reserved for EME, CW expansion
1296.0-1296.05	EME-exclusive
1296.07-1296.08	CW beacons
1296.1	CW, SSB calling frequency
1296.4-1296.6	Crossband linear translator input
1296.6-1296.8	Crossband linear translator output
1296.8-1297.0	Experimental beacons (exclusive)
1297-1300	Digital Communications

Above and Beyond

All modes and licensees (except Novices) are authorized on the following bands:

2300-2310 MHz	10.0-10.5 GHz (Pulse not permitted)	
2390-2450	24.0-24.25	165.0-170.0
3300-3500	48.0-50.0	240.0-250.0
5650-5925	71.0-76.0	All above 300

Amateur allocations in a number of these bands were in a state of flux at press time. Amateurs considering operation above 1300 MHz should contact ARRL Hq. for the latest information.

(Note: 1 GHz = 1000 MHz)

The Emissions

Radio emissions are transmissions from your Amateur Radio station. The FCC Rules use a number of symbols for the various types of emission used in Amateur Radio. These emission symbols indicate how your transmitter reference frequency (the carrier) is modulated, the nature of the signal modulating the carrier, and the type of information transmitted. As a result of WARC '79, the familiar two-character emission designators (A1 for CW, F3 for FM phone, for example) have been replaced with new three-character designators. The new designators allow much more specific description of the characteristics of emissions.

The first character describes the type of modulation of the main carrier.

N — Emission of an unmodulated carrier
A — AM double sideband
H — Single sideband, full carrier
R — Single sideband, reduced carrier
J — Single sideband, suppressed carrier
B — Independent sidebands
C — Vestigial sidebands
F — Frequency modulation
G — Phase modulation

Sequence of pulses

P — Unmodulated
K — Modulated in amplitude
L — Modulated in width/duration
M — Modulated in position/phase
Q — In which the carrier is angle modulated during the period of the pulse
V — Which is a combination of the above, or produced by other means
X — Cases not otherwise covered

The second character describes the nature of the signal modulating the main carrier:

0 — No modulating signal
1 — A single channel carrying quantized or digital information without the use of a modulating subcarrier
2 — A single channel carrying quantized or digital information with the use of a modulating subcarrier
3 — A single channel containing analog information
7 — Two or more channels containing quantized or digital information
8 — Two or more channels containing analog information
9 — Composite system with one or more channels containing quantized or digital information, together with one or more channels containing analog information
X — Cases not otherwise covered

The third character describes the type of information to be transmitted:

N — No information transmitted
A — Telegraphy for aural reception
B — Telegraphy for automatic reception
C — Facsimile
D — Data transmission, telemetry, telecommand
E — Telephony
F — Television
W — Combination of the above
X — Cases not otherwise covered

Here are a few examples of how the new designators describe emissions used by amateurs:

J3E — Single-sideband suppressed-carrier telephony
A1A — Continuous-wave (CW) telegraphy
F1B — Frequency-shift-keyed radioteletype (RTTY)
F3E — Frequency-modulated telephony

There is no precise one-to-one correlation between the old emission designators and the new designators, and there are some problems with the FCC's list of authorized emission types in Part 97. As this book goes to press, ARRL staff is working with the FCC to clear up these problems.

Chirps, Clicks and Good Engineering Practice

The mandate of Section 97.78 of the Rules is that each amateur station must be operated in accordance with good engineering practice. This means signals should be free of harmonics, chirps, key clicks, splatter and hum. Operate a clean machine! Your friends will thank you for it.

Band Edges

"How close can I set my dial to the band edge?" is a question asked not only by the beginner, but by experienced amateurs as well. We'll tell you how close you can go to get that rare DX QSL card — and avoid that rare FCC "QSL" card.

Q. I'm an active HF phone DXer. How close to the band edges can I set my VFO?

A. Many factors are involved. AM double-sideband signals occupy about 6 to 7 kHz of band space, or *bandwidth* — 3 kHz on each side of the carrier (center) frequency. Most amateurs, though, use single-sideband emissions on the popular DX phone bands. Properly generated single-sideband signals have only one discernible sideband and no audible carrier because of strong suppression of the carrier and the unwanted sideband. Thus, to determine where you may set your VFO in relation to the band edge, you must consider (1) which band edge you're near (upper or lower) and (2) which sideband is suppressed. For example, if you're an Extra Class licensee working near the bottom edge of the 20-meter phone band (14.150 MHz) and using the upper sideband, your VFO can be set just inside the band edge if the unwanted lower sidebands are suppressed by at least 40 dB (97.73[a]). The carrier frequency is the frequency of operation and is required to be within the authorized frequency band (97.63[a]). Always allow a margin of safety for possible inaccuracy of your frequency readout.

If you're operating near the top edge (14.350 MHz) with the upper sideband, you must set your VFO dial at least 3 kHz away to accommodate your sideband. Remember, all of your sidebands must be confined within the amateur bands and subbands as applicable (97.63[b]).

Morse Code

Q. When operating CW, how close to the band edge can I go?

A. The answer depends upon how fast you send your code. The bandwidth of a CW signal in hertz depends on the rise and fall time of the note, and is approximately four times the sending speed in words per minute. For example, if you're honking along at 25 WPM, the signal occupies about 100 Hz of spectrum. So, keep your VFO at least half of the bandwidth away from the band edge: 50 Hz or more. Also, most rigs offset the transmit signal from the receive by 600 to 800 Hz, so this factor should be considered in your final frequency determination. Remember, the faster your fist, the greater space you're taking up on the band!

Bandwidth Limitations

Q. How wide can my voice signal be?

A. For AM double sideband voice, bandwidth should not be greater than 7 kHz to be consistent with good engineering and amateur practice. You should take precautions to avoid overmodulating your transmitter so you don't "splatter" and make your signal wider than necessary. Single-sideband signal bandwidth should normally be confined to 3 kHz per good engineering practice (97.78, 2.202). Incidentally, the Commission defines *bandwidth* as the width of the frequency band outside of which the mean power of any emission is at least 26 dB below the average power level of the total emission (97.65[e][3]).

Q. How about my FM voice signal?

A. The bandwidth of an FM voice signal is determined by the audio frequency employed and its amplitude. The only FCC restrictions on FM voice signals apply to operation below 29 MHz, where their bandwidths may not exceed that of a double-sideband voice emission with the same audio characteristics: about 6 to 7 kHz. Wider FM bandwidths are permitted above 29 MHz. Common FM repeater and repeater-user signals occupy 15 to 25 kHz (16 kHz is the norm) of spectrum, usually depending on the attenuation character of the filter preceding the modulated stage. That is, the carrier frequency deviates off center by 5 kHz on either side, with the rest of the bandwidth occurring from sidebands of the input signal based on the Bessel function distribution. This type of FM operation is generally referred to as 16F3 narrow-band FM and is used almost exclusively by gentlemen's agreement below 450 MHz on the popular repeater areas.

Some repeater transmitters use 7 or 8 kHz of deviation from the center frequency. But, such operation is generally frowned upon by the fm community because more space than necessary is used to carry out the desired communications. The FCC 29-MHz cutoff rule for FM voice bandwidth is found in Section 97.65(c).

TV and Facsimile

Q. Why is fast-scan television not found on the HF bands?

A. Fast-scan television, a mode in which images appear in the same manner as a home broadcast TV, is not found at HF because of the bandwidth limitations. To get across all the information necessary for a fast-moving TV picture, much spectrum is required; so much, in fact, that on the relatively small HF bands other modes of communication would be precluded. Thus, bandwidth limits restrict HF TV operation to the slow-scan variety, whereby images appear as a photograph, or "stop-action," and do not require oodles of band space.

When using AM or FM TV and facsimile (FAX is a method of sending pictures and words for permanent display on paper) below 50 MHz, signals must not be wider than a single-sideband voice emission, about 3 kHz (97.65[d]).

Between 50 and 225 MHz, AM FAX and TV *single-sideband* signals may not be wider than a voice SSB signal, about 3 kHz. AM FAX and TV *double-sideband* signals may not be wider than an AM double-sideband voice signal, about 6 to 7 kHz, when operating between 50 and 225 MHz. On FM at this segment, 20 kHz is the limit for FAX and TV (97.65[e]).

No special bandwidth limits apply above 420 MHz, so you'll find wider bandwidth modes, such as fast-scan television, there. But, remember that in all cases not specifically covered by the rules, the various signals must be used in accordance with good engineering practice. Use state-of-the-art equipment that is properly adjusted. Conserve spectrum!

Ham Radio Power!

Think minimum, not maximum. If every ham were to "use the minimum amount of transmitter power necessary to carry out the desired communications," as mandated by the Rules, the bands would be a happier place for all (97.67[a]).

How many fellow amateurs do you know who violate this rule every day? Like the guy who checks into his local 75-meter traffic net running his new nuclear-powered amplifier to the meltdown point. Think before flipping on the Big Switch.

Think output, not input. In marginal communications conditions when more power is required to get information across to the other party, bear in mind the maximum power limits of the FCC Rules. These limits are now expressed in terms of peak envelope power (PEP) *output*. The former terms were expressed as direct power input to the plate circuit of the transmitter final amplifier. The move brings the power terms into consonance with modern transmitter technology.

General

In the general case, ham transmitters may never be operated with a peak envelope power (PEP) output of more than 1500 W (97.67[b]).

AM double sideband users, however, may still use the old measure of 1000-W dc *input* to the transmitter's final amplifier until the year 1990. At that time, FCC may revisit the issue (97.67[f]). The reason for this "grandfathering" is that the new 1500-W PEP output limit would mean an approximate 3-dB reduction in maximum power permitted for AM operations. FCC wanted to minimize the impact on these operations, but could not justify the additional expense of training personnel to measure power under the old system. Also, safety factors are involved with the old system of measurement. No longer will FCC inspectors have to stick their hands into a 5000-V power-supply cage for measurements!

Novice Bands

Novices and higher-class licensees inhabiting the Novice class subbands may never operate their transmitters with a peak envelope power (PEP) output in excess of 200 W (97.67[d]).

Other

Repeaters, beacons and 450-MHz transmitters near certain military installations have special power limits that are now expressed in terms of PEP output.

Repeaters. ERP (effective radiated power) is the term used for defining the power limits for stations in repeater operation. ERP is defined as the product of the transmitter PEP output in watts delivered to the antenna, and the gain of the antenna over that of a half-wave dipole antenna.

Beacons. These special stations are limited to 100 W of peak envelope power output.

450 MHz. Special 50-W PEP output limits apply to stations operating at this region when they are located near certain military installations in the U.S. See Sec.

97.61(b)(7). Telecommand and earth stations must also observe special power restrictions in these military areas: 611-W ERP (1000-W equivalent isotropically radiated power) is the maximum (97.421[c] and 97.422).

Q. What is peak envelope power?

A. Peak envelope power (PEP) is the average power during one radio frequency cycle at the crest of the modulation envelope, taken under normal operating conditions (97.3[t][l]).

Q. How do I measure PEP output to determine if my transmitter is operating within FCC rules?

A. The Commission has chosen and published the following standards of measurement: (1) Read an in-line peak-reading RF wattmeter that is properly matched (commercial units are available), and (2) calculate the power using the peak RF voltage as indicated by an oscilloscope or other peak-reading device. Multiply the peak RF voltage by 0.707, square the result and divide by the load resistance (SWR must be 1).

Q. Is it required that I have a means of measuring power output from my transmitter?

A. FCC does not require you to provide such measurement equipment and techniques. Hams are simply required to abide by the power limits, period. The standards listed in the answer above simply indicate how the Commission would measure your transmitter's output during a station inspection.

As a practical matter, most hams don't have to worry about special equipment to check their transmitter's output because they never approach the 1500-W PEP output limit. Many common amateur amplifiers aren't capable of generating this much power. However, if you *do* have a planet-destroyer amplifier and *do* operate close to the limit on those rare occasions when you need the extra power, then you'd better be prepared to measure your output along the lines of the standards reproduced above!

Q. What are the power limits for repeaters?

A. The repeater power limits are spelled out in Section 97.67. If your repeater operates at 420 MHz (with HAAT below 105 feet) or on the 1240-MHz band and above (with any HAAT), 1500-W PEP output may be used *except* that, in all cases, the minimum amount of power necessary to carry out the desired communications must be used.

An example: Your repeater is sitting atop a tall peak in the Berkshire Mountains. You've marked out the radials on your map and have determined that the height of average terrain is 1000 feet. From the contour lines, you've also determined that your antenna's height above mean sea level is 1600 feet. Thus, your antenna's height above average terrain (HAAT) is 600 feet.

Now, to ERP: Your transmitter PEP output is 100 W, with losses in the feed line and duplexers totaling 3 dB. Antenna gain is 6 dB, giving an ERP of 200 W (100 W at a net gain of 3 dB = 200 W). Your repeater operates at 220 MHz, and thus your transmitter operates at the maximum allowable ERP of 200 W.

Digital Codes Deciphered

With the advent of the home computer, interest among amateurs for digital communications is on the rise. ASCII, a popular computer code, is allowing hams to trade programs on the air and to facilitate computer-to-computer conversations directly. In recent times, the FCC has addressed rulemaking in the digital arena — ASCII was approved, additional digital codes were authorized for experimental purposes and AMTOR is now allowed. Let's take a look at digital codes in Amateur Radio today, and what may be in store for hams in the near future.

Q. What is RTTY?

A. RTTY means *radioteletype,* a form of telegraphic communication using typewriter-like machines or small home computers with alphanumeric keyboards. Two things happen when an RTTY message is sent: (1) a *coded* message is generated from electrical impulses made when typewriter keys are pressed for the desired words, and (2) the message is transmitted in this code to a distant receiver that converts the code back to plain language for the message recipient. So, you can easily talk to your friends on the air by typing out your message, pressing the transmit button, and then awaiting the response to appear on your TV screen or printout. It's not all that complicated.

Q. What kinds of codes are used for coding these messages?

A. *Baudot* (also called *Murray* and *International Telegraph Alphabet No. 2*) is a code used to encode the alphabet, numbers and some special symbols into five-level binary code. Binary is a number system consisting of only two digits, 0 and 1. The binary system is used for ease in computer operations. There are only two states to deal with: *on* and *off*, or "mark" and "space" (two discrete frequencies) in RTTY applications. For example, the letter "D" in Baudot is "10010." An RTTY transmitter/encoder sends a "mark" (on one frequency) for each "1" and a "space" (on the other frequency) for each "0." The receiver/decoder at a distant station subsequently receives the coded "D" and converts it back into English. See Fig. 1 for a "picture" of Baudot letter "D."

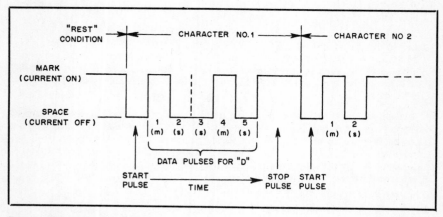

Fig. 1 — Baudot character "D."

Q. What is ASCII?

A. Like Baudot, *ASCII* is a binary code, but it has *seven* levels instead of five (an eighth parity bit allows for error checking). ASCII (American Standard Code for Information Interchange) is becoming popular because of a few key advantages: More punctuation and commands can be encoded, and many modern computers use ASCII, thus simplifying computer/ham activities.

Q. What's AMTOR?

A. AMTOR, a digital teleprinter code that produces copy less prone to errors, is now authorized in the Amateur Service. Under marginal conditions, amateur stations using conventional codes often lose transmitted data, and must engage in time-consuming repeats. With AMTOR, the equipment checks itself periodically for errors and repeats only when necessary, thus increasing communications efficiency. Microprocessor circuitry is used to generate AMTOR signals. Lower power can be used, and interference will be reduced. See "AMTOR, an Improved Error-Free RTTY System," June 1981 *QST*, for more information.

Q. What about sending speeds? What's baud rate?

A. ASCII, AMTOR and Baudot code speeds can be given in terms of *baud rate,* which equals the reciprocal of the time of a unit or data pulse. For example, if you're using a data pulse 22 ms long in a Baudot character, your baud rate is 45 (1/0.022 = 45), safely within the FCC rules. For the Baudot code, 45 bauds is by far the most common amateur data rate. The lowest standard ASCII data rate in common usage is 110 bauds. Data rates up to 300 bauds are allowed on frequencies below 28 MHz. Rates up to 1200 bauds are okay between 28 and 50 MHz; up to 19.6 kilobauds between 50 and 220 MHz; and up to 56 kilobauds above 220 MHz.

ASCII-encoded characters normally have shorter data pulses, and higher baud rates. The 110-baud rate is the most practical for HF use because of readily available equipment, as well as the increased susceptibility of the higher data rates to noise, static interference and so forth. VHF FM activity finds 110 and 300 bauds useful for terminal-to-terminal communications, and 300 and 1200 bauds best for computer-related activities, such as exchanging programs.

Q. What modes and frequencies are used for ASCII, AMTOR and Baudot RTTY?

A. On the VHF bands where A2A and F2A transmission is permitted, *audio-frequency-shift keying* is generally used. In this case, the steady RF carrier is transmitted continuously, the pulses being transmitted by frequency-shifted *tone modulation.* The two tones are fed into the audio stage of the transmitter; the microphone, for example. In AFSK "shift" is of the modulating audio frequency, not the carrier. Below 50 MHz, *frequency-shift keying* is used. The carrier is on continuously, but in this case, it is the carrier frequency itself that is shifted. FCC permits shifts up to 1000 Hz below 50 MHz. Above 50 MHz, the frequency shift for AFSK or FSK in the hertz must not be greater than the sending speed, in bauds, of the transmission or 1000 Hz, whichever is greater. A 170-Hz shift is most commonly used. In AFSK the tones may not exceed 3000 Hz.

Q. How can I use my SSB transmitter for RTTY at HF?

A. Amateurs operating RTTY in the HF bands frequently use audio tones fed into the microphone input of an SSB transmitter. With properly designed and constructed equipment that is correctly adjusted, this provides a satisfactory method of obtaining F1B-like emission and is okay with the FCC. The user should make certain, however, that audio distortion, the carrier and unwanted sidebands are not present to the degree of causing interference in receiving equipment of good engineering design.

Q. Can I use CW for ASCII?

A. Yes. CW may be used where RTTY is permitted. Novices (and Technicians using Novice subbands) may *not* use RTTY because they are restricted to radiotelegraphy code only.

In practice, however, *frequency-shift keying* is preferred because it gives definite pulses on both mark and space, an advantage in printer operation. And, since FSK can be received by methods similar to those used for fm reception, there is considerable discrimination against noise. Both factors make for increased reliability in printer operation.

Q. Are other codes allowed in Amateur Radio?

A. Yes, the FCC permits the use of experimental digital codes on amateur frequencies *above 50 MHz,* except those frequencies on which only CW emission is permitted (50.0-50.1 and 144.0-144.1 MHz). "An amateur radio communication may include digital codes which represent alphanumeric characters, analogue measurements or other information." Communications using such digital codes are allowed within the U.S. only, unless special provisions have been made between the U.S. and another country.

Bandwidth may not exceed 20 kHz between 50 and 220 MHz, and 100 kHz between 220 and 1215 MHz. Above 1215 MHz, any bandwidth may be used, provided the sidebands are confined within the amateur band and all spurs are reduced or eliminated according to good engineering practice. A description of the experimental code must be kept.

Q. How do I identify my station when transmitting RTTY?

A. You may identify by using Morse code or voice. If using Baudot, ASCII or AMTOR, stations may identify using the particular code being used for communication. If you are using other digital codes above 50 MHz, ASCII, Baudot or AMTOR may be used for ID.

Q. What is Packet Radio?

A. Packets are individual bursts of data (digitally encoded). A user's *packet* is made up at his or her "Terminal Node Controller," addressed, then transmitted to another station, which accepts packets, performs an error check on them and, if there are no errors, sends a confirmation. Members of a Local Area Network (LAN) can talk to each other by this system. Many QSOs can take place at the "same" time (the "time sharing" characteristic of computer use is employed) on a single channel, thus conserving spectrum. A packet compresses information into short "bursts" that take only milliseconds to send, allowing this frequency sharing. Packet Radio is rapidly gaining popularity; packet systems are up all over the country, and there are many packet repeaters, or digipeaters, on the air. To learn more about packet radio, subscribe to the ARRL packet radio newsletter, *Gateway*. Write to ARRL Hq. for details.

Spurious Emissions

Spurious emissions are unwanted transmissions that are outside an authorized amateur frequency band. Refer to Graph 1. An operator is required to reduce or eliminate any spurious emissions that cause harmful interference to reception at another station. Additionally, if your transmitter or RF power amplifier was built after April 14, 1977, or first marketed after December 31, 1977, and transmits on frequencies —

below 29.7 MHz — the mean power (MP) of any spurious emissions must
- never be more than 50 mW;
- be at least 30 dB below the MP of the fundamental emission, if the MP output is less than 5 W; and
- be at least 40 dB below the MP of the fundamental emission, if the MP output is 5 W or more.

between 50 and 225 MHz — any spurious emission must
- never be more than 25 μW MP;
- be at least 40 dB below the MP of the fundamental emission, if the MP output is less than 25 W, but may be as much as 10 μW; and
- be at least 60 dB below the MP of the fundamental emission if the MP output is 25 W or more, but may be as much as 10 μW.

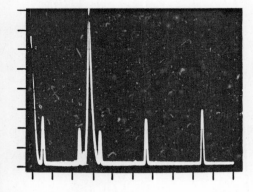

Graph 1 — Worst-case spectral display of a modern transceiver. Vertical divisions are each 10 dB and horizontal divisions are each 5 MHz. Output power is approximately 90 W on 20 meters. All spurious emissions are at least 50 dB below peak fundamental output. The rig complies with current FCC specifications for spectral purity.

Amplifiers and Type Acceptance

The Tech Standards subpart includes type-acceptance standards and requirements for RF power amplifiers. This set of questions and answers will provide a good understanding of the basis for these rules, and of their impact on the average amateur.

Amplifier Ban Amplified

In April 1978, the Federal Communications Commission banned the manufacture and marketing of any external radio frequency power amplifier or amplifier kit that is capable of operation on any frequency below 144 MHz unless the FCC has issued a grant of type acceptance for that model amplifier. Since that time, scores of amateurs have written ARRL and FCC with questions regarding this ban. In December 1978, FCC issued a Public Notice that included the most frequently asked questions, and their answers.

Q. Is it illegal to use amplifiers on 10 meters?

A. No. Amateurs may use amplifiers capable of operating on 10 meters. While this ruling may make it difficult to buy a new amplifier capable of operation on 10 meters, the FCC said it will allow those amateurs with the appropriate class of license to modify an amplifier to restore or include 10-meter capability. However, an amateur may modify no more than one unit of the same model amplifier in any year, without a grant of type acceptance.

Of course, as in the past he could also build his own amplifier, or convert equipment from any other radio service for this use, or buy a used amplifier. He can do this without regard to either the type-acceptance requirements or to the 24- to 35-MHz frequency ban, as long as the individual amateur does not intend to market this equipment, and the amplifier is used at a licensed amateur station. (Amplifiers may be sold on an individual level; see below.

Q. Can a dealer modify amplifiers to restore their 10-meter capability if they are sold only to licensed amateurs?

A. No. These modifications can only be performed by an individual amateur for specific use by the licensed owner of the amplifier at his licensed Amateur Radio station. Note that you can ask another amateur to modify the amplifier for you, but you are responsible for ensuring that the equipment complies with all the technical requirements contained in the amateur regulations.

Q. What type of amplifiers may a dealer sell?

A. All external amplifiers capable of operation below 144 MHz must be type accepted by the FCC in order to be marketed. A number of amplifiers, manufactured prior to the April 28, 1979, cutoff date, were issued a waiver of the effective date of the new regulations.

Q. May I buy or sell a used amateur amplifier that has not been issued either a grant of type acceptance or a waiver, or has been modified so that the grant is no longer valid? What about one that was originally marketed before these regulations were announced, or one that was built from scratch — neither of these two would have a grant nor waiver.

A. You may buy or sell an amplifier under those conditions, but there are restrictions that would be valid regardless of whether the amplifier was capable of operation in the 24 to 35-MHz range. Some amplifiers marketed before April 28, 1978, are covered under the waiver if they are the same model that was granted a waiver. An individual amateur may sell his amplifier regardless of grants or waivers, provided that he sells it only to another amateur operator. He may also sell it to a bona fide amateur-equipment dealer. The dealer could sell only those amplifiers that he purchased *used* from an individual amateur operator, and then only if he sold it to another ham.

While the FCC said it does not require proof of licensing at this time, it is the responsibility of the seller of the equipment, whether he is an individual or a dealer (whoever currently owns the amplifier), to ensure that the buyer is indeed a licensed amateur operator, or a bona fide amateur equipment dealer.

Q. What does type acceptance mean?

A. Type acceptance is an equipment authorization granted by the FCC, based on equipment data submitted by the manufacturer, to be used in the proper manner of the service for which it has been accepted (FCC rules and regulations, Subpart J, section 2.905a). This acceptance applies to all identical units marketed by the grantee. Amplifiers capable of operating below 144 MHz are the only sort of amateur equipment requiring type acceptance, by the way. Of course, other equipment must meet the FCC standards for purity of emission (97.73). But the manufacturer of amateur transmitting equipment other than HF amplifiers does not need to submit the "specs" or an actual unit for testing purposes unless the Commission decides the model is not meeting FCC standards, and wants to inspect the equipment.

Q. Under what circumstances would FCC dismiss or deny an application for type acceptance of an external RF amplifier?

A. Some features which may cause a denial are (1) any accessible wiring which, when altered, would permit operation in a manner contrary to FCC rules, (2) circuit boards or similar circuitry to facilitate the addition of components to change the amplifier's operating characteristics in a manner contrary to FCC rules, (3) instructions for operation or modification of the amplifier in a manner contrary to FCC rules, (4) any internal or external controls or adjustments to facilitate operation of the amplifier in a manner contrary to FCC rules, (5) any internal radio-frequency sensing circuitry or any external switch, the purpose of which is to place the amplifier in the transmit mode, (6) the incorporation of more gain than is necessary to operate in the Amateur Radio Service, and (7) any attenuation in the input of the amplifier, which when removed or modified, would permit the amplifier to function at its designed output power when driven by an RF input of less than 50 watts mean power.

Q. Why was the 10-meter ban imposed?

A. In a news release dated December 1978, FCC said that this action had been taken to "stem the flow of large quantities of amplifiers which were being distributed for . . . illegal use on frequencies in and around the Citizen's Band Radio Service."

Table 1

The International Table of Frequency Allocations, Radio Regulations (Geneva, 1982)

(Amateur Radio extracts)
Services listed in capital letters denote Primary allocations, and have priority over secondary services listed in normal characters. Stations of a secondary service may not cause harmful interference to Primary service stations, nor may they claim protection from harmful interference from Primary stations.

  Footnotes contain special cases in allocations. Significant footnotes affecting U.S. amateurs appear below each of the following tables. These tables are extracts from the IRR Table where Amateur Radio is allocated. The U.S. is in ITU Region 2.

kHz

Region 1	Region 2	Region 3

1800-1810
RADIOLOCATION
	1800-1850
	AMATEUR
		1800-2000
		AMATEUR
		FIXED
		MOBILE except
		  aeronautical
		  mobile

1810-1850 AMATEUR	489	RADIONAVIGATION Radiolocation

1850-2000
FIXED
MOBILE except
  aeronautical
  mobile
	1850-2000
	AMATEUR
	FIXED
	MOBILE except
	  aeronautical mobile
	RADIOLOCATION
	RADIONAVIGATION
	489
		489

Note: Frequencies are in kilohertz.

489 In Region 2, Loran stations operating in the band 1800-2000 kHz shall cease operation by 31 December 1982. In Region 3, the Loran system operates either on 1850 kHz or 1950 kHz, the bands occupied being 1825-1875 kHz and 1925-1975 kHz, respectively. Other services to which the band 1800-2000 kHz is allocated may use any frequency therein on condition that no harmful interference is caused to the Loran system operated on 1850 or 1950 kHz.

Region 1	Region 2	Region 3

3500-3800
AMATEUR 510
FIXED
MOBILE except
  aeronautical
  mobile
	3500-3750
	AMATEUR 510
		3500-3900
		AMATEUR 510
		FIXED
		MOBILE

3800-3900
FIXED
AERONAUTICAL
  MOBILE (OR)
LANDMOBILE
	3750-4000
	AMATEUR 510
	FIXED
	MOBILE except
	  aeronautical
	  mobile (R)	

3900-3950
AERONAUTICAL
  MOBILE (OR)
		3900-3950
		AERONAUTICAL
		  MOBILE
		BROADCASTING

3950-4000 FIXED BROADCASTING	514 515	3950-4000 FIXED BROADCASTING

510 For the use of the bands allocated to the amateur service at 3.5 MHz, 7.0 MHz, 10.1 MHz, 14.0 MHz, 18.068 MHz, 21.0 MHz, 24.89 MHz and 144 MHz in the event of natural disasters, see Resolution 640.

514 Additional allocation: in Canada, the band 3950-4000 kHz is also allocated to the broadcasting service on a primary basis. The power of broadcasting stations operating in this band shall not exceed that necessary for a national service within the frontier of this country and shall not cause harmful interference to other services operating in accordance with the Table.

515 Additional allocation: in Greenland, the band 3950-4000 kHz is also allocated to the broadcasting service on a primary basis. The power of the broadcasting stations operating in this band shall not exceed that necessary for a national service and shall in no case exceed 5 kilowatts.

Region 1	Region 2	Region 3
7000-7100	AMATEUR 510 AMATEUR-SATELLITE	
7100-7300 BROADCASTING	7100-7300 AMATEUR 510 528	7100-7300 BROADCASTING

528 The use of the band 7100-7300 kHz in Region 2 by the amateur service shall not impose constraints on the broadcasting service intended for use within Region 1 and Region 3.

Region 1	Region 2	Region 3
10,100-10,150	FIXED Amateur 510	
14,000-14,250	AMATEUR 510 AMATEUR-SATELLITE	
14,250-14,350	AMATEUR 510	
18,068-18,168	AMATEUR 510 AMATEUR-SATELLITE 537	

537 The band 18,068-18,168 kHz is allocated to the fixed service on a primary basis subject to the procedure described in Resolution 8. The use of this band by the amateur and amateur-satellite services shall be subject to the completion of satisfactory transfer of all assignments to stations in the fixed service operating in this band and recorded in the Master Register, in accordance with the procedure described in Resolution 8.

21,000-21,450	AMATEUR 510 AMATEUR-SATELLITE	
24,890-24-990	AMATEUR 510 AMATEUR-SATELLITE 543	

543 The band 24,890-24,990 kHz is allocated to the fixed and land mobile services on a primary basis subject to the procedure described in Resolution 8. The use of this band by the amateur and amateur-satellite services shall be subject to the completion of the satisfactory transfer of all assignments to fixed and land mobile stations operating in this band and recorded in the Master Register, in accordance with the procedure described in Resolution 8.

MHz

Region 1	Region 2	Region 3
28-29.7	AMATEUR AMATEUR-SATELLITE	
47-68 BROADCASTING	50-54 AMATEUR	
144-146	AMATEUR 510 AMATEUR-SATELLITE	
146-149.9 FIXED MOBILE except aeronautical mobile	146-148 AMATEUR	146-148 AMATEUR FIXED MOBILE

```
Region 2
220-225
AMATEUR
FIXED
MOBILE
Radiolocation
627
```

627 In Region 2, the band 216-225 MHz is also allocated to the radiolocation service on a primary basis until 1 January 1990. On and after 1 January 1990, no new stations in that service may be authorized. Stations authorized prior to 1 January 1990 may continue to operate on a secondary basis.

Region 1	Region 2	Region 3
420-430	FIXED MOBILE except aeronautical mobile Radiolocation 651 652	
430-440 AMATEUR RADIOLOCATION	430-440 RADIOLOCATION Amateur 664	
440-450	FIXED MOBILE except aeronautical mobile Radiolocation 651 652	

652 Additional allocation: in Australia, the United States, Jamaica and the Philippines, the bands 420-430 MHz and 440-450 MHz are also allocated to the amateur service on a secondary basis.

651 Different category of service: in Australia, the United States, India, Japan and the United Kingdom, the allocation of the bands 420-430 MHz and 440-450 MHz to the radiolocation service is on a primary basis (see No. 3432/141).

664 In the bands 435-438 MHz, 1260-1270 MHz, 2400-2450 MHz, 3400-3410 MHz (in Regions 2 and 3 only), 5650-5670 MHz the amateur-satellite service may operate subject to not causing harmful interference to other services operating in accordance with the Table. Administrations authorizing such use shall ensure that any harmful interference caused by emissions from a station in the amateur-satellite service is immediately eliminated. The use of the bands 1260-1270 MHz and 5650-5670 MHz by the amateur-satellite service is limited to the Earth-to-space direction.

```
Region 2
902-928
FIXED
AMATEUR
Mobile except
   aeronautical mobile
Radiolocation
705 707
```

705 Different category of service: in the United States, the allocation of the band 890-942 MHz to the radiolocation service is on a primary basis.

707 In Region 2, the band 902-928 MHz (centre frequency 915 MHz) is designated for industrial, scientific and medical (ISM) applications. Radiocommunication services operating within this band must accept harmful interference which may be caused by these applications.

1215-1240	RADIOLOCATION RADIONAVIGATION-SATELLITE (space-to-Earth)
1240-1260	RADIOLOCATION RADIONAVIGATION-SATELLITE (space-to-Earth) Amateur 714
1260-1300	RADIOLOCATION Amateur 714

714 Additional allocation: in Canada and the United States the bands 1240-1300 MHz and 1350-1370 MHz are also allocated to the aeronautical radionavigation service on a primary basis.

Region 1	Region 2	Region 3
2300-2450 FIXED Amateur Mobile Radiolocation 752	2300-2450 FIXED MOBILE RADIOLOCATION Amateur 752	

752 The band 2400-2500 MHz (centre frequency 2450 MHz) is designated for industrial, scientific and medical (ISM) applications. Radio services operating within this band must accept harmful interference which may be caused by these applications.

Region 1	Region 2	Region 3
3300-3400 RADIOLOCATION	3300-3400 RADIOLOCATION Amateur Fixed Mobile	3300-3400 RADIOLOCATION Amateur
3400-3600 FIXED FIXED-SATELLITE (space-to-Earth) Mobile Radiolocation	3400-3500 FIXED FIXED-SATELLITE (space-to-Earth) Amateur Mobile Radiolocation 664	

Region 1	Region 2	Region 3
5650-5725	RADIOLOCATION Amateur Space Research (deep space) 664	
5725-5850 FIXED-SATELLITE (Earth-to-space) RADIOLOCATION Amateur 806 808	5725-5850 RADIOLOCATION Amateur 806 808	

5850-5925
FIXED
FIXED-SATELLITE
  (Earth-to-space)
MOBILE
 	
806
	5850-5925
	FIXED
	FIXED-SATELLITE
	  (Earth-to-space)
	MOBILE
	Amateur
	Radiolocation
	806
		5850-5925
		FIXED
		FIXED-SATELLITE
		  (Earth-to-space)
		MOBILE
		Radiolocation
		
		806

806 The band 5725-5875 MHz (centre frequency 5800 MHz) is designed for industrial, scientific and medical (ISM) applications. Radiocommunication services operating within this band must accept harmful interference which may be caused by these applications.

808 The band 5830-5850 MHz is also allocated to the amateur-satellite service (space-to-Earth) on a secondary basis.

GHz

Region 1	Region 2	Region 3
10-10.45 FIXED MOBILE RADIOLOCATION Amateur 828	10-10.45 RADIOLOCATION Amateur 828	10-10.45 FIXED MOBILE RADIOLOCATION Amateur 828
10.45-10.5	RADIOLOCATION Amateur Amateur-Satellite	

828 The band 9975-10,025 MHz is also allocated to the meteorological-satellite service on a secondary basis for use by weather radars.

24-24.05	AMATEUR
	AMATEUR-SATELLITE
	881
24.05-24.25	RADIOLOCATION
	Amateur
	Earth Exploration-Satellite
	(active)
	881

881 The band 24-24.25 GHz (centre frequency 24.125 GHz) is designated for industrial, scientific and medical (ISM) applications. Radiocommunication services operating within this band must accept harmful interference which may be caused by these applications.

47-47.2	AMATEUR
	AMATEUR-SATELLITE
75.5-76	AMATEUR
	AMATEUR-SATELLITE
76-81	RADIOLOCATION
	Amateur
	Amateur-satellite
	912

912 In the band 78-79 GHz radars located on space stations may be operated on a primary basis in the earth exploration-satellite service and in the space research service.

116-126	EARTH EXPLORATION
	SATELLITE (passive)
	FIXED
	INTER-SATELLITE
	MOBILE
	SPACE RESEARCH (passive)
	915

915 The band 119.98-120.02 GHz is also allocated to the amateur service on a secondary basis.

142-144	AMATEUR
	AMATEUR-SATELLITE
144-149	RADIOLOCATION
	Amateur
	Amateur-satellite
	918

918 The bands 140.69-140.98 GHz, 144.68-144.98 GHz, 145.45-145.75 GHz and 146.82-147.12 GHz are also allocated to the radio astronomy service on a primary basis for spectral line observations. In making assignments to stations of other services to which the bands are allocated, administrations are urged to take all practicable steps to protect the radio astronomy service from harmful interference. Emissions from space or airborne stations can be particularly serious sources of interference to the radio astronomy service.

241-248	RADIOLOCATION
	Amateur
	Amateur-Satellite
	922
248-250	AMATEUR
	AMATEUR-SATELLITE

922 The band 244-246 GHz (center frequency 245 GHz) is designated for industrial, scientific and medical (ISM) applications. The use of this frequency band for ISM applications shall be subject to special authorization by the administration concerned in agreement with other administrations whose radiocommunication services might be affected. In applying this provision administrations shall have due regard to the latest relevant CCIR Recommendations.

Chapter 5

Standard Operating Procedure — The Basics

I*n all respects not specifically covered by these regulations each amateur station shall be operated in accordance with good engineering practice and good amateur practice (97.78).*

This rule is one of the most significant in Part 97. It gives the FCC wide latitude in dealing with problems of poor operating and engineering habits of some operators on the bands. Although the rule is quite general, it carries much clout with the Commission. In fact, it's the first rule to be found in Subpart D of the Rules — Operating Requirements and Procedures — the subject of Chapters 5 and 6.

Types of Operation

As an active radio amateur, you'll be bumping into different kinds of operation. Here's an overview of these operations so you'll be able to talk intelligently with your ham friends, and understand Part 97 a bit better.

Fixed operation. Radiocommunication conducted from the specific geographical land location shown on the station license. Your home shack, normally.

Portable operation. Radiocommunication conducted from a specific geographical location other than that shown on the station license. A vacation home, or friend's house, for example.

Mobile operation. Radiocommunication conducted while in motion or during halts at unspecified locations (Note: It's important to make the distinction between *portable* and *mobile* operation. Mobile refers to talking on your 2-meter rig while driving your pick-up truck, while jogging or while backpacking in the Green Mountains. *Portable* means operation for an extended period of time at a specific, definable location, such as your retreat cabin on Lake Indian Name.

Control Operator: The Concept

The concept of station control in Amateur Radio is fundamental, yet may be complex enough to stump the most ardent repeater/auxiliary system operator. More amateurs are remotely controlling their stations all the time; more and more repeaters are linked by more sophisticated means. Some *person* must be responsible in each case for the proper operation of each transmitter; Amateur Radio operator licenses are not granted to machines! Let's find out exactly who a control operator is, and exactly what is meant by "control."

Q. Who is responsible for the proper operation of an amateur station?

A. The licensee and the control operator of the station share responsibility. The station licensee is the person whose name appears on the station license. The control operator is the person who sits at the controls (control point) to perform the immediate operation of the station. Usually, the station licensee and the control operator are the same person—you normally operate your own rig. But occasionally you will invite a ham friend over to your shack to, say, help share operating duties in a contest. When your friend is controlling the station, he or she is the control operator, and you both share responsibility for the rig's proper operation.

The FCC always assumes you are the control operator of your station unless a written record exists to the contrary. So, when your friend is CO, jot down a note to this effect in a record or log book. If he or she breaks an FCC rule while operating, you'll both be responsible.

Q. When my friends are operating my rig, whose call sign is used? What frequencies and privileges may they use?

A. The control operator is *always* limited to the privileges of his or her own operator license, even if the station licensee's are greater. If, for example, the station licensee is a Novice and the control operator is a General class licensee, the CO may use his or her General class privileges, provided proper ID is made. If the Novice's station call is used, the CO must add his/her own call at the end: KA1KOW/K8CH, for example (97.79[c]) (97.84[b]). Of course, the control operator may simply use his or her own call sign at your shack to ID the operations. This point was clarified in a report from ARRL's Washington Area Coordinator, detailing a conversation with John Johnston, W3BE, Chief of FCC's Personal Radio Branch:

> In August 1984 QST, Washington Mailbox dealt with the issue of which call to sign. The statement, "Of course, the control operator may simply use his or her own call sign at your shack to ID the operations" was challenged by several amateurs, who see it as in conflict with Section 97.84. The copy had been read by John before publication, so it seemed wise and natural to ask his views again. Now that transceivers can be passed from hand to hand, the interpretation he has been using for some time is based on physical control being the important criterion. Thus, John believes that the call sign of the person having physical control of the station equipment may always be used. The original rule was written in another era for different equipment conditions. Yet there are cases, such as W1AW, other club stations and central stations for emergency service, in which the identity of the station should be preserved—as indeed it is in the language of Section 97.84. Summing up, the present interpretation as reported in August 1984 QST poses no unreasonable limits and provides maximum flexibility to the Amateur Service.

Q. What stations need control operators?

A. Every station must have a control operator when in operation. The control operator must be present at the control point of the amateur station, except when the station is operated by automatic control (97.79[b]). Automatic control is permitted for stations in repeater, auxiliary, space and beacon operation only.

Q. What is automatic control?

A. This type of control allows the control operator to be away from the control point of the station provided there is assurance that the station is operated legally. Devices and procedures must be used to prevent unauthorized tampering with the control functions or the physical equipment itself. It's used mainly for repeaters when it's not feasible to have the control operator on duty at the control point at all times (97.3[m][3]).

Q. What types of control are used for other stations?

A. Most stations are locally controlled; that is, manual control with the control operator monitoring the operation on duty at a control point of the transmitter with the knobs and dials directly accessible (97.3[m][1]). In other words, he or she sits right in front of the rig to twiddle the knobs and watches the lights blink to make sure it is operated properly. More and more stations are being operated by remote control.

Q. How does remote control work?

A. In some cases, it's not easy to have a control operator sit right at the transmitter controls, or you want to operate your home station when you're not at home. For example, a station placed at the top of a mountain to gain better signal transmission and reception can be operated from one's home in the valley by *remote control*. This is manual control, too, but the control operator performs the control function at a distant control point of the station. Control is established through a *control link* to the transmitter (97.3[m][2]). The transmitter doing the controlling—transmitting control signals in the link—is in *auxiliary operation*. It's important to point out that the remotely controlled transmitter is *not* a "repeater" as defined in 97.3(l). This means that an operator controlling a remote base must not operate the remotely controlled transmitter beyond the privileges allowed by his or her license class.

The CO must be able to control the station from the remote control point just as well as if he/she was at a control point physically in front of the transmitter. It's important to remember that if the control link fails, the station's transmissions must cease after three minutes. Most hams install three-minute timers in the control circuitry of the remotely controlled station to meet this requirement (97.88[d]).

Q. What kinds of techniques are used for remote control links?

A. Some hams use wire or telephone lines to send their control commands to the station. Others use radio, or auxiliary operation of a station, to transmit control commands to the remote station. Auxiliary control links must be placed on frequencies above 220.5 MHz, except 431-433 MHz and 435-438 MHz (97.61[d]).

Q. Do I have to monitor the frequencies used by my remote control station?

A. Yes. Immediately before and during the station's operation, the frequencies employed must be monitored by the control operator. He or she must terminate all transmissions immediately if a rule violation occurs (97.88[c]).

Q. Do I have to protect my remote station from tampering?

A. Yes. You must take steps to ensure that your station cannot be operated by unauthorized individuals either by activation through the control link or by some other means. This is accomplished often by using padlocks on the station's housing and keeping command codes and control link frequencies as secret as possible (97.88[g]).

Q. What are MSOs, and how are they controlled?

A. MSO, Message Storage Operations, are on-the-air "mailboxes" where hams can leave and receive messages for storage and retrieval. A station is activated by a command and, using digital or other techniques, a message is stored or retrieved from the mailbox memory system.

Just as with any amateur station, an MSO system and transmitter must be controlled either manually or remotely. Most MSOs are not in repeater operation, so they cannot be controlled automatically. Thus, a control operator must be on duty at a control point of the MSO transmitter at all times it is in operation (97.79[b]).

Q. When my repeater is automatically controlled with no control operator on duty at a control point, who's responsible for the station's transmissions?

A. Again, the station licensee is responsible for the proper operation of the station. The key to automatic control is that the station perform just as if the control operator were present at a control point. You must be able to effect control immediately.

Unlicensed Persons

One of the enjoyable parts of our avocation is watching the grin of an unlicensed person's face as he participates in Amateur Radio by talking to a station across the country or on the other side of the world. The important term in that sentence is *participates*. An unlicensed person may never *operate* an amateur station, but he may *participate* in Amateur Radio. This means that, as a third party, he may speak over a microphone, use the keyboard of a radioteletype station, or a telegraph key or camera, depending on the mode used.

One point is very important. When a third party (which, by the way, may even be an amateur if he isn't *operating* the station) is participating in Amateur Radio at an amateur station, the station can only be in contact with countries which have third-party agreements with the U.S.

Let's give an example. You have an amateur license, but your brother-in-law, who's speaking over the microphone of your station, is your unlicensed guest. He's busy talking to a station in the States, when an amateur in Spain tries to contact your station. Your brother-in-law may not contact that Spanish station because Spain and the U.S. do not have a third-party agreement. He may, if possible, contact a station in Brazil, because the two countries involved have third-party agreements. The current list of countries that have third-party agreements with the U.S. appears at the end of this chapter. Updates are reported in *QST*, in League Lines or Happenings.

Q. Is it okay to let my unlicensed friend operate my rig? Who's responsible for his operations?

A. Any licensee may permit any third party (someone other than the two control operators—the first and second parties — involved in the communication) to *participate* in your Amateur Radio operations, as long as the third party did not once hold an amateur operator license subsequently suspended, or a station license subsequently revoked (97.114[c][2]). The key word is *participate*. A third party may never operate (control) a station, but may speak into a mic or use a key or keyboard to communicate with the ham on the other end (or the nonham, if there's another third party at the other station). The control operator (first party) must be present to ensure that the station is operating properly during the third-party messages (97.79[d]). The station licensee/control operator assumes full responsibility for the third party's actions.

Q. How closely must the control operator control?

A. Although there is no specific rule about how close the control operator must be to the transmitter's controls, he or she must be "present at a control point." Practically speaking, the CO should not leave the control point with a third party engaged in communication. While it would be okay to allow the third party to press the PTT switch on the mic, the control op should make all operating adjustments to the transmitter.

The third-party-participation rules were never intended to allow quasi-amateur operation by unlicensed individuals.

Where Do I Keep My Amateur Radio License?

A fundamental question, certainly. An amateur station license authorizes the use, under the control of the licensee, of all the transmitting equipment at the fixed location specified on the station license. And, it also authorizes the use under control of the licensee of portable and mobile transmitting equipment at other locations. The station license (the original or a photocopy) must be posted in a conspicuous place in the room occupied by the licensed operator while the station is being operated at a fixed location. If you choose, however, you may also simply keep it in your personal possession — in your wallet or purse, for example.

When the station is operated away from the fixed location, at your vacation home, for example, the station license (again, original or photocopy) must be kept in the personal possession of the station licensee or a licensed representative, when the station is operated portable or mobile. Note, however, that your original station license must be available upon demand of the Commission (except if it has been forwarded for renewal or modification, or has been lost, mutilated or destroyed and request has been made for a duplicate license.)

The operator license must be kept in the personal possession of the licensee when operating an amateur station. A photocopy is sufficient, but the original must be available upon request by the FCC. Of course, the station and operator licenses are on the same piece of paper, so most amateurs simply keep their licenses in their wallet with a copy taped to the wall of their shack.

Points of Communications

A few basics. Amateur stations may communicate with other amateur stations

— except those in countries on the so-called "banned countries list." In the late '60s, for example, Cambodia, Indonesia, Thailand and Vietnam forbade radio communication between their amateur stations and amateur stations in other countries, under this provision of the ITU Radio Regulations:

Article 32, Section 1

Radiocommunications between amateur stations of different countries shall be forbidden if the administration of one of the countries concerned has notified that it objects to such radio communications.

As this is written, however, U.S. amateurs may communicate with any foreign amateur station, as there are no "banned countries." Of course, this may change in the future.

Amateur stations may also communicate with stations in other services licensed by the Commission in emergencies and, on a temporary basis, for test purposes. Amateurs may communicate with U.S. Government stations for civil defense purposes in accordance with RACES (see Chapter 6). Amateurs may communicate with any other station authorized by the Commission to communicate with amateur stations.

Amateur Radio stations may also be used for observation of propagation, radio control of model crafts and similar experimental purposes, and for certain one-way communications covered in Chapter 6. *Beacons* are amateur stations that fall into these categories — stations that are used to measure propagation and ionospheric conditions. (See Chapter 6).

Logs Axed

There is no longer any requirement that radio amateurs keep a record of their operations in a station logbook. The FCC said it made little use of the information kept in hams' logs so the requirements for station logbooks were felled under their deregulatory blade. Goodbye, Sections 97.103 and 97.105!

Let's quickly point out that hams are still encouraged to keep records of their operations, especially of experiments and other activities that may contribute to advances in the radio art. Still other hams will continue to keep track of their QSOs and nets for sentimental or practical reasons. Logs will remain as autobiographies of hams at the helms of their stations.

We should also point out that some information pertaining to specialized operations such as repeater, auxiliary and remote control activity will still have to be kept as "station records." We'll discuss this topic in Chapter 6.

Radio Frequency Interference

Q. First things first: What is RFI?

A. Radio frequency interference (RFI) occurs, or has the potential to occur, whenever an electronic device finds itself surrounded by a field of radio frequency (RF) energy. The source of this RF might be an amateur, CB, police, broadcast or television transmitter, or any other device capable of generating RF energy and causing interference. The electronic device being interfered with and picking up the unwanted RF energy could be a television set, a hi-fi system, a garage-door opener or other sensitive receiver. RFI actually occurs when the electronic device in the midst of the RF field behaves or responds in an undesirable manner because of the presence of the radio frequency field. Sometimes the transmitter is at fault, but usually the fault lies with the electronic device itself, because of insufficient shielding or filtering.

Q. Who is responsible for RFI?

A. The FCC specifies standards for amateur emissions. Amateurs must make sure that their transmitted signals are within these standards, or rules, found in Part 97.

These include limitations on the fundamental signal and harmonics (multiples of the fundamental frequency) and parasitic or spurious emissions (radiations from a transmitter that are outside the authorized amateur band being used). If an amateur signal does not meet these standards and is causing interference, it is the responsibility of the station licensee or control operator of the transmitter to eliminate it. Similarly, if the transmitter is producing a signal that exceeds FCC power limitations, the responsibility for any problems lies with the transmitter operator. If, however, the transmitter is being operated in accordance with the rules and radiating RF energy only on its fundamental frequency, any RF susceptibility that results is caused by design deficiencies such as insufficient shielding and filtering in home-entertainment devices (TVs, stereos and so forth). The responsibility in this case lies with the owner who must modify the equipment to make it immune to unwanted RF energy.

Q. What is meant by "quiet hours"?

A. "Quiet hours" refer to periods of restricted operation, an administrative sanction found in Section 97.131:

"(a) If the operation of an amateur station causes general interference to the reception of transmissions from stations operating in the domestic broadcast service when receivers of good engineering design including adequate selectivity characteristics are used to receive such transmission and this fact is made known to the amateur station licensee, the amateur station shall not be operated during the hours from 8 P.M. to 10:30 P.M., local time, and on Sunday for the additional period from 10:30 A.M. until 1 P.M., local time, upon the frequency or frequencies used when the interference is created.

(b) In general, such steps as may be necessary to minimize interference to stations operating in other services may be required after investigation by the Commission."

Additional quiet hours and further administrative sanction may be imposed in the event of multiple violations of technical standards. In these cases, an amateur must prove to the Commission that problems have been corrected before full privileges will be reinstated (§§97.133, 97.135, 97.137).

Q. What must I do if I receive a Notice of Violation?

A. You must reply to the FCC office issuing the Notice within 10 days of receipt (unless you have a valid excuse for a tardy response). If the Notice relates to a physical or electrical problem, you must state fully what steps you have taken to correct the situation to ensure future compliance with the rules. This information should include manufacturers' names of remedial equipment installed. The reply should be complete in itself and may not be abbreviated by reference to other communications or notices. If the notice relates to some lack of attention to or improper operation of the transmitter, the name of the operator in charge must be given (§97.137). It is very important to reply to a Notice of Violation — FCC will initiate license-revocation proceedings should you choose not to respond!

A Break For Station Identification

Score another victory in the win column for unregulation. Recently, the FCC relaxed station identification requirements so amateurs are no longer required to identify the station with which they were in contact. The sole exception applies to *international* third-party traffic: i.e., when amateurs are engaged in phone patching, or any other third-party-traffic activity involving foreign stations, *both* call signs must still be given. This provision also applies to RTTY stations. (Prior to the FCC action, RTTY operators were not required to ID the other station at any time.)

Response to the commission's action has been generally favorable, and perhaps may be typified by the following excerpt from the *Murphy Message,* newsletter of the Murphy's Marauders Contest Club: "The former requirement of signing both calls was an unnecessary burden to contesters and DXers for a long time . . . The previous rule was totally impractical for high-volume QSO situations, and even though it took FCC four years to act, let's be glad that it finally happened, especially in time for this year's contest season.''

Let us now turn to a subject close to home of the active amateur — station ID.

Q. What is the language of the new ID rule?

A. Part 97 of the Commission's rules was amended as follows:

In section 97.84, paragraph (a) is amended and paragraph (h) is added to read:

§97.84 *Station Identification*

(a) Each amateur radio station shall give its call sign at the end of each communication, and every ten minutes or less during a communication.

(h) At the end of an exchange of third-party communications with a station located in a foreign country, each amateur radio station shall also give the call sign of the station with which third-party communications were exchanged.

Q. Does this new rule mean that amateurs don't have to give their call sign at the beginning of the contact?

A. Affirmative. Legally, amateurs may give their calls only at the end of the contact, and at least once every 10 minutes during the course of the QSO. As a practical matter, however, most amateurs will continue the tradition of IDing often to promote efficient, effective communications. The new rules carry the most impact for contesters and DXers where brevity is their bread, and swiftness their butter. Also, the Commission felt that the simpler ID requirement would mean smoother-flowing communications in emergencies and in emergency-preparedness exercises such as nets and round-tables. To a large extent, this should be true. Amateurs will no longer have to give lengthy IDs when engaged in high-speed emergency traffic handling.

Q. What is this "Temporary AA" I keep hearing in the bands?

A. A few years ago, the FCC eliminated the need for amateurs who are upgrading to endure the wait for the new license before commencing operation with their new privileges. Volunteer examiners issue temporary permits that authorize use of the applicant's newly won privileges immediately.

In the period after passing the exam and before the new ticket arrives from Gettysburg, amateurs must add a special designator to their call signs when identifying operation with the new privileges. For example, a station operating in the Advanced portion of the band with a new Advanced class temporary permit must give his call followed by "temporary AA"; the AA is the VEC designator for Advanced class temporary permits. On CW, the slant bar is transmitted after the call sign, followed by the VEC designator.

Q. I frequently conduct my QSOs in Spanish. Is it okay if I identify my station in this language?

A. No. The rules specifically say that the ID must be made in the English language.

Q. In what manners may I identify my station?

A. You may use Morse code telegraphy and English language telephony. You may also use AMTOR, ASCII or Baudot when the particular code is used for transmission of all or part of the communication or when the communication is transmitted in any digital code on frequencies above 50 MHz.

Video may be used for identifying fast-scan TV signals when the standard 525-scan-line-format is employed. Facsimile and slow-scan TV communications must still be identified in Morse or phone.

Q. Is it okay to give my call sign in phonetics when identifying?

A. Yes. The Commission encourages the use of a nationally or internationally recognized standard phonetic alphabet as an aid for correct telephone identification. The International Telecommunication Union (ITU) has developed such a list:

A — Alfa	N — November
B — Bravo	O — Oscar
C — Charlie	P — Papa
D — Delta	Q — Quebec
E — Echo	R — Romeo
F — Foxtrot	S — Sierra
G — Golf	T — Tango
H — Hotel	U — Uniform
I — India	V — Victor
J — Juliette	W — Whiskey
K — Kilo	X — X-Ray
L — Lima	Y — Yankee
M — Mike	Z — Zulu

For example, Linda, KA1GQJ, may identify her operation by transmitting the words "Kilo Alfa One Golf Quebec Juliette." Cute IDs should be avoided when fulfilling the station ID requirements.

Q. Is it legal to use "tactical" call signs when engaged in public service communications?

A. Yes; amateurs may use such "tactical" call signs as "Unit One" or "Checkpoint Charlie" to promote efficiency and coordination in public service communication activities. However, these types of identifiers are *not* substitutes for station call signs when fulfilling the identification requirements of §97.84. Amateurs must *always* identify their station's operation with its FCC-assigned call sign.

Operation Away From Home

While most of your ham radio activity will take place, logically, at your home shack, opportunities will arise for operation at other locations — in your car, at your vacation home, at Field Day or even outside the country. Amateurs are permitted to operate their stations portable or mobile under their station licenses anywhere in the United States, its territories and possessions (see table at the end of this chapter for a list). There is no longer any need to notify the FCC, or make a log notation, of your portable operation.

When there is a permanent change in station location, however, the Commission must be notified on a Form 610 so the station license may be modified accordingly.

International and Maritime Mobile Operation

Good amateur practice and strict rules compliance have always characterized the operations of the vast majority of U.S. hams. In fact, on several occasions the Commission itself has lauded the amateur community for its self-policing abilities and adherence not only to the rules but to unwritten ethics dictating high standards of conduct.

However, pockets of problems do crop up from time to time. They usually stem from misinterpretations and myths surrounding so-called "gray areas" in the rules. Nowhere is this more true than in the case of maritime mobile operation in and around foreign ports. Well-intentioned U.S. hams often have trouble in determining just whose rules they're supposed to follow when sailing the seven seas.

There is a darker side, too. Unscrupulous yachters who do not hold ham tickets use our amateur frequencies for such purposes as ordering parts and supplies for their vessels, and conducting stateside business affairs. They harbor the ill-conceived notion that, because they're on the high seas, somehow the rules don't apply to them. Still others forgo the standard marine mobile emergency communications gear, relying instead solely on an unlicensed ham transceiver — a dangerous proposition in a maritime emergency. Unfortunately, some ham sailors disregard international and domestic law, complicating U.S. and foreign efforts to reach important third-party and reciprocal-operating agreements.

Administrations unfriendly to international Amateur Radio are the first to cite these instances as reasons for removing privileges and frequencies at worldwide allocation conferences such as WARC-79. With another general WARC possible in just a few short years, now is the time for all amateurs to come to grips with these problems so that international Amateur Radio will remain the shining star it is.

Q. Soon my wife and I will set sail on a luxury liner for a cruise among the Caribbean islands. I'd like to bring a rig with me. When operating, whose rules do I follow?

A. The first determinant is the country of registry for the vessel. When operating on the high seas (in international waters) on a U.S.-registered vessel, you will follow Part 97 of the FCC Rules. This means that if you are an alien (other than a Canadian citizen) licensee, you must obtain either a U.S. Amateur Radio license by passing the required examination, or a reciprocal operating permit from the FCC prior to your operation aboard the U.S. ship. U.S. licensees and Canadian DOC licensees need no special permit or authorization other than their own licenses. Canadian and U.S. hams enjoy automatic reciprocal operating privileges.

Q. Whose rules do I follow when my U.S. ship sails into the waters of another country?

A. When sailing or anchored in the territorial waters of another country, you must check the rules of that country prior to your operation of an amateur station. You must comply with those rules and obtain any required license or permit from that country's government. It is recommended that you study the country's requirements well in advance of your departure date, as some administrations can take as long as six months to issue the necessary operating paperwork. Plan ahead!

Q. What if the vessel is of non-U.S. origin?

A. If you are sailing in international waters aboard a non-U.S. vessel, check the rules of the country of the ship's registry. You must obey those rules, and obtain any necessary license or permit from that country's government prior to your operation. If you are sailing in the waters of a foreign government's territory, then you must observe the rules of that government. You must obtain any necessary license or permit from that government prior to your operation in its territory.

Q. What do foreign Amateur Radio rules encompass?

A. When your operation is governed by the rules of a foreign country, be sure you obey *all* of them. This means you should review those rules carefully, as there may be requirements that differ widely from your home country's rules. Make sure you observe the frequency bands permitted, station ID requirements, third-party traffic restrictions, and so forth.

Part 97 on the High Seas

Q. When U.S. rules apply, what provisions pertain specifically to international and maritime mobile operation?

A. Concerning your equipment aboard a ship, (1) the installation and operation must be approved by the master of the ship; (2) it must be separate from and independent of all other radio equipment, if any, installed aboard the ship; (3) its electrical installation must be in accord with the rules applicable to ships as put forth by the appropriate government agency; (4) no interference must result to the efficient operation of any radio equipment installed onboard the same ship; and (5) your equipment and any associated gear must not cause a hazard to the safety of life or property (97.101).

For stations in ITU Region 2 frequencies used must be consistent with U.S. frequency bands and, if a U.S. station, the privileges of the control operator's license class. Outside Region 2 and subject to the limitations of the control operator's license class, the frequency segments listed in 97.7 may be employed.

Q. What ITU Region do I reside in?

A. If your station is in Europe or Africa, it's in Region 1. North and South America comprise Region 2. And the rest of the world makes up Region 3. See map below.

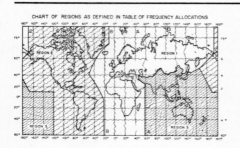

CHART OF REGIONS AS DEFINED IN TABLE OF FREQUENCY ALLOCATIONS

Note: Region 2 is defined as follows: On the east, a line (B) extending from the North Pole along meridian 10° of Greenwich to its intersection with parallel 72°; thence by Great Circle Arc to the intersection of meridian 50° W and parallel 40° N; thence by Great Circle Arc to the intersection of meridian 20° W and parallel 10° S; thence along meridian 20 degrees west to the South Pole. On the west, a line (C) extending from the North Pole by Great Circle Arc to the intersection of parallel 65°, 30' N with the international boundary in Bering Strait; thence by Great Circle Arc to the intersection of meridian 165° East of Greenwich and parallel 50° N; thence by Great Circle Arc to the intersection of meridian 170° West and parallel 10° N; thence along parallel 10° N to its intersection with meridian 120° West thence along meridian 12° West to the South Pole.

Q. Can I pass third-party traffic?

A. In cases where U.S. rules apply, you may pass third-party traffic, including phone patches with the U.S. mainland. You may *not* handle or pass such traffic with other countries, *except* those with whom the U.S. holds third-party-traffic agreements. There are never any exceptions to these rules, and even thoughtless violations can cost the good reputation hams have earned over the years.

There has been a great amount of abuse of third-party-traffic privileges. These privileges are tenuous, at best, and subject to swift revocation. Do *not* use phone patches and traffic nets for ordering parts and supplies, delivering business messages or making arrangements for accommodations at ports of call. Third-party messages and remarks must be limited to those of a personal nature — general greetings, for example. Of course, if an emergency presents a threat to the safety of life or property, then use whatever means you can to get help.

Make a special effort to inform other hams of the gravity of the third-party-traffic situation. Let's put our self-policing powers to work to curb abuses.

Q. I am an alien licensee and want to operate in U.S. waters. What kind of authorization do I need? What rules do I follow?

A. In order to operate when you are in U.S. jurisdiction including aboard a U.S. vessel in international waters and on any vessel or land in U.S. territory, you must obtain either an FCC Amateur Radio license by passing the required exams or a reciprocal operating permit. The only exception applies to Canadian citizens with DOC licenses because of U.S.-Canadian automatic reciprocity. (97.303)(97.41)

Any alien may apply for a U.S. ham license, and is encouraged to do so by the FCC if he/she will be spending a considerable length of time in the U.S. Applications for U.S. licenses are made on the Form 610.

Application for a reciprocal operating permit is made on the FCC Form 610-A, and sent to FCC, Gettysburg, PA 17325. The application should be filed at least 60 days in advance of the planned operation. Normally, a permit will expire one year after issuance, but in no event after the expiration of the license issued to the alien amateur by his or her government (97.307). Reciprocal operating permits will be issued *only* to non U.S. citizens.

Alien operation under the FCC permit will be governed by Part 97, the terms of the reciprocal-operating agreement between the U.S. and the alien's home country, and the provisions of the alien's home license. FCC may also impose additional conditions on the alien's operation. (97.311)

Station ID consists of the alien's home call sign followed by the U.S. call sign letter prefix and number for the location of his or her operation — G3CE/W1, for example. At least once during each contact with another amateur station, the alien amateur shall indicate, in English, the geographical location of his station as nearly as possible by city and state, commonwealth or possession — G3CE/W1 Boston, Massachusetts, for example. (97.313)

Third-Party-Traffic Countries List

Alphabetical by country

V2	Antigua & Barbuda	YS	El Salvador	ZP	Paraguay
LU	Argentina	C5	The Gambia	OA	Peru
VK	Australia	9G	Ghana	VR6	Pitcairn Island*
V3	Belize	J3	Grenada	V4	St. Christopher (St. Kitts)
CP	Bolivia	TG	Guatemala		and Nevis
PY	Brazil	8R	Guyana	J6	St. Lucia
VE	Canada	HH	Haiti	J8	St. Vincent
CE	Chile	HR	Honduras	3D6	Swaziland
HK	Colombia	4X	Israel	9Y	Trinidad & Tobago
TI	Costa Rica	6Y	Jamaica	GB	United Kingdom**
CO	Cuba	JY	Jordan	CX	Uruguay
J7	Dominica	EL	Liberia	YV	Venezuela
HI	Dominican Rep.	XE	Mexico	4U1ITU	ITU, Geneva
HC	Ecuador	YN	Nicaragua	4U1VIC	VIC, Geneva
		HP	Panama		

*Informal Temporary

**Limited to special-event stations with callsign prefix GB; GB3 excluded

Alphabetical by prefix

CE	Chile	J3	Grenada	V4	St. Christopher (St. Kitts)
CO	Cuba	J6	St. Lucia		and Nevis
CP	Bolivia	J7	Dominica	XE	Mexico
CX	Uruguay	J8	St. Vincent	YN	Nicaragua
C5	The Gambia	LU	Argentina	YS	El Salvador
EL	Liberia	OA	Peru	YV	Venezuela
GB	United Kingdom**	PY	Brazil	ZP	Paraguay
HC	Ecuador	TG	Guatemala	3D6	Swaziland
HH	Haiti	TI	Costa Rica	4U1ITU	ITU, Geneva
HI	Dominican Rep.	VE	Canada	4U1VIC	VIC, Geneva
HK	Colombia	VK	Australia	4X	Israel
HP	Panama	VR6	Pitcairn Island*	6Y	Jamaica
HR	Honduras	V2	Antigua & Baruda	8R	Guyana
JY	Jordan	V3	Belize	9G	Ghana
				9Y	Trinidad & Tobago

*Informal Temporary

**Limited to special-event stations with callsign prefix GB; GB3 excluded

Reciprocal Operating Permits

You will need to have a reciprocal operating permit to operate your station in the territory of a foreign government, except Canada. Follow these guidelines to allow smooth sailing for your application.

1) Submit your application via air mail as long in advance of your trip as possible. Allow at least 60 to 90 days for processing of your application (forms and information on specific countries are available from the Information Services Dept., ARRL Hq., upon request with s.a.s.e.).

2) Send a letter with your application giving the purpose of your trip, dates of stay, passport number and an address where you may be reached in the host country.

3) Attach a photocopy of your current amateur license to your application or letter.

4) For those countries for which the ARRL does not have formal application papers, you should request them in your cover letter described above.

5) Ask the consulate or embassy in the U.S. of the country or countries you intend to visit regarding their policy of importing your amateur equipment; policies vary from country to country. This can save you much grief when you arrive at your destination. Remember that although the customs officers are generally quite polite, they will never bend rules or violate them.

For amateurs trying to obtain permission to operate in a country with which the U.S. does not hold a reciprocal operating agreement, these additional steps should be taken:

1) Take along three or four passport-size photos of yourself. Some countries require them before processing applications.

2) Have three extra photocopies of your U.S. license(s) with you.

3) Present a letter attesting to your character, signed by the chief of police (or equivalent) in your home city. Have extra copies with you.

4) Include photocopies of your residence permit, visa or tourist card with your cover letter.

Many of the countries not holding reciprocity with the U.S. and Canada will grant permits on a courtesy basis. But you may have to wait until your arrival to apply. Obviously, it would not be to such a country's advantage — or yours — to process an application for periods of stay of less than 30 days. If you plan ahead — and follow these instructions — you should find the process of applying to operate an amateur station overseas to be pleasant and uncomplicated.

Canadian and U.S. Reciprocal Operating

A few years ago, the FCC, and the Canadian counterpart, the Department of Communications (DOC) agreed to automatic reciprocity. Thus, Canadian radio amateurs visiting the U.S. and United States amateurs visiting Canada no longer need reciprocal operating permits from the country they are visiting.

Visiting amateurs must confine themselves to both the host country's restrictions *and* their home restrictions. When you travel across the U.S./Canadian border, it's always a good idea to have your original license with you.

Special reciprocal operating agreements between the U.S. and other countries exist to facilitate applications and granting of permits. These countries are:

LU	Argentina	V3	Belize	HK	Colombia
VK	Australia	CP	Bolivia	TI	Costa Rica
OE	Austria	A2	Botswana	OZ	Denmark
C6	Bahamas	PY	Brazil	HI	Dominican Rep.
8P	Barbados	VE	Canada	HC	Ecuador
ON	Belgium	CE	Chile	YS	El Salvador
3D2	Fiji	6Y	Jamaica	DU	Philippines
OH	Finland	JA	Japan	CT	Portugal
F	France	JY	Jordan	J6	St. Lucia
DL	Germany	T3	Kiribati	9L	Sierra Leone
SV	Greece	9K	Kuwait	H4	Solomon Islands
J3	Grenada	EL	Liberia	ZS	South Africa
TG	Guatemala	LX	Luxembourg	EA	Spain
8R	Guyana	3A	Monaco	PZ	Suriname
HH	Haiti	PA	Netherlands	SM	Sweden
HR	Honduras	PJ	Neth. Antilles	HB	Switzerland
TF	Iceland	ZL	New Zealand	9Y	Trinidad & Tobago
VU	India	YN	Nicaragua	T2	Tuvalu
YB	Indonesia	LA	Norway	G	United Kingdom*
EI	Ireland	HP	Panama	CX	Uruguay
4X	Israel	ZP	Paraguay	YV	Venezuela
I	Italy	OA	Peru	YU	Yugosalvia

*Includes the following territories: VP2A, VP2D, VP2M, VP2V, VP5, VP8, VP9, VS6, ZB2, ZD7 and ZF.

The following is a list of the territories and possessions of the United States:

KH1	Baker and Howland Islands	KH7	Kure Island
KH2	Guam	KH8	American Samoa
KH3	Johnston Island	KH9	Wake Island
KH4	Midway Island	KH0	Northern Marianas
KH5	Palmyra and Jarvis Islands (except KH5K)	KP1	Navassa
		KP2	Virgin Islands
		KP4	Puerto Rico
KH5K	Kingman Reef	KP5	Desecheo Island

Chapter 6

Specialized Operating Practices

In the last chapter, we examined the general operating rules as they affect operation of all amateur stations. In this section, we'll take a look at some of the more specialized operating activities and rules. We'll examine repeaters and auxiliary stations, remote control, RACES, satellites, beacons, emergency communications and more. As your interests in Amateur Radio blossom, you'll want to know how to take part in a manner consistent with the rules.

Repeaters

Repeater communication is one of the most popular activities in Amateur Radio today...Just what is the basic appeal of the repeater?

First, let's look at the functions of a "machine." A repeater normally consists of a transceiver, an antenna, a control box and a duplexer (to allow use of a single antenna for both transmitting and receiving). Operation generally occurs on the VHF amateur bands although there is some 10-meter repeater activity. The most popular band for repeaters is 144 MHz (2 meters) with 220 MHz and 450 MHz following in popularity. FM is widely used.

A typical machine sits atop a mountain or tall building and automatically retransmits the "user's" signal from a small hand-held or mobile rig. The result is an increase in communications coverage for the user — some repeaters will extend coverage to entire states and more! Because of this unique characteristic of repeaters, many other radio services use them. Police and fire departments, forest services, taxis and other so-called land mobile services make great use of repeaters.

The FCC Rules define repeater operation as "radio communication, other than auxiliary operation, for retransmitting automatically the radio signals of other Amateur Radio stations." With this definition in mind, we'll turn now to a discussion of some important rules affecting operation of repeaters.

Control

Just as with any Amateur Radio station, a control operator must be present at a control point to ensure that the repeater is operating within the Rules. There is one exception called, "automatic control," which we'll talk about shortly.

As we've seen from the discussion of control in Chapter 5, there are many ways to effect control of ham stations. Because repeaters are generally found on hilltops and tall buildings, *local* control is not practical. Thus, many repeaters are controlled remotely through the use of a control link. This link can take the form of a telephone line or dedicated line from the control point to the repeater. Or, radio remote control may be employed whereby a second Amateur Radio station is used to transmit control commands to the repeater. This second station, usually found at the home or office of the station trustee and/or control operator, is in *auxiliary operation*. And many auxiliary stations can be used to control the repeater — one or two for each control operator. When the repeater is controlled remotely, transmissions must be stopped within *three minutes* if a malfunction occurs in the control link system.

Amateurs often install a three-minute timer so, if the control link should fail, the repeater will shut off automatically in three minutes.

Most repeaters are operated under still another type of control, *automatic control*. Even though no control operator is required to be present at a control point, the repeater must operate properly just as if one were present under other types of control. Make sure procedures and devices are used to prevent unauthorized tampering — either physically at the repeater site, or by the use of the control link functions. Use "secret" control link frequencies. Put padlocks on your repeater housing. Make sure you get the word quickly if something is wrong, and then have quick access to the repeater turn-off function. Protect your feed lines and antennas whenever possible. And don't allow autopatch operation when the repeater is operated by automatic control — when third parties participate in ham radio communication, a control operator *must always be present* to ensure rules compliance.

The station license must be posted at the transmitter site of the remotely controlled station. Also, station records must include the names, addresses and call signs of all authorized control operators, and a functional block diagram of the control link sufficient to describe its operation. If radio remote control is employed, don't forget to include a system network diagram showing the relationship of the associated stations. All remotely controlled stations must be protected against unauthorized use, either physically or through the control link.

Repeater Power Limits and Station Records

Special power limits apply to stations in repeater operation because of their unique

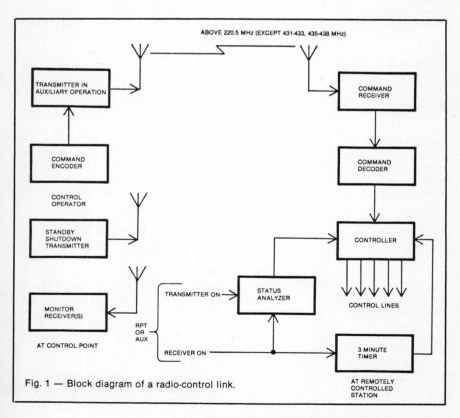

Fig. 1 — Block diagram of a radio-control link.

characteristics of height above average terrain and power combining to influence the "coverage" area directly. The higher and stronger they are, the greater the coverage. FCC specifies power limits in terms of effective radiated power that vary depending on the height above average terrain of the machine. The higher the repeater, the lesser the amount of ERP allowed. See Section 97.67 for repeater ERP limits. See Chapter 4 for information on how to compute HAAT and ERP.

If your repeater transmits an ERP higher than 100 watts between 29.5 and 420 MHz, or 400 watts between 420 and 1215 MHz, then you must include the following information in your station records: (1) location of the station transmitting antenna marked upon a topographic map having contour intervals and having a scale of 1:250,000 (indexes and ordering information for suitable maps are available from the U.S. Geological Survey, Washington, DC 20242, or from the Federal Center, Denver, CO 80255; (2) the transmitter's HAAT; (3) ERP in the horizontal plane for the main lobe of the antenna pattern, calculated for the maximum transmitter output power that occurs during operation; (4) the loss in the transmission feed line between the transmitter and the antenna (including devices such as duplexers, cavities or circulators), expressed in decibels; and (5) the relative gain in the horizontal plane of the transmitting antenna.

Repeater Station Identification

Repeaters may be identified by CW or voice. On CW, send your call followed by /RPT or /R. On voice use the word "repeater." Repeaters can also be identified by telegraphy using ASCII, Baudot or AMTOR when that particular code is used for all or part of the communication or when the communication is transmitted in any digital code above 50 MHz. Amateur television repeaters may identify with video as long as the U.S. standard 525-line system is used. The same applies to auxiliary stations, except that /AUX, /A or "auxiliary" should be added to your call sign.

Repeater Frequency Segments

Repeater operation is permitted on the following frequency segments:

29.5-29.7 MHz	220.5-225.0 MHz
52.0-54.0 MHz	420-431 MHz and 433-435 MHz
144.5-145.5 and 146.0-148.0 MHz	Any amateur frequency above 438.0 MHz

Band Plans

Got a renegade ham on your hands? You know the type: He operates simplex on the input of the local repeater. Or worse, he puts *his* repeater on a frequency pair of *his* choosing despite what the local frequency coordinator has to say. Some renegades enjoy setting up shop on FM in popular EME and terrestrial weak-signal areas, creating havoc with communications of good spectrum citizens.

The renegade writes off his "operation" as being in strict accordance with the letter of the law in Part 97. "Sure, wideband FM is permitted at 144.15 — check it out in the regs" and "I was here first — who cares if this happens to be some dumb repeater's input?" are popular retorts from the renegade.

These retorts, however, don't wash with the Commission. And thanks to a recent communique, the FCC's feelings are down on paper. Let's take a look at the meaning of good amateur practice, and how it affects operation in accord with nationally recognized band plans.

Q. How does the Commission feel about the amateur community's own frequency planning and coordination?

A. In a repeater rules proceeding a while back, FCC said:

"The Commission is persuaded by the comments and by observation that regional and national frequency planning and coordination by amateur radio operators themselves can result in the best spectrum utilization appropriate to the service." We'll add that "best spectrum utilization" means amateurs operating in accordance with "good amateur practice" — a requirement found in Section 97.78 of the Rules.

Q. How does FCC view amateurs who place their repeaters on frequency pairs in disregard of repeater band plans?

A. In an April 27, 1983, letter to a major repeater council, FCC said:

> The only national planning for Amateur Radio Service frequencies that has come to our attention is that done by the American Radio Relay League. The 1982-83 edition of the *ARRL Repeater Directory* lists over 5600 stations in repeater operation all over the United States and Canada. In view of this widespread acceptance of their band plans, we conclude that any amateur who selects a station transmitting frequency not in harmony with those plans is not operating in accord with good amateur practice. [For example] The *ARRL Repeater Directory* lists the frequency pair 144.83/145.43 MHz as a repeater channel. Therefore, designation of this channel by the regional frequency coordinator in [an] area is in accord with the ARRL national band plan.

The bottom line is that if stations transmit on frequencies 144.83 or 145.43 (to use the Commission's example above), in a manner that creates interference to coordinated repeaters, then sufficient cause would exist for issuance of an Official Notice of Violation of Section 97.78. And, such operation could mean an additional Notice for deliberate and malicious interference (97.125).

There are good reasons why simplex operation should be moved from repeater frequencies. The FCC has labeled three: (1) Repeater operation is not permitted on some Amateur Radio bands; (2) on those bands where repeater operation is permitted, such operation is confined to a limited portion — a subband — of the band; and (3) the nature of repeater operation necessitates some form of channelization; haphazard frequency selection would result in poor spectrum use, and constant frequency change is impractical.

Simplex stations do *not* have such limitations; thus, they have much greater flexibility in frequency choice. They must avoid repeater channels found in widely accepted band plans. Such avoidance constitutes good amateur practice.

Q. Do band plans exist for other bands and activities?

A. Yes; in fact, there are band plans for just about every amateur band.

For example, the 450-MHz band harbors many amateur activities: satellite, television, weak-signal terrestrial and EME commmunications, and FM and repeater operation. Sure, there's a lot of space in this segment, 420-450 MHz. But there are many activities that would collide with each other if it were not for this plan.

Let's be quick to point out that these plans are not unilateral decisions made in a vacuum. With *lots* of input from the VRAC, the VUAC and other leading groups, they develop and evolve over a period of several years, sometimes decades. Each plan is designed to promote the greatest spectrum efficiency possible.

All amateurs should make every effort to operate in concert with these plans, which have the approval of the ham community and the FCC. In fact, "good amateur practice" dictates compliance with these community standards.

Q. Where can I find copies of band plans?

A. You won't find them in Part 97. As mentioned above, band plans are generated within the amateur ranks, not from the desks of the FCC. You will find these plans in Chapter 4.

Q. Why are band plans so crucial?

A. Since the beginning, amateurs have maintained a fine tradition of keeping their own shop in order. For years, the Commission has lauded our Service for its effective self-policing abilities. There is no clearer demonstration of this tradition than amateurs' own development of band plans.

As every active ham knows, there is a myriad of special interests in Amateur

Radio. Band plans are in place, in lieu of regulations to allow the array of operating activities to function with a minimum of QRM and frustration. They keep Amateur Radio on the straight and narrow path to coordinated and orderly progress. And most important, if we as amateurs can't keep order to prevent chaos, no one can!

Auxiliary Operation

When a repeater is controlled remotely by radio, there is another station involved — the station doing the controlling. This station is said to be in *auxiliary operation*. In FCC Rules, an auxiliary station is used, among other things, to send transmissions to control other amateur stations in a system of stations. The control link is a radio signal of the auxiliary station to the station in repeater operation being controlled. Tones are transmitted on the link to the control board of the repeater, and are decoded and implemented. The repeater is turned on and off by this means.

The auxiliary station's transmissions (the control link) must be on amateur frequencies above 220.5 MHz (except 431-433 and 435-438 MHz to protect satellite operations here). Fig. 1 on page 6-2 shows a block diagram of a typical radio-control link. The repeater input must *not* be used for control link command purposes.

Auxiliary stations are also used as remote receivers for repeaters to bring in distant users' signals. And, occasionally, auxiliary stations are used to "link" two repeaters to broaden the coverage area of any given user's signals. In this case, the auxiliary station may use an input (receiving) frequency in the auxiliary bands, repeater bands, or both.

The important fact to remember is that auxiliary stations are *point-to-point* in nature. An auxiliary station is used to facilitate communication between two designated points within a system of stations.

Auxiliary stations are not limited to use with repeaters. Another application of an auxiliary station is *remote control* of conventional amateur stations. For example, a ham who lives in a valley between two mountains may put a 2-meter station atop one of the mountains and remotely control it with an auxiliary station at the control point at his home in the valley. Hams may use this method to relay their signals into distant repeaters (see Fig. 2).

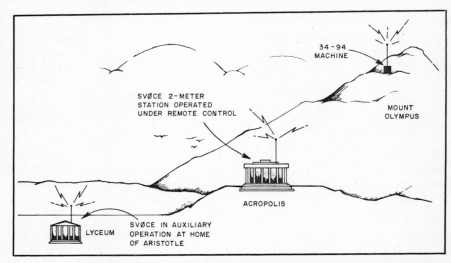

Fig. 2 — In ancient Athens, Aristotle, SVØCE, used an auxiliary link to remotely control his 2-meter station atop the Parthenon. This system enabled him to check into the nightly Philosophy Net on the distant Mount Olympus repeater to discuss the issues of the day with fellow hams Theophrastus, Eudemus and Alexander The Great.

More and more, conventional amateur stations remotely controlled in the manner just described are becoming known as *remote bases*. The transmitter controlling the remote base is in auxiliary operation, but the remote base is not in auxiliary operation unless auxiliary links operate in both directions. And it's important to point out, as mentioned in Chapter 5, that the remotely controlled transmitter or remote base is not a repeater as defined by the FCC rules. This means that an operator controlling a remote base must not operate the remotely controlled transmitter beyond the privileges allowed by his or her license class. (In other words, although, for example, it is acceptable for the 2-meter signals of a Technician Class licensee to be repeated on 10 meters if the license class of the repeater's control operator affords operation on the 10-meter repeater subband, it is not acceptable for a Technician to control a remote base with an output on a "non-Technician" frequency. Once again, the reason for this is that the remote base is not a repeater; the person controlling the remote base is the control operator of a conventional amateur station.)

Questions and Answers

Q. What frequencies must be used by a relay station operating as a link between two repeaters?

A. The relay station is a "station in auxiliary operation" and must be operated on frequencies available for auxiliary operation. Its input (receiving) frequencies, however, may be frequencies available for auxiliary operation, repeater operation, or both (§97.86[b]), (§97.3[1]).

Q. Is it permissible to incorporate additional inputs (receivers) and outputs (transmitters) in my repeater?

A. Yes, with certain limitations. Additional receivers and transmitters may be incorporated, as long as they are used on frequencies available to repeaters. There is a further restriction on transmitters — "A station in repeater operation shall not concurrently retransmit Amateur Radio signals on more than one frequency in the same amateur frequency band, from the same location" (§97.85[c]).

Q. Are "closed" repeaters legal?

A. Yes. "Provisions to limit automatically the access to a station in repeater operation may be incorporated but are not mandatory" (§97.85[a]). Repeaters are often operated under this provision when incidental signals on the input frequency interfere with repeater transmissions.

Q. A local repeater has a special provision whereby it automatically retransmits a local NOAA (National Oceanic and Atmospheric Administration) weather reporting station broadcast on the hour. Is this legal?

A. No. The Commission specifically prohibits retransmission by automatic means of programs or signals emanating from any class of station other than amateur (§97.113).

However, there are at least two ways you can legally make this information available. If the weather service has a recorded *telephone* message, you can have one of the autopatch functions encoded to dial that telephone number. Thus, it would not be a retransmission by automatic means, since it was never transmitted in the first place.

The other way is to have someone record the weather from a script onto a tape, updating the information every so often, and making the recording available to repeater station users. And, of course, it should be made available *only* to amateurs so that the transmission of the information is not intended to be a one-way communication to be received by the general public (§97.113).

Q. Our repeater system incorporates a link by which an operator may have his 2-meter signals retransmitted on 10 meters. A Technician class licensee often avails himself of this function. Is it legal for his signals to be retransmitted by our repeater on frequencies not assigned to Techs?

A. The Commission says "As long as the control operator of the transmitting station is authorized (see §97.7) for the frequency privileges being used, the fact that the station may retransmit from frequencies authorized to both higher and lower operator classes is of no consequence. For example, there is no prohibition, per se, for those types of operations where retransmission is permitted (repeater, auxiliary and space) to retransmitting the signals from a station with a Technician class control operator on frequencies not authorized for the Technician class." In a nutshell, the above clarification allows Technician class amateur signals to be retransmitted automatically by stations in repeater operation in the 10-meter subband not authorized to Techs.

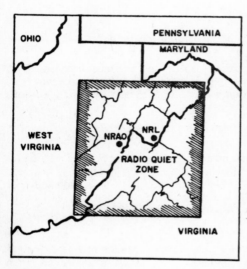

The National Radio Quiet Zone

If you're modifying an existing repeater, or are thinking about placing your station in repeater operation in the National Radio Quiet Zone, you must give written notification of your proposal to the Director, National Radio Astronomy Observatory, P.O. Box 2, Green Bank, WV 24944. Station modification is any change in frequency, power, antenna height or directivity, or the location of the station. The notification must include the geographical coordinates of the antenna, antenna height, antenna directivity (if any), proposed frequency, emission type and power.

If the Commission receives an objection to the proposed operation from the National Radio Astronomy Observatory at Green Bank, for itself, or on behalf of the Naval Research Laboratory at Sugar Grove, within 20 days from the date of notification, the Commission will consider all aspects of the problem and take appropriate action.

The National Radio Quiet Zone is the area bounded by 39° 39' N on the north, 78° 30' W on the east, 37° 30' N on the south and 80° 30' W on the west.

Emergency Communications

Emergency communications is defined in the rules (Section 97.3[w]) as "a non-directed request for help or a distress signal directly relating to the immediate safety of human life or the immediate protection of property." Section 97.107 of the rules deals with amateur operation in emergencies. If an emergency strikes a widespread area, disrupting the normal lines of communication, the FCC engineer-in-charge of the area may designate certain frequencies for use by stations assisting the stricken area only. All amateur transmissions with, or within, the designated area conducted on the FCC-designated emergency frequencies must pertain directly to relief work, emergency service or the establishment and maintenance of efficient networks for handling emergency traffic. Also, the Commission may designate certain amateur stations to police the emergency frequencies, warning noncomplying stations operating there. The emergency conditions imposed by the FCC under Section 97.107 of its rules can be lifted only by the FCC or its authorized representative. Amateurs desiring a declaration of a communication emergency should contact the FCC engineer-in-charge of the area concerned.

Permissible One-Way Transmissions

Amateurs generally conduct two-way communications with other amateur stations. Broadcasting is not allowed. To clarify its position on broadcasting by amateurs, however, the Commission has listed in §97.113(d) of its rules four types of one-way transmissions that *are* permitted and that it will not construe as broadcasting. These

---

Repeater Operating Practices

1) Monitor the repeater to become familiar with any peculiarities in its operation.

2) To initiate a contact simply indicate that you are on frequency. Various geographical areas have different practices on making yourself heard, but, generally, "This is W1AW monitoring" will suffice. One practice that is looked upon with disfavor universally is calling a long CQ on a repeater.

3) Identify legally; you must identify at the end of a transmission or series of transmissions and at least once each 10 minutes during the communication.

4) Pause between transmissions. This allows other hams to use the repeater (someone may have an emergency). On most repeaters a pause is necessary to reset the time.

5) Keep transmissions short and thoughtful. Your monologue may prevent someone with an emergency from using the repeater. If your monologue is long enough, you may *time out* the repeater. Your transmissions are being heard by many listeners including non-hams with "public service band" monitors; don't give a bad impression of our hobby.

6) Use simplex whenever possible. If you can complete your QSO on a direct frequency, there is no need to tie up the repeater and prevent others from using it.

7) Use the minimum amount of power necessary to maintain communications. This FCC regulation minimizes the possibilities of accessing distant repeaters on the same frequency.

8) Don't break into a contact unless you have something to add. Interrupting is no more polite on the air than it is in person.

9) Repeaters are intended to facilitate mobile operation. During the commuter rush hours, base stations should relinquish the repeater to mobile stations; some repeater groups have rules that specifically address this practice.

10) Many repeaters are equipped with autopatch facilities which, when properly accessed, connect the repeater to the telephone system to provide a public service. The FCC forbids using an autopatch for anything that could be construed as business communications. Nor should an autopatch be used to avoid a toll call. Do not use an autopatch where regular telephone service is available. Abuses of autopatch privileges may lead to their loss.

11) All repeaters are assembled and maintained at considerable expense and inconvenience. Usually an individual or a group is responsible and those who are regular users of a repeater should support the efforts of keeping the repeater on the air.

Tracking Down Repeater Jammers

Repeaters, which of course are fixed-frequency devices, are vulnerable to abuse by the lunatic fringe among us who find some perverse pleasure in destroying the pleasure of others by disrupting repeater communications. The ARRL has been making a concerted effort to feature more articles on direction-finding techniques in *QST*. We have also produced a selected bibliography of radio direction-finding articles.

If you or your repeater group is plagued with malicious interference, please write the Field Services Department, VOLMON Program, ARRL, 225 Main St., Newington, CT 06111 for assistance.

---

are: (1) Beacon or radio control operation; (2) information bulletins consisting solely of subject matter relating to Amateur Radio; (3) transmissions intended for persons learning or improving proficiency in the International Morse Code; and (4) emergency communications (see above). In addition, roundtable discussions or net operations where more than two amateur stations are in communication with one another are not considered broadcasting (Section 97.113[e]).

Secion 97.89 of the rules permits amateur stations to be used for measuring radio emissions, propagation studies, controlling remote objects (such as model airplanes), and other experimental purposes. Amateur Radio beacon stations, which are used to learn if a band is open, are another example of permissible one-way communications.

To make life for the radio remote-control enthusiast a little easier, the FCC has simplified identification. If the mean output power of the transmitter, controlling the model craft does not exceed 1 watt and the transmitter has affixed to it a transmitter-identification card (either FCC Form 452-C or a durable, homemade card with the station call sign and licensee's name and address), on-the-air identification is not required. Also, the signals will not be construed as codes or ciphers, which are prohibited under other circumstances.

The Net Game

Nets are on-the-air clubs, folks coming together to discuss or engage in favorite activities of mutual interest. There are nets for traffic handlers, ragchewers, computer fans, DXers, historians, aviators, philosophers, county hunters and hosts more for countless other hams.

Nets meet regularly on prearranged days, times and frequencies, and can attract scores of members and passersby at any time. One merely must open the pages of the ARRL *Net Directory* to see just how much formal net activity exists for public-service-minded hams alone!

Let's examine that curious creature of the forest, the net operator, and his habitat, the net.

Q. I noticed that there are quite a few nets meeting regularly on 75 meters. Do these nets have exclusive rights to a specific frequency?

A. There is nothing in the Rules that recognizes a net's special privilege to any specific frequency. It's generally a case of first come, first served. Before starting a net, the net-control station should take precautions to avoid using a frequency occupied by other stations. This should be accomplished by asking politely "Is this frequency in use?" Conversely, individual operators should ask the same question before engaging in operation to determine if another QSO or net is in progress on that frequency.

The bottom line is that no one owns a frequency. Whoever is on any given frequency first should, if possible, be protected from interference by other stations. Net-control stations should tell their charges that the net will convene on the prearranged net frequency "plus or minus the QRM," for example.

Q. If I am in QSO with another ham on a net frequency prior to net time, am I supposed to move to accommodate the net when it convenes?

A. Because there are so many hams on one frequency during a net, there must be a regularly scheduled, prearranged net frequency and time. Remember: These net members must *find* the net in the first place. Net operations are a bit more unwieldy than individual operations because nets involve so many stations. It is far easier for individuals to look out for nets than it is for nets to move 10 or 100 hams to other frequencies in a crowded band. There are no hard-and-fast rules concerning this policy. Indeed, it is not formally recognized by FCC as "good amateur practice." It's simply a matter of courtesy, nothing more. After all, nets are good ways to meet and exchange ideas with other hams having similar interests; and they occupy only one frequency. Many hams making use of but one frequency is efficient and sound spectrum usage.

Q. How does one identify while engaged in net operations?

A. The Rules say you must identify your station once every 10 minutes. The problem is that most net check-ins are idle for 10 or more minutes at a time. Thus, most check-ins give their call after every transmission or brief communication on the net to ensure that they will not have to identify while another station is transmitting (97.84).

If you're handling third-party traffic with a foreign ham on the net, you must also give his or her station's call sign as part of your ID [97.84(h)].

Q. Do I have to log my net operations?

A. No, the Commission no longer requires any log entries for amateur operations. If your station is operated by remote control, or is in auxiliary or repeater operation, certain station *records* must be kept, however.

Q. In the United States there are many nets that cater to hams selling and buying their ham radio equipment. Are these so-called "swap and shop" nets legal?

A. Yes, within certain constraints. Amateurs may use their stations from time to time to discuss the availability of a piece of Amateur Radio equipment, but such activity would be limited to that of an occasional nature. It's best not to discuss price on the air. Instead, swap phone numbers with the interested party and finish the dickering off the air. Activities could not include any items of a personal nature, such as a camera or ordinary broadcast radios. Hams should not engage in regular "flea market" or business activities on swap nets so as to derive a profit by buying and selling ham gear on a regularly scheduled basis (97.112).

Q. Where can I find a list of traffic and emergency communications nets?

A. The ARRL publishes an annual *Net Directory*, available for $1 from ARRL Hq.

RACES

Those of you who think that RACES operation takes place on Sunday afternoons at the local Dragway are right — it does. But, those of you who think it has something to do with emergency communications are right, too. Founded in 1952 with the help of the ARRL, the Radio Amateur Civil Emergency Service is fed and cared for by the Federal Emergency Management Administration (FEMA). RACES works principally at the local level through local and state civil defense agencies organized by state government to provide emergency communications in the event the FCC authorizes its use. Part 97, subpart (F), is totally devoted to this very important part of the Amateur Radio Service.

Emergency communications preparation is rapidly becoming one of the top priorities for many radio amateurs. Government agencies are beginning to realize the potential service that hams who are familiar with emergency communications procedures can provide. Get ready, Get set, *Go!*

Q. What is RACES, and what does it have to do with me?

A. The Radio Amateur Civil Emergency Service, as part of the Amateur Rado Service, provides radio communications for civil defense purposes *only*, during periods of local, regional or national civil emergencies. These emergencies are not limited to war-related activites, but can include natural disasters such as fires, floods and earthquakes. As defined in the Rules, RACES is a radiocommunication service, conducted by *volunteer* licensed amateurs, designed to provide emergency radiocommunications to local, regional or state civil defense organizations. It is important to note that RACES operation is authorized by the FCC upon request of a state or federal official, and is strictly limited to official civil defense activity in the event of an emergency communications situation (97.161, 97.163).

Q. Does this mean that I can volunteer as a RACES station?

A. At the present time there is a freeze on the issuance of new RACES licenses. RACES operation is conducted by amateurs using their own primary station licenses, and by existing RACES stations (97.163[b]).

Q. Then to volunteer as a RACES control operator, all I need is a valid Amateur Radio license?

Table 1

RACES Frequencies

kHz		MHz	
1800-1825	3984-4000	14.047-14.053	52-54
1975-2000	7079-7125	14.220-14.230	
3500-3550	7245-7255	14.331-14.350	144.50-145.71
3930-3980		21.047-21.053	146-148
		21.228-21.267	220-225
		28.550-28.750	420-450
		29.237-29.273	1240-1300
		29.450-29.650	2390-2450
		50.350-50.750	

A. Well, not quite. You must *also* be officially enrolled in a civil defense organization (97.177).

Q. While engaged in RACES operation, does my license class limit me as to frequency use?

A. Affirmative. Operator privileges in RACES are dependent upon, and identical to, those for the class of license held in the Amateur Radio Service.

Q. What frequencies are available to an operator conducting communications in RACES?

A. All of the authorized frequencies and emissions allocated to the Amateur Radio Service are also available to RACES on a shared basis. But in the event that RACES is activated by the FCC following a request from a local, state or federal official, Amateur Radio stations engaged in RACES operation will be limited to the frequencies listed in Table 1. Additionally, there are specific operating limitations with respect to these frequencies (listed in Part 97.185 of the Commission's rules). At this point, it should be noted that in all cases not specifically covered by the provisions in Subpart (F), amateurs engaging in RACES operation will be governed by the provisions of the rules governing Amateur Radio stations and operators (Subparts A through E of this part) (97.165).

Q. As an operator in RACES, what types of other stations can I communicate with?

As a RACES operator, you may communicate with: (1) Amateur Radio stations certified as being registered with a civil defense organization, (2) stations in the Disaster Communications Service, (3) stations of the U.S. Government authorized by the responsible agency to conduct communications with stations engaged in RACES operation and (4) any other station in any other service regulated by the FCC, whenever that station is authorized by the Commission to exchange communications with stations in RACES operation (97.189).

Q. Is there anything else I should keep in mind while engaged in RACES operation?

A. It is important to bear in mind that any communication you make while operating in RACES *must* be specifically authorized by the civil defense organization for the area served. Furthermore, RACES stations may transmit only civil defense communication of the following types: "Communications concerning impending or actual conditions jeopardizing public safety, or national defense or security during periods of civil emergencies including: (1) communications directly concerning the immediate safety and protection of life, property and the maintenance of law and order; the alleviation of human suffering and need, and the combating of armed attack or sabotage; (2) communications directly concerning the accumulation and dissemination of public information or instructions to the civilian population. Also permitted are communications for the purpose of training (drills and tests) when necessary to establish and maintain the orderly and efficient operation of RACES as ordered by the responsible civil defense organization. However, these communications must not exceed a total time of one hour per week." Additionally, brief one-way transmissions for testing and adjusting equipment are allowed (97.191).

Q. Will I be paid for this work by the civil defense agency?

A. No. Just as in the Amateur Radio Service, no compensation of any form is permitted (97.193).

Q. I thought the emergency communications aspect of Amateur Radio was provided for in ARES. What is the difference between RACES and ARES?

A. This is an important distinction. ARES, the Amateur Radio Emergency Service, is the "emergency" division of the ARRL Field Organization. It consists of licensed amateurs who have voluntarily registered their qualifications and equipment for communication duty in the event of a disaster. Every licensed amateur, whether or not a member of ARRL or any other local or national organization, is eligible for membership in ARES. ARES is administered on a local, section-wide and national basis. RACES, on the other hand, is sponsored by the federal government and is under the jurisdiction of the FCC. It is a means by which amateurs may serve civil defense agencies in disaster communications on an organized basis, using their own bands and, to a large extent, their own equipment. It is intended that RACES, when properly authorized, will remain on the air in the event of any officially declared emergency, although the rest of Amateur Radio may be silenced.

RACES is a separate entity from ARES, although we advocate dual membership in and cooperative efforts between both groups whenever possible. In fact, the Federal Emergency Management Agency has recommended that civil defense organizations throughout the country affiliate with already-existing ARES groups in their state.

Satellite Service Rules

In 1971, member nations of the International Telecommunication Union sat down at the conference table to fashion regulations for the burgeoning commercial and noncommercial satellite technologies. Rules were needed for international coordination of satellite frequencies, locations and purposes, given the proliferation of hardware floating virtually over every nation on earth. The 1971 Space WARC (World Administrative Radio Conference) delegates arrived at a number of agreements and requirements, and the FCC was obligated to carry them out. Accordingly, the Amateur Radio Service witnessed the introduction of a new subpart in Part 97: the Amateur-Satellite Service (ASAT).

So, if you're a satellite fan thinking about getting more involved with this state-of-the-art technology, you'll want to take the following crash course on the ASAT rules.

Q. First things first — why is there a separate Amateur-Satellite Service?

A. The Amateur-Satellite Service was created by the Commission in response to the 1971 Space WARC. It provides for procedures of notification so FCC can meet its obligations to the international telecommunications community for advance notice of new satellites, international coordination and the general maintenance of records. In the event of an interference problem, the Commission can check its records quickly — determining which satellite is where, and who operates it — to effect a termination of the satellite's transmissions until the problem is resolved. The rules found in Subpart H are based largely on the agreements reached at the 1971 Space WARC, and on the experience the Commission has had with the OSCAR satellites (OSCAR stands for Orbiting Satellite Carrying Amateur Radio.)

Q. How does the FCC define this service?

A. The FCC rules define the purpose of the Amateur-Satellite Service as a "radiocommunication service using stations on earth satellite for the same purpose as those of the Amateur Radio Service" (97.401). In plain language, amateur satellite communications are authorized for the same bases and purposes as the parent Amateur Radio Service.

Q. What is meant by space operation?

A. Space operation is space-to-earth and space-to-space transmission by an Amateur Radio station that is, or is on, an earth satellite. An earth satellite is a body that revolves around (or *with,* in the case of geostationary satellites) the planet earth. A satellite's motion is determined by the force of the earth's gravity (97.403[a]).

Q. How about earth operation?

A. This type of operation is much more down-to-earth! It is earth-to-space transmission by an amateur station of communications intended to be retransmitted space-to-earth by an amateur station in space operation (an OSCAR satellite, for example). Earth operation is a fancy term for "working the bird" (97.403[b]).

Q. What is telecommand operation?

A. Telecommand operation is earth-to-space transmissions of control commands intended to turn on, change or turn off the functions of a satellite transponder (station in space operation) (97.403[c]). Just as any amateur station must be controlled properly, so too must an amateur station in space be told what to do so that it operates within the rules. Control of a station in space operation is called telecommand operation.

A station in telecommand operation may transmit one-way control messages to a station in space operation using special codes intended to obscure the meaning of the messages (97.421[a]). This special provision aids satellite owners and telecommand operators in guarding against unauthorized tampering and sabotage. An improper command could result in the destruction of a satellite!

Stations in telecommand operation are exempt from the station ID rules. They don't have to be identified (97.421[b]).

Q. Are there any frequency limitations for ASAT operation?

A. Yes. First, of course, you're limited to operation on frequencies prescribed by the class of your license. Furthermore, ASAT operation is restricted to the following bands: 7000-7100 kHz, 14,000-14,250 kHz, 21.00-21.45 MHz, 24.89-24.99 MHz, 28.00-29.7 MHz, 144-146 MHz, 435-438 MHz and 24.00-24.05 GHz. These ASAT subbands apply to all space, earth and telecommand operation. [Note: ASAT stations must not interfere with other stations operating in other services between 435 and 438 MHz].

Q. How does OSCAR operate in space?

A. The transponder aboard an OSCAR is an Amateur Radio station in space operation. Accordingly, it may transmit from anywhere beyond the major portion of earth's atmosphere for sending telemetry, retransmitting signals of stations in earth operation live or delayed, and retransmitting communications of other stations in space operation live or delayed (97.417).

Stations in space operation are exempt from station ID, and control operator requirements (97.417) — *but* the FCC must be notified formally of prespace, space and post-space operation with detailed information (97.423).

In addition, a sufficient number of telecommand stations must be in place to turn off the space station if the FCC says so (97.413). This is a very important provision in that, if the ITU says a satellite is causing interference, the FCC can quickly stop the satellite from transmitting by ordering the owner and/or the telecommand operator to effect termination. The FCC has an obligation to the international satellite communications community, and the ASAT rules help it meet this obligation.

Q. What do the notification requirements involve?

A. The license of every station in space operation must notify the FCC in writing of such operation as noted above. The FCC must be notified prior to space operation of (1) the expected date that space operations will start, along with a prediction of the duration of the operation; (2) the name of the satellite (OSCAR, for example); (3) the service area that will be covered in the satellite; (4) the orbital parameters (where in space the satellite will travel); and (5) the technical parameters (frequencies, emissions, powers and so forth) (97.423). This information serves to assist the FCC in coordinating space activities with its international counterparts.

Q. Are other notifications required?

A. Yes. An *in-space* notification is required after space operation is initiated to update the information contained in the *pre-space* notification (97.423[c]). And, a *post-space* notification is required no later than three months after termination is complete; 24 hours if the termination is ordered by the Commission (97.423[d]).

Q. What are telemetry messages?

A. Telemetry messages are space-to-earth transmissions from a station in space operation that contain technical information about the condition of the satellite and the station. The measurements transmitted must be restricted to those of an electrical and mechanical nature (97.403[d]).

Telemetry messages may be encoded to simplify their transmission and reception (97.419[a]). Information often transmitted includes satellite temperature, solar cell current, battery temperature and voltage, and other parameters that describe the electrical and mechanical condition of the space vehicle and station.

Q. Who is eligible to be the licensee of a station in space operation?

A. Extra Class licensees *only* are eligible to place their stations in space operation. However, the licensee may permit any Amateur Radio operator to be the control operator, subject to the privileges of the control operator's license class (97.407).

Any amateur station may conduct earth operation, subject to the limitations of the control operator's license class (97.409).

Any amateur station designated by a space station licensee may conduct telecommand operation with the station in space operation, subject to the limitations of the control operator's license class privileges (97.411).

Beacon Operation

A beacon station is simply a transmitter that alerts listeners to its presence. In the Radionavigation Service beacons are used to provide navigational guidance. In the Amateur Service, beacons are used primarily for the study of radio-wave propagation — to allow amateurs to tell when a band is open to different parts of the country or world.

The Rules define beacon operation as one-way communication conducted in order to facilitate measurement of radio equipment characteristics, adjustment of radio equipment, observation of propagation or transmission phenomena, or other related experimental activities. Automatically controlled beacon stations are limited to the following frequencies (in megahertz):

28.20-28.30	220.05-220.06	all amateur bands above 450 MHz
50.06-50.08	222.05-222.06	
144.05-144.06	432.07-432.08	

Beacons that are manually controlled are not frequency restricted. Emissions authorized for automatically controlled beacon operation are NØN, A1A, F1B or J2A (when type F1B or J2A emissions are used below 450 MHz, the radio or audio frequency shift, as appropriate, must be less than 1000 Hz.) All amateur frequency bands above 450 MHz are available for automatically controlled beacon operation with the general emission limitations specified for each band. The minimum amount of power necessary to fulfill the function of the beacon must be used, provided peak envelope power output does not exceed 100 watts.

Beacons are identified with the letters BCN or B at the end of the call sign — K1CE/BCN, for example. On phone, the word "beacon" is added to the phone ID. Phone beacons must be manually controlled. Identification must be made at least *once* per minute.

A station in beacon operation must not operate concurrently on more than one frequency in the same frequency band from the same location.

A station in beacon operation may be controlled automatically (that is, no control operator is present) if devices and procedures are used to prevent rules violations. Such devices and procedures include locked cabinets or doors, and limited disclosure of command codes.

Duplex and Crossband Operation

When two or more stations are in communication with each other and are using different frequencies (or even different amateur bands), and the transmitter carrier remains on during periods of reception, we call this type of operation *duplex*. For a good reason, duplex operation is permitted only in the amateur bands above 51 MHz (where NØN emissions are allowed). It reduces congestion in the bands where "skip" communication is common.

On the other hand, where two or more stations are communicating, and each operator turns off the carrier while listening, this is *crossband* operation. This is legal on any of the amateur bands and modes in the U.S. Let's say you're a Novice class licensee using cw (telegraphy) on 7140 kHz. You may communicate with an Amtaeur Extra Class station transmitting phone on 3780 kHz.

Chapter 7

Thou Shalt Not . . .

In previous chapters, we've seen just what Amateur Radio operators *can* do. We've seen how stations may be operated, and what frequencies and emissions can be used. Thus, we've reviewed the *do's* of Amateur Radio. Now, for the *don'ts:* 13 Thou Shalt Nots found in Subpart E of the Rules — "Prohibited Practices and Administrative Sanctions." This chapter will focus on a few specific, and critical, areas of the Rules — the prohibition against compensation for amateur operation and broadcasting, retransmitting signals, third-party traffic, business communications and FCC violation notices. But we'll also look at some areas that are less in the "gray" area and more black-and-white. These are just as important — music, codes and ciphers, malicious interference and more.

Direct and Indirect Payment

No remuneration for use of station (or, no bucks in the bands). A quick review of the bases and purposes of Amateur Radio from Part 97 will explain why:

> Recognition and enhancement of the value of the amateur service to the public as a *voluntary noncommercial communication service,* particularly with respect to providing emergency communications. (emphasis added)

So, if your club is lending communications support to the town of Needham, make sure you don't accept payment for your public service. In fact, you should never accept anything for your Amateur Radio work. FCC prohibits operation of an amateur station "for material compensation, direct or indirect, paid or promised" (97.112) This includes *direct payment* (money, goods, food, and so forth) and *indirect payment* (goodwill, publicity, advertising, and so on). This rule is quite clear, and is interpreted strictly by the Commission. Well, then, how is it that W1AW (the League Hq. station) operators are compensated? A good question deserving a good answer: The rules provide for just such an activity.

Control operators of a club station may be compensated when the club station is operated primarily for code practice transmissions or for transmitting bulletins consisting of Amateur Radio news having direct interest to hams. To qualify under this provision, however, the station must conduct telegraphy practice sessions *for at least 40 hours per week,* schedule operations on *at least six medium- and high-frequency amateur bands,* and *publish the schedule* of operating times and frequencies at least 30 days in advance of the actual transmissions. Control operators may accept compensation only when the station is transmitting code practice and bulletins. A control operator may not be paid at any other time that the station is transmitting material other than code practice and bulletins (97.112).

Broadcasting

Broadcasting must be left to those services that are directly authorized to do so by the FCC — television and radio, for example. "Broadcasting" refers to transmissions that are intended to be received by the general public.

Broadcasting is specifically prohibited in Amateur Radio: " . . . an amateur station shall not be used to engage in any form of broadcasting, that is, the dissemination of radio communications intended to be received by the public directly or by intermediary relay stations . . . '' It's important to note the difference, however, between broadcasting and the permitted one-way communications of bulletins. As we've seen, bulletins dealing directly with Amateur Radio matters may be transmitted one-way to amateurs only, and may not be transmitted for the benefit of the general public. For example, an amateur may recite the latest ARRL bulletin over his local repeater, but *may not* give a rundown on the Middle East situation on the repeater intended for the ears of the general public who have home scanners.

Nor may Amateur Radio be used for the retransmission of "programs or signals emanating from any class of station other than amateur except for emergency communications (see §97.3[w])'' (97.113[c]). For example, a local repeater may not automatically retransmit a local NOAA weather broadcast picked up from a VHF weather radio. Amateurs may not retransmit fm broadcast programs, or television soundtracks.

Occasionally, at a Field Day, or other operating activity, a local broadcast station may ask you to let them record your station's transmissions and receptions for the local evening news. This is fine. You may consent to the retransmission, either live or delayed, of your amateur station transmissions by a radio or television broadcast station. However, you must not allow your amateur station to be used for any activity directly related to program production or newsgathering for broadcast purposes (97.113[b]).

FCC completed a sweeping review of the relationship between broadcasting and Amateur Radio in June 1985. In its *Report and Order* in BC Docket 79-47, a number of longstanding rules were modified or overturned, and our own Section 97.113 ("Broadcasting and broadcast related activities prohibited") was heavily modified. One change was the deletion of the requirement that broadcasters obtain permission from amateurs to rebroadcast amateur signals: Such permission is no longer required, and broadcasters are no longer obligated to advise FCC that any such retransmission has occurred. This arises from Amateur Radio's exemption from the secrecy of communications provisions of Section 705 of the Communications Act of 1934, as amended (see Chapter 2). A prohibition against broadcast use of amateur repeaters was adopted (97.85[d]). Otherwise, FCC felt that "the new 97.113" itself provides enough protection against Amateur Radio stations being used for broadcast program production and newsgathering.

Third-Party Traffic

Third-party traffic is Amateur Radio communication by or under the supervision of the control operator at an Amateur Radio station to another Amateur Radio station on behalf of anyone other than the control operator. A third-party message is one the control operator (first party) of your station sends to another station (second party) for anyone else (third party). Third-party messages include those that are spoken, written, keystroked, keyed, photographed or otherwise originated by or for a third party, and transmitted by your Amateur Radio station live or delayed. A third party may also be a person permitted by the control operator to *participate* in Amateur Radio communications.

Third-party traffic is one of the so-called "gray" areas where there is much room for interpretation. It is one of the lesser understood concepts in Amateur Radio today. Accordingly, this discussion will clear up some of the confusion often associated with this area of the rules.

There are three main types of third-party traffic. The first deals with third-party *messages,* those sent via traffic nets or other means. Message fairs and displays at shopping malls provide sources of these types of routine messages. Not all messages are as formal as this, however. A third-party message may be no more than a "Gee, you're in Birmingham, please say hello to Tyrone Shoelaces for me . . .''

The second type of third-party traffic deals with phone-line interconnection, or so-called "phone patch" and "autopatch." These operations allow third parties to communicate directly with second and first parties via the telephone system.

The third type of third-party traffic is the direct participation by interested third parties in actual Amateur Radio communication. The rules provide for this type of operation as long as the control operator supervises the third party and makes transmitter adjustments to ensure proper operation. At no time may a control operator leave a third party unattended at a transmitter that is on the air. Such an act would amount to a serious relinquishing of control duties. Section 97.114(c)(2) prohibits participation in this type of third-party traffic by "a prior Amateur Radio licensee whose license was revoked; suspended for less than the balance of the license term and the suspension is still in effect; suspended for the balance of the license term and relicensing has not taken place; surrendered for cancellation following notice of revocation, suspension or monetary forfeiture proceedings; or who is the subject of a cease and desist order which relates to amateur operation and is still in effect."

The third-party-traffic rules are quite clear: International third-party traffic is prohibited except in cases where the U.S. has a special third-party-traffic agreement with other countries (see page 5-11) for a list of these countries); third-party traffic involving material compensation to any party is not allowed; and business communications are not permitted unless for a bona fide emergency.

With all of this in mind, let's examine some common questions about third-party traffic.

Q. Our traffic net often serves as an outlet for incoming and outgoing international traffic. Is this legal, and what regulations should we be aware of?

A. The handling of international third-party traffic is forbidden except under certain conditions:

1) The country must have a third-party agreement with the United States.

2) When handling third-party traffic with these countries, amateurs may handle messages on behalf of third parties provided the messages are of a character that would not normally be sent by any existing means of electrical communications, except for the availability of the amateur station. Messages shall be limited to those of a technical nature and to remarks of a personal nature for which, *by reason of their unimportance,* recourse to the public telecommunications service is not justified. It is *very* important for amateurs to heed this international law to preserve and enhance respect for Amateur Radio throughout the world.

So, sending a message that says HI RINALDO X HAVE YOU INSTALLED YOUR NEW TRIBANDER YET QUERY would be okay; but sending the message HI STANLEY X DO YOU NEED ANY HELP WITH INSTALLING YOUR NEW GOVERNMENT QUERY would definitely not be okay!

Q. What about the legality of sending a message to a nonprofit organization such as the ARRL Hq.?

A. Chances are, such a message could be construed to be facilitating the normal business affairs of the League. In this case, the League is a "business," and by sending the message DID NOT GET MY APRIL QST X 73, you are involving material compensation and the commercial affairs of Hq. (97.114[c]). The same applies to requests for the *Repeater Directory,* contest forms, operating aids and so forth. *Don't* send a message to FCC via the National Traffic System asking for 500 610 Forms for the Heavy Hitters Amateur Radio and Taxidermy Society.

Q. How about a message requesting medical supplies from the Red Cross during an emergency? Wouldn't this message be considered to be facilitating the normal course of business of the Red Cross?

A. The key word is *emergency.* Emergency communications must relate directly to the *immediate* safety of life of individuals or to the *immediate* protection of property (97.3[w]). In an *emergency* situation, the FCC does not prohibit U.S. amateurs from handling traffic relating to the saving of life and property. Requests for emergency supplies from a Red Cross center would be permitted under these circumstances. Normally, however, such communications would not be permitted.

Q. What if I'm talking to someone in a country with whom we have a third-party agreement, and he wants to talk with a relative in my town. I don't speak their language — what do I do?

A. You have two choices: You can tell the relative what he can and cannot talk about, and hope he understands — and complies! However, the better choice is to *decline to cooperate,* including terminating the conversation in progress, if you think there is a possibility that the communication may be questionable. There are two reasons for this. You may have your license revoked for allowing illegal traffic to pass through your station. But on a broader scale, isn't it better to risk hurting someone's feelings than to risk the revocation of a third-party agreement? It could happen, if a telecommunication authority in another country decides that its amateurs are conducting illegal traffic.

Q. May I, a General class licensee, retransmit via my station the transmissions of a Technician's 2-meter signal over the 20-meter General phone band?

A. When a Technician's signals enter the 14-MHz band at a General class licensee's station, the operation involves third-party traffic to the General class licensee. Such operation is permitted under Sections 97.79(d) and 97.114 of the Rules, which do not specify the manner in which the third-party traffic is received for relay: by mail, telephone, in person, *or by 2 meters.* All third-party-traffic rules apply, of course, so the Technician (for the record, a third party at the General's transmitter) could not communicate with countries not holding third-party agreements with the U.S. via this operation (§§ 97.79[d] and 97.114). This applies to *manual* retransmission only; e.g., holding the 20-meter transmitter mike to the 2-meter receiver speaker. Retransmission by *automatic* means is permitted for stations in repeater or auxiliary operation only (§ 97.126[a]).

Q. On checking into a traffic net the other night, I was asked to handle a message originated in the U.S. and bound for a person living in a country that does not have a third-party agreement with the U.S. I realize, of course, that I must not relay the message via a ham in that country. But, may I route it for ultimate delivery to a ham in another country that holds an agreement with the U.S. and with the addressee's country?

A. Yes. The FCC, and the third-party-traffic rules, are concerned with the *borders* of the countries involved. That is, as far as you're concerned, the third-party message crosses the U.S. border, and the border of the second party's country that holds an agreement with the U.S. The FCC is not concerned about the location of the message's origination or destination; they are concerned with the manner in which the third-party traffic is handled over the air (§ 97.114).

Field Day

Q. Our Field Day group uses a member's Extra Class call sign. Does this mean all operators may use Extra Class privileges at the FD station even though their own license classes may be lower than Extra?

A. In every case, a station control operator is limited to his or her own license class privileges. For example, say one of your FD operators is licensed as a General. Accordingly, he or she may operate the Extra Class FD station only to the extent of General Class privileges. However, *any person,* amateur or nonamateur, may participate in Amateur Radio communication *as a third party.* This means that anyone may speak their third-party messages directly into the mike of the FD station provided a control operator is present to supervise and control the operation. And, again, the operation may be only to the extent of that particular control operator's license privileges regardless of the fact that the FD station is identified with an Extra Class call sign. Another example: A General class licensee may *participate* as a third party in the Advanced portion of the band provided an Advanced or Extra Class control operator is present to supervise the operation. The distinction here is one of semantics — the participant, although an amateur, is a third party, not a control operator. The fact that he or she is a General class licensee is irrelevant in this case (§ 97.79).

Q. May the third-party participant identify the station?

A. Yes — the station-identification requirements of the FD activity (§ 97.84) may be met by having the third party give the ID. However, and this is important, a third-party participant may communicate only with U.S. stations (which is usually the case in Field Day) and other countries that have third-party agreements with the U.S. For example, a third-party participant may not communicate with a station in France (§ 97.114).

Business Communications

Q. Is it okay for our local ham club, the Rehobeth Radio Ruminators, to provide communications in the upcoming Ajax Halibut Company's "Run-For-The-Halibut" Marathon?

A. For the public's benefit, yes; for the direct benefit of the sponsor, no. Business communications are strictly out-of-bounds in Amateur Radio. Sections 97.110 and 97.114 mandate that third-party traffic involving business communication and material compensation, either tangible or intangible, direct or indirect, to any person is prohibited. Emergency communication (any Amateur Radio communication directly relating to the immediate safety of the life of an individual or the immediate protection of property) is the *only* exception to this rule. This point was clarified in a letter from FCC Private Radio Branch Chief Robert Foosaner to Steven Mendelsohn, WA2DHF, regarding amateur participation in the New York City marathon:

This is in response to your letter of October 15, 1984, concerning providing amateur radio communications at the New York Road Runners Club marathon. The Commission addressed the matter of business communications in the Amateur Radio Service in the Order released July 12, 1983. You will note that the term *business communications*, as defined in Section 97.3(bb) of the Rules, is used in the broadest context. It includes all types of communications which are intended to facilitate the regular business affairs of any party, whether for-profit or not-for-profit, etc. Thus, the determination as to the types of amateur radio communications that your group could provide at a marathon would not be affected by the profit objectives of the sponsor, nor by the pay status of other participants.

A fundamental guideline that should be observed in these instances is also stated in the Order: "...the Amateur Radio Service should not be used as an alternative to the land mobile, broadcast, maritime or common carrier radio services, all of which have been established by appropriate regulatory processes." To the extent that these other radio services can be used to perform the necessary communications, such communications should not be transmitted by amateur radio.

Section 97.110 of the Rules, which prohibits business communications by amateur radio, does not prohibit amateur radio operators from participating in a marathon as a public service activity. Although some communications transmitted could incidentally benefit a sponsor, we do not view such communications as violations of the rules where their main purpose is to provide a service to the public.

In your letter you describe three specific services which amateur radio could provide. The first is a medical network, by which race authorities could be notified of a runner's need for medical attention. This medical network is, of course, acceptable.

The second service is logistical. Amateur radio operators would provide the communications necessary to facilitate the public's safe observation of the event. Clearly there is benefit to the race sponsor, but it is incidental; the principal beneficiaries of this would be the runners and the public.

Finally, there is the lead-runner position network. As you acknowledge, the purpose of this is to faciliate a system whereby the public, including, presumably, the news media, are informed of the progress of the race via amateur radio. This runs afoul of Section 97.113 of the Rules, which prohibits the dissemination of radio communications intended to be received by the public. If you wish to provide this service, we recommend you do it on commercial frequencies with other equipment. Amateur radio operators could participate in this phase, but not by virtue of their amateur licenses.

Please inform your group that their licenses are not endangered by participating in the marathon. They have my support and my personal thanks for serving the public.

Q. How about using autopatch to call a service station to have a tow truck come out to remove a disabled vehicle from the shoulder of the highway. Isn't this facilitating the day-to-day functions of the service station?

A. Calls made concerning highway safety in cases where there is an immediate threat to the safety of life or property are permitted. In fact, this ability to eliminate delay in reaction time is exactly what makes autopatch so useful in emergencies. The ability to call the police, or an ambulance, without having to depend on the necessary condition that another amateur is monitoring the frequency, can save precious minutes. Autopatch, when used responsibly, is a valuable asset to the community.

Phone Patch and Autopatch Guidelines

Radio amateurs in the United States enjoy a great privilege: the ability to inter connect their individual stations and repeaters with the public telephone system. The wisdom of the federal government in permitting, and even in defending, this freedom has been demonstrated time and again. There is no way to calculate the value of the lives and property that have been saved by the intelligent use of phone patch and autopatch facilities in emergency situations. The public interest has been well served by amateurs with interconnect capabilities.

As with any privilege, this one can be abused, and the penalty for abuse could be the loss of the privilege for all amateurs. What constitutes abuse of phone patch and autopatch privileges? In the absence of specific regulations governing their use, the answer to this question depends on one's perspective. Consider these facts: To other amateurs, phone patching activities that result in unnecessary frequency congestion or which appear as a commercialization of Amateur Radio operation are an abuse of their privilege to engage in other forms of amateur activities.

To the telephone company, which needs to protect its massive investment in capital equipment, anything that endangers its equipment, its personnel or its revenues is an abuse.

To the Federal Communications Commission, which is responsible for the efficient use of the radio spectrum by the services it regulates, any radiocommunication that could be handled more appropriately by wire is an unnecessary use of a valuable resource.

To the commercial suppliers of radiocommunication for business purposes (Radio Common Carriers), competition from a noncommercial service constitutes a possible threat to their livelihood.

At one time or another, threats to radio amateur's interconnect privileges have come from each of these sources. And threats may come from another quarter: the governments of certain nations that prohibit amateurs from handling third-party messages internationally in competition with government-owned telecommunications services. If illegal phone patching to and from their countries cannot be controlled, they reason, the solution may be to ban *all* international third-party traffic by amateurs and to permit no such special arrangements.

The question facing amateurs is this: Should phone patches and autopatches be subject to reasonable voluntary restraints, thereby preserving most of our traditional flexibility, or should we risk forcing our government to define for us specifically what we can and cannot do? Experience has shown very clearly that when specific regulations are established, both innovation and flexibility are likely to suffer.

The Amateur Radio Service is not a common carrier, and its primary purpose is not handling of routine messages on behalf of nonamateurs. However, third-party communications as an incidental part of Amateur Radio adds an important dimension to our public service capability.

It is the policy of the American Radio Relay League to safeguard the prerogative of amateurs to interconnect their stations, including repeaters, to the public telephone system. An important element of this defense is encouraging amateurs to maintain a high standard of legal and ethical conduct in their patching activities. It is to this end that these guidelines are addressed. They are based on several sets of standards that have been in use for several years on a local or regional basis throughout the country. The ideas they represent have widespread support within the amateur community. All amateurs are urged to observe these standards carefully so our traditional freedom from government regulation may be preserved as much as possible.

1) International phone patches must be conducted *only* when there is a special third-party agreement between the countries concerned. The only exception is when the *immediate safety of life or property* is endangered.

2) Phone patches or autopatches involving the business affairs of any party must not be conducted *at any time*. The content of any patch should be such that it is clear to any listener that business communications is *not* involved. Particular caution must be observed in calling any business telephone. Calls to place an order for a commercial product must not be made, nor may calls be made to one's office to receive or to leave business messages. However, calls made in the interests of highway safety, such as for the removal of injured persons from the scene of an accident or for the removal of a disabled vehicle from a hazardous location, are permitted.

3) All interconnections must be made in accordance with telephone company tariffs. If you have trouble obtaining information about them from your telephone company representatives, the tariffs are available for public inspection at your telephone company office.

4) Phone patches and autopatches should *never* be made solely to avoid telephone toll charges. Phone patches and autopatches should *never* be made when normal telephone service could just as easily be used.

5) Third parties should not be retransmitted until the responsible control operator has explained to them the nature of Amateur Radio. Control of the station must *never* be relinquished to an unlicensed person. Permitting a person you don't know very well to conduct a patch in a language you don't understand amounts to relinquishing control.

6) Phone patches and autopatches must be terminated *immediately* in the event of any illegality or impropriety.

7) Autopatch facilities must not be used for the broadcasting of information of interest to the general public. If a repeater has the capability of transmitting information, such as weather reports, which is of interest to the general public, such transmissions must occur only when requested by a licensed amateur and must not conform to a specific time schedule. The retransmission of radio signals from other services is not permitted in the Amateur Radio Service. However, the retransmission of taped material from other sources is permitted.

8) Station identification must be strictly observed. In particular, U.S. stations conducting international phone patches must identify in English at least once every 10 minutes, and must also give their call sign and the other station's call sign at the end of the exchange of transmissions.

9) In selecting frequencies for phone-patch work, the rights of other amateurs must be considered. In particular, patching on 20 meters should be confined to the upper portion of the 14,200-14,350 kHz segment in accordance with the IARU Region 2 recommendation, Miami, April 1976.

10) Phone patches and autopatches should be kept as *brief as possible,* as a courtesy to other amateurs; the amateur bands are intended to be used primarily for communication among radio amateurs.

11) If you have any doubt as to the legality or advisability of a patch, *don't make it.*

Compliance with these guidelines will help ensure that our interconnection privilege will continue to be available in the future, which will in turn help us contribute to the public interest.

The Simpatch

Q. The big question: Is the simplex autopatch legal? If so, how can I operate my device legally?

A. It is possible to use a simplex autopatch device in a limited manner that complies with the Amateur Rules, even though its use is not specifically provided for in the Rules.

Most importantly, a control operator must be present at *both* stations' control points (97.79[b]). The operation involves third-party traffic in that a third party is "participating" in amateur radiocommunication. This "participation" is permitted as long as the control operator is present and monitors and supervises the radiocommunication continuously to insure compliance with the Rules (97.79[d]). This provision limits the mobile station operator to placing calls; incoming calls from third parties must be answered and screened off the air by the other station control operator, before being placed on the air.

Q. Is it legal to operate the home simplex autopatch transmitter by remote control from my mobile rig?

A. Remote-control operation is permitted within specific constraints. In this case, the mobile station in contact with the fixed home station is actually controlling the simpatch. This means that the mobile station, when it is used to turn the fixed station on and off and transmit other control function signals, is in *auxiliary operation* ("Radiocommunication for remotely controlling other amateur radio stations . . ." 97.3[1]). Accordingly, the mobile station in auxiliary operation must confine the control link frequency to 220.5 MHz and above (except 431-433 and 435-438 MHz) where auxiliary operation is permitted. Thus, when the home fixed simplex autopatch transmitter is being remotely controlled by the mobile auxiliary station, 2-meter operation is precluded.

Amateurs should have a good working knowledge of auxiliary operation, remote control and control-operator requirements before attempting to employ a remotely controlled station with simplex-autopatch capability.

Q. What about the legality of the so-called reverse autopatch?

A. Section 97.79 of the Rules concerning control-operator requirements makes it clear *no* unlicensed person may initiate an amateur transmission. Incoming calls, as previously mentioned, must be answered and screened off the air by the control operator to ensure rules compliance. Reverse autopatch is permitted only under these strict conditions.

Q. Are simplex autopatches appropriate in the Amateur Service?

A. The Commission is aware that simplex-autopatch devices can be used easily in a way that violates the Rules. But even when the device is operated within the Rules, the appropriateness of the operation is an open question. The Commission has not received any requests asking that simplex autopatch devices be either prohibited or expanded. The Commission is, however, interested in learning how the amateur community feels about the appropriateness of these devices in the Amateur Radio Service.

Malicious Interference

A malignancy by a minority, malicious interference continues to plague the amateur bands. Although the problem has always existed to some degree, it has become a crisis in recent times. Amateurs have faced crises before, such as the RFI problem of the 1950s — but unlike RFI, the crisis of malicious interference has been generated from within our own ranks. And like the problem itself, the solution will be generated from within. The amateur community, after all, is still one of the best self-policed services under FCC jurisdiction.

Q. What are the rules concerning malicious interference?

A. The specific rule prohibiting interference is §97.125: *"No licensed radio amateur shall willfully or maliciously interfere with or cause interference to any radio-communication or signal."*

Q. Rules are one thing, but how can I fight malicious interference at an individual level?

A. When experiencing malicious interference, use the most effective means of combatting it at your disposal — *ignore it* on the air. Call your Section Manager and alert him or her to the situation. (A list of ARRL Section Managers appears on page 8 of every issue of *QST*.) Simply give the facts — frequency and stations involved. Follow through with a brief written letter to your Section Manager noting dates, times, frequencies and call signs. Encourage others to do the same.

Above all, keep your on-the-air operation strictly above board. Don't make the Commission's job more difficult by engaging interfering stations in their own game. And, by ignoring the offending stations, you deprive them of their one need — attention.

Q. What about the Volunteer Monitoring Program?

A. Self-sufficiency is the prevailing philosophy for the modern Amateur Radio Service. This is epitomized by the volunteer monitoring (VOLMON) program. The Amateur Auxiliary to the FCC's Field Operations Bureau, an outgrowth of the Official Observer program, is the organized way that we as caring radio amateurs keep our own on-the-air house in order. In view of diminished federal resources, Uncle Sam has made it "perfectly clear" that we are to resolve our own operating matters. Writing or calling the FCC about every questionable on-the-air event or dreaming up abstract regulatory hypotheticals is precisely the wrong way to show the FCC that we have the maturity and good judgment to deal with our own affairs. The best approach is to contact your ARRL Section Manager, who is the chief administrator of the Amateur Auxiliary in your section/state. Your Section Manager can unleash the Amateur Auxiliary program solvers to bring about direct, cooperative solutions.

Q. What can we do about repeater jamming?

A. Interference problems generated on VHF/UHF are essentially local problems requiring local resolution. The Amateur Auxiliary mechanism for dealing with local amateur-to-amateur interference is the Local Interference Committee, specifically authorized by the ARRL Section Manager. The FCC has indicated its willingness to enter into agreements with Local Interference Committees as an effective means of dealing with problems that might be encountered on VHF repeaters. The Local Interference Committee will operate at all times in an impartial manner, and can respond to complaints and allegations while emphasizing cooperative "no fault" solutions. For further information on establishing a Local Interference Committee, contact your ARRL Section Manager.

Q. Our net is often inundated with malicious interference. What can we do to suppress it?

A. Nets are often singled out for abuse because of their "ownership" of a particular frequency. Of course, no one has any special privilege to any part of a band. Keeping this in mind, use extra caution when choosing a frequency to engage your net. If you experience difficulties with interference, have net members contact your Section

Manager and as mentioned earlier, keep operation legal and follow up with written documentation (length dissertations are not necessary — just the facts).

Apply peer pressure If a known bad apple tries to check into your net — ignore him or her; chances are, the offender will go away.

Q. What is the role of the Federal Communications Commission?

A. The Commission's role in *our* fight against malicious interference will be to enforce its rules. There are severe penalties for violations of federal rules: If the FCC finds that you have violated the Communications Act, FCC rule or 18 U.S.C. 1464 (which prohibits the transmission of obscene, indecent or profane language), you may have to pay as much as $2000 in fines. If FCC rules, it may revoke or suspend your license. Violations of FCC rules are *serious.* Many repeat offenders have already been dealt with harshly.

Q. What can the amateur community do collectively to combat malicious interference?

A. Education is a large part of the solution — amateur clubs and organizations should spread the word about proper operating standards among their members. Point out effective means of dealing with interference. The exertion of peer pressure through club committees is helpful.

Other Prohibited Practices

Music is strictly prohibited in the amateur bands. For example, expect some mail from the FCC if you transmit Rossini's *William Tell Overture* on your favorite 75-meter phone net. Note that the FCC mail will *not* be a critical review of the performance; it will, however, be a notice of violation for your station requiring a formal reply within 10 days of receipt.

Amateur Radio may not be used "for any purpose, or in connection with any activity, that is contrary to Federal, State or local law." This means that if you use your 2-meter hand-held for communications to perform a bank heist, you can expect to lose your license. (Of course, you won't have use for one anyway because the cement walls and iron bars at San Quentin are somewhat less than conducive to VHF propagation.)

Amateurs may not obscure the meaning of their communications by putting them into codes or ciphers. This restriction carries out the Commission's obligations under the international regulations that amateur communications be made in plain language. Abbreviations may be used, however, when the intention is *not* to hide the meaning of the transmission. You can expect an inquisitive letter from the FCC if they monitor your station engaged in the following exchange:

"The sun sets in the west."

"Yes, but the birds of the east can see in the dark."

Obscenity, indecency and profanity are strictly prohibited. Many amateurs have lost their licenses for violating this rule. It's more than rule, though. It's simply common sense, and courtesy. There may be countless listeners to the transmissions of your station. At HF, these listeners are found at all points of the globe. Don't make off-color remarks, because (1) we want others to have a good impression of Amateur Radio, and of U.S. amateurs, and (2) we do *not* want an anti-Amateur Radio administration to play a tape of indecent U.S. amateur transmissions during a critical period of the next international spectrum allocation conference!

False signals are clearly prohibited in the amateur bands. You may not use someone else's call sign without authorization, or transmit a communication that is intended to deceive listeners.

Amateurs must not transmit unidentified radio communications or signals. The so-called "kerchunkers" violate this rule every time they press their push-to-talk mike button to "see if they're within repeater range" without any intention of seeking a QSO.

Amateurs must never obtain, attempt to obtain or assist another person to obtain or attempt to obtain, an operator license by fraudulent means. It's likely that an attempt to cheat on your exam, or to help someone else cheat, will bring about an FCC revocation proceeding. It's difficult to make a case that holding an amateur license under these circumstances would be in the best interest of the public.

An amateur must never willfully damage, or permit to be damaged, any radio equipment in any licensed radio station. So, if you don't like the fact that your ham neighbor has more DXCC countries than you, don't sneak over to his yard in the dark and put a pin through his coax!

Retransmitting Radio Signals

Radio amateurs may retransmit Amateur Radio signals *only*, except for emergency communications (see §§97.3[w] and 97.113). Often, amateurs find that retransmitting a friend's 20-meter signal over the local repeater adds some variety to their day-to-day activities. No problem, as long as this is done manually (with control operator present). *Automatic* retransmission of amateur signals may be done *only* by stations in repeater or auxiliary operation, and by certain remotely controlled stations (§97.126).

Citations

Occasionally an amateur will be found violating some amateur regulation. In minor cases, such as harmonics falling within another amateur band, the amateur will receive only an "advisory notice" from the Commission to point out what was done wrong. This notice does not require a reply. It serves only to warn the amateur that the questionable operation is not allowed according to the strictest sense of the rules. It's not considered a serious violation. In more serious matters, the Commission will send the offending amateur an official citation, which does require a reply within 10 days.

Both notices, the advisory notice and the official citation, are sent to the licensee of the station being operated. In other words, should some amateur friend of yours operate your station improperly, *you* will receive the Commission's notice, and you may have to reply to the FCC, depending on the citation.

Suppose you do receive an advisory notice. Act quickly to clear up the problem. In the case of an official citation, follow its instructions to the letter. The Commission will usually accept any good explanation of a rule infraction as long as the reply spells out that steps are being taken to prevent any further similar problems. Nothing is more serious, though, than ignoring a citation or failing to answer it altogether. In fact, some amateurs have had their licenses revoked, mainly for not answering a citation and the FCC's followup letter. In addition, the FCC now has the power to fine amateurs who willfully or repeatedly violate certain regulations up to $2000. The FCC can fine an amateur without having to go through the federal court system.

An amateur allegedly causing television interference (TVI) may receive form letters from the FCC, probably based on a complaint by a neighbor, asking him to cooperate in clearing up the trouble. Receiving such a letter doesn't mean the FCC points its finger at you. The letter is simply attempting to advise you of the complaint and to obtain your cooperation in working with your neighbor on this trouble (the neighbor, or whoever complained, also receives a form letter). Several such notices may arrive, especially if you're located in a fringe area for television. Simply answer each notice promptly and completely. The Commission will often judge the situation depending on how cooperative you are and how quickly you reply to the notice.

Q. What Are the Penalties for Violating these Rules?

A. If the FCC finds that you have willfully or repeatedly violated the Communications Act, FCC Rules or 18 U.S.C. 1464 (which prohibits the transmissions of obscene, indecent or profane language), you may have to pay as much as $2000. (See Section

503[b] of the Communications Act.)

If the FCC finds that you have willfully or repeatedly violated the Communications Act or FCC Rules, it may revoke your license. (Other grounds for revoking a license are listed in Section 312[a] of the Communications Act).

If the FCC finds that you have violated any section of the Communications Act or the FCC Rules, you may be ordered to stop whatever action caused the violation (see Section 312[b] of the Communications Act).

If a federal court finds that you have willfully and knowingly violated any FCC Rule, you may be fined up to $500 for each day you committed the violation. (See Section 502 of the Communications Act.)

If a federal court finds that you have willfully and knowingly violated any provision of the Communications Act, you may be fined up to $10,000, or you may be imprisoned for one year, or both. (See Section 501 of the Communications Act.)

If the FCC finds that you have violated any section of the Communications Act or the FCC Rules, your Amateur Radio operator license may be suspended (see Section 303[m][1][A] of the Communications Act).

APPENDIX

CONTENTS—PART 97

Authority: §§ 97.1 to 97.313 issued under 48 Stat. 1066, 1082, as amended; 47 U.S.C. 154, 303. Interpret or apply 48 Stat. 1064-1068, 1081-1105, as amended; 47 U.S.C. Sub-chap. I, III-VI.

Subpart A—General

§ 97.1 Basis and purpose.

The rules and regulations in this part are designed to provide an amateur radio service having a fundamental purpose as expressed in the following principles:

(a) Recognition and enhancement o` the value of the amateur service to the public as a voluntary noncommercial communication service, particularly with respect to providing emergency communications.

(b) Continuation and extension of the amateur's proven ability to contribute to the advancement of the radio art.

(c) Encouragement and improvement of the amateur radio service through rules which provide for advancing skills in both the communication and technical phases of the art.

(d) Expansion of the existing reservoir within the amateur radio service of trained operators, technicians, and electronics experts.

(e) Continuation and extension of the amateur's unique ability to enhance international goodwill.

§ 97.3 Definitions.

(a) *Amateur radio service.* A radio communication service of self-training, intercommunication, and technical investigation carried on by amateur radio operators.

(b) *Amateur radio communication.* Non-commercial radio communication by or among amateur radio stations solely with a personal aim and without pecuniary or business interest.

(c) *Amateur radio operator* means a person holding a valid license to operate an amateur radio station issued by the Federal Communications Commission.

(d) *Amateur radio license.* The instrument of authorization issued by the Federal Communications Commission comprised of a station license, and in the case of the primary station, also incorporating an operator license.

Operator license. The instrument of authorization including the class of operator privileges.

Station license. The instrument of authorization for a radio station in the Amateur Radio Service.

(e) *Amateur radio station.* A station licensed in the amateur radio service embracing necessary apparatus at a particular location used for amateur radio communication.

(f) *Primary station.* The principal amateur radio station at a specific land location shown on the station license.

(g) *Military recreation station.* An amateur radio station licensed to the person in charge of a station at a land location provided for the recreational use of amateur radio operators, under military auspices of the Armed Forces of the United States.

(h) *Club station.* A separate amateur radio station licensed to an amateur radio operator acting as a station trustee for a bona fide amateur radio organization or society. A bona fide Amateur Radio organization or society shall be composed of at least two persons, one of whom must be a licensed amateur operator, and shall have:

(1) A name,

(2) An instrument of organization (e.g., constitution),

(3) Management, and

(4) A primary purpose which is devoted to amateur radio activities consistent with §97.1 and constituting the major portion of the club's activities.

(i) *Line A.* Line A begins at Aberdeen, Washington, running by great circle arc to the intersection of 48 °N., 120 °W., thence along parallel 48 °N., to the intersection of 95 °W., thence by great circle arc through the southernmost point of Duluth, Minn., thence by great circle arc to 45 °N., 85 °W., thence southward along meridian 85 °W., to its intersection with parallel 41 °N., thence along parallel 41 °N., to its intersection with meridian 82 °W., thence by great circle arc through the southernmost point of Bangor,

Maine, thence by great circle arc through the southernmost point of Searsport, Maine, at which point it terminates.

(j) *Terrestrial location.* Any point within the major portion of the earth's atmosphere, including aeronautical, land and maritime locations.

*(k) *Coordinated station operation.* The repeater or auxiliary operation of an amateur station for which the transmitting and receiving frequencies have been implemented by the licensee in accordance with the recommendation of a frequency coordinator.

*(k) *National Radio Quiet Zone.* The area bounded by 39° 15 ′ N on the north, 78° 30 ′ W on the east, 37° 30 ′ N on the south and 80° 30 ′ W on the west.

(l) *Amateur radio operation.* Amateur radio communication conducted by amateur radio operators from amateur radio stations, including the following:

Fixed operation. Radio communication conducted from the specific geographical land location shown on the station license.

Portable operation. Radio communication conducted from a specific geographical location other than that shown on the station license.

Mobile operation. Radio communication conducted while in motion or during halts at unspecified locations.

Repeater operation. Radio communication other than auxiliary operation, for retransmitting automatically the radio signals of other amateur radio stations.

Auxiliary operation. Radio communication for remotely controlling other amateur radio stations, for automatically relaying the radio signals of other amateur radio stations in a system of stations, or for intercommunicating with other amateur radio stations in a system of amateur radio stations.

Beacon operation. One-way radio communication conducted in order to facilitate measurement of radio equipment characteristics, adjustment of radio equipment, observation of propagation or transmission phenomena, or other related experimental activities.

Radio control operation. One-way radio communication for remotely controlling objects or apparatus other than amateur radio stations.

(m) *Control* means techniques used for accomplishing the immediate operation of an Amateur Radio station. Control includes one or more of the following:

(1) *Local control.* Manual control, with the control operator monitoring the operation on duty at the control point located at a station transmitter with the associated operating adjustments directly accessible. (Direct mechanical control, or direct wire control of a transmitter from a control point located on board any aircraft, vessel, or on the same premises on which the transmitter is located, is also considered local control.)

(2) *Remote control.* Manual control, with the control operator monitoring the operation on duty at a control point located elsewhere than at the station transmitter, such that the associated operating adjustment are accessible through a control link.

(3) *Automatic control* means the use of devices and procedures for control without the control operator being present at the control point when the station is transmitting.

(n) *Control link.* Apparatus for effecting remote control between a control point and a remotely controlled station.

(o) *Control operator.* An amateur radio operator designated by the licensee of an amateur radio station to also be responsible for the emissions from that station.

(p) *Control point.* The operating position of an amateur radio station where the control operator function is performed.

(q) *Antenna structures.* Antenna structures include the radiating system, its supporting structures, and any appurtenances mounted thereon.

(r) *Harmful interference.* Interference which seriously degrades, obstructs or repeatedly interrupts the operation of a radiocommunication service.

(s) *Transmitter.* Apparatus for converting electrical energy received from a source into radio-frequency electromagnetic energy capable of being radiated.

(t) *Transmitting power.* The radio frequency (RF) power generated by operations of an amateur radio station, including the following:

(1) *Transmitter power.* The peak envelope power (output) present at the antenna terminals (where the antenna feedline, or if no feedline is used, the antenna, would be connected) of the transmitter. The term "transmitter" includes any external radio frequency power amplifier which may be used. Peak envelope power is defined as the average power during one radio frequency cycle at the crest of the modulation envelope, taken under normal operating conditions.

(2) *Effective radiated power.* The product of the transmitter (peak envelope) power, expressed in watts, delivered to an antenna, and the relative gain of the antenna over that of a half-wave dipole antenna.

(u) *System network diagram.* A diagram showing each station and its relationship to the other stations in a network of stations, and to the control point(s).

(v) *Third-party traffic.* Amateur radio communication by or under the supervision of the control operator at an amateur radio station to another amateur radio station on behalf of anyone other than the control operator.

(w) *Emergency communication.* Any amateur radio communication directly relating to the immediate safety of life of individuals or the immediate protection of property.

(x) *Automatic retransmission.* Retransmission of signals by an amateur radio station whereby the retransmitting station is actuated solely by the presence of a received signal through electrical or electro-mechanical means, i.e., without any direct, positive action by the control operator.

(y) *External radio frequency power amplifier.* Any device which, (1) when used in conjunction with a radio transmitter as a signal source, is capable of amplification of that signal, and (2) is not an integral part of the transmitter as manufactured.

(z) *External radio frequency power amplifier kit.* Any number of electronic parts, usually provided with a schematic diagram or printed circuit board, which, when assembled in accordance with instructions, results in an external radio frequency power amplifier, even if additional parts of any type are required to complete assembly.

(aa) *Frequency coordinator.* An individual or organization recognized in a local or regional area by amateur operators whose stations are eligible to engage in repeater or auxiliary operation which recommends frequencies and, where necessary, associated operating and technical parameters for amateur repeater and auxiliary operation in order to avoid or minimize potential interference.

(bb) *Business communications.* Any transmission or communication the purpose of which is to facilitate the regular business or commercial affairs of any party.

(cc) *Spread spectrum transmission.* An information bearing transmission in which information is conveyed by a modulated RF carrier and where the bandwidth is significantly widened, by means of a spreading function, over that needed to transmit the information alone.

*Editor's Note: At the time of this writing, both of these definitions have been erroneously issued the same number by the FCC. HQ understands the Commission will correct this shortly.

Subpart B—Amateur Operator and Station Licenses

§97.5 Classes of operator licenses

Amateur Extra.
Advanced.
General.
Technician.
Novice.

§97.7 Frequency privileges.

The following transmitting frequency bands are available to amateur radio stations having a control operator of the license class designated, subject to the limitations of paragraph (g) of this section:

(a) Novice class:

Meter band	Terrestrial location of the amateur radio station			Limitations (see para. (g))
	ITU Region 1	ITU Region 2	ITU Region 3	
		kilohertz		
80	3700-3750	3700-3750	3700-3750	1, 3, 32
—	—	5167.5	—	2
40	7050-7075	7100-7150	7050-7075	1, 3, 32
15	21100-21200	21100-21200	2100-21200	1, 32
10	28100-28200	28100-28200	28100-28200	1

(b) Technician class: All of the frequency bands listed in paragraph (f), as well as the frequency bands in the following table:

Meter band	Terrestrial location of the amateur radio station			Limitations (see para. (g))
	ITU Region 1	ITU Region 2	ITU Region 3	
		kilohertz		
80	3700-3750	3700-3750	3700-3750	1, 3, 32
—	—	5167.5	—	2
40	7050-7075	7100-7150	7050-7075	1, 3, 32
15	21100-21200	21100-21200	21100-21200	1, 32
10	28100-28200	28100-28200	28100-28200	1

(c) General class: All of the frequency bands listed in paragraph (f), as well as the frequency bands in the following table:

Meter band	Terrestrial location of the amateur radio station ITU Region 1	ITU Region 2	ITU Region 3	Limitations (see para. (g))
	kilohertz			
160	1810-1850	1800-2000	1800-2000	3, 5, 21
80	3525-3750	3525-3750	3525-3750	3, 32
75	—	3850-4000	3850-3900	3, 32
—	—	5167.5	—	2
40	7025-7100	7025-7150	7025-7100	3, 32
40	—	7225-7300	—	3, 32
30	10100-10150	10100-10150	10100-10150	28, 32
20	14025-14150	14025-14150	14025-14150	32
20	14225-14350	14225-14350	14225-14350	32
15	21025-21200	21025-21200	21025-21200	32
15	21300-21450	21300-21450	21300-21450	32
12	24890-24990	24890-24990	24890-24990	29, 32
10	28000-29700	28000-29700	28000-29700	

(d) Advanced class: All of the frequency bands listed in paragraph (f), as well as the frequency bands in the following table:

Meter band	Terrestrial location of the amateur radio station ITU Region 1	ITU Region 2	ITU Region 3	Limitations (see para. (g))
	kilohertz			
160	1810-1850	1800-2000	1800-2000	3, 5, 21
80	3525-3750	3525-3750	3525-3750	3, 32
75	3775-3800	3775-4000	3775-3900	3, 32
—	—	5167.5	—	2
40	7025-7100	7025-7300	7025-7100	3, 32
30	10100-10150	10100-10150	10100-10150	28, 32
20	14025-14150	14025-14150	14025-14150	32
20	14175-14350	14175-14350	14175-14350	32
15	21025-21200	21025-21200	21025-21200	32
15	21225-21450	21225-21450	21225-21450	32
12	24890-24990	24890-24990	24890-24990	29, 32
10	28000-29700	28000-29700	28000-29700	

(e) Amateur Extra class: All of the frequency bands listed in paragraph (f), as well as the frequency bands in the following table:

Meter band	Terrestrial location of the amateur radio station ITU Region 1	ITU Region 2	ITU Region 3	Limitations (see para. (g))
	kilohertz			
160	1810-1850	1800-2000	1800-2000	3, 5, 21
80/75	3500-3800	3500-4000	3500-3900	3, 32
—	—	5167.5	—	2
40	7000-7100	7000-7300	7000-7100	3, 32
30	10100-10150	10100-10150	10100-10150	28, 32
20	14000-14350	14000-14350	14000-14350	32
15	21000-21450	21000-21450	21000-21450	32
12	24890-24990	24890-24990	24890-24990	29, 32
10	28000-29700	28000-29700	28000-29700	

(f) Frequency bands available to all amateur stations having a control operator of the Technician, General, Advanced or Amateur Extra class:

Meter band	*Terrestrial location of the amateur radio station*			Limitations (see para. (g))
	ITU Region 1	ITU Region 2	ITU Region 3	
		megahertz		
6	—	50-54	50-54	3
2	144-146	144-148	144-148	3, 32
1.25	—	220-225	—	3, 4, 5
0.70	430-440	420-450	420-450	3, 5, 6, 7, 10, 30
0.35	—	902-928	—	3, 5, 8, 9
0.23	1240-1300	1240-1300	1240-1300	5, 11, 22
—	2300-2310	2300-2310	2300-2310	3, 5, 12, 13
—	2390-2450	2390-2450	2390-2450	3, 5, 13, 14
			gigahertz	
—	—	3.3-3.5	3.3-3.5	3, 5, 15, 16, 17
—	5.650-5.850	5.650-5.925	5.650-5.850	3, 5, 18, 19, 20
—	10.0-10.5	10.0-10.5	10.0-10.5	5, 21, 22, 23, 31
—	24.00-24.25	24.00-24.25	24.00-24.25	3, 5, 22, 24, 26
—	47.0-47.2	47.0-47.2	47.0-47.2	
—	75.5-81	75.5-81	75.5-81	5, 21, 22
—	119.98-120.02	119.98-120.02	119.98-120.02	15, 25
—	142-149	142-149	142-149	5, 15, 21, 22
—	241-250	241-250	241-250	5, 21, 22, 27
—	above 300	above 300	above 300	15

(g) Limitations:

(1) Novice and Technician class radio operators are limited to the use of international Morse code when communicating in this band.

(2) This band may only be used by Amateur stations in the State of Alaska or within fifty nautical miles of the State of Alaska for emergency communications with other stations authorized to use this band in the State of Alaska. This frequency band is shared with licensees in the Alaska-private fixed service who may use it for certain non-emergency purposes.

(3) Where, in adjacent regions or subregions, a band of frequencies is allocated to different services of the same category, the basic principle is the equality of right to operate. Accordingly, the stations of each service in one region or subregion must operate so as not to cause harmful interference to services in the other regions or subregions. (See International Telecommunication Union Radio Regulations, RR 346 (Geneva, 1979).)

(4) This band is allocated to the amateur, fixed and mobile services in the United States on a co-primary basis. The basic principle which applies is the equality of right to operate. Amateur, fixed and mobile stations must operate so as not to cause harmful interference to each other.

(5) Amateur stations in the 1900-2000 kHz, 220-225 MHz, 420-450 MHz, 902-928 MHz, 1240-1300 MHz, 2300-2310 MHz, 2390-2450 MHz, 3.3-3.5 GHz, 5.650-5.925 GHz, 10.0-10.5 GHz, 24.05-24.25 GHz, 76-81 GHz, 144-149 GHz and 241-248 GHz bands must not cause harmful interference to stations in the Government radiolocation service and are not protected from interference due to the operation of stations in the Government radiolocation service.

(6) No amateur station shall operate north of Line A (see § 97.3(i)) in the 420-430 MHz band.

(7) The 420-430 MHz band is allocated to the Amateur service in the United States on a secondary basis, but is allocated to the fixed and mobile (except aeronautical mobile) services in the International Table of Allocations on a

primary basis. Therefore, amateur stations by other nations in the fixed and mobile (except aeronautical mobile) services and are not protected from interference due to the operation of stations authorized by other nations in the fixed and mobile (except aeronautical mobile) services.

(8) In the 902-928 MHz band, amateur stations shall not operate within the States of Colorado and Wyoming, bounded by the area of: latitude 39° N to 42° N, and longitude 103° W to 108° W. This band is allocated on a secondary basis to the Amateur service subject to not causing harmful interference to the operations of Government stations authorized in this band or to Automatic Vehicle Monitoring (AVM) systems. Stations in the Amateur service are not protected from any interference due to the operation of industrial, scientific and medical (ISM) devices, AVM systems or Government stations authorized in this band.

(9) In the 902-928 MHz band, amateur stations shall not operate in those portions of the States of Texas and New Mexico bounded on the south by latitude 31° 41 ′N, on the east by longitude 104° 11 ′W, on the north by latitude 34° 30 ′N, and on the west by longitude 107° 30 ′W.

(10) The 430-440 MHz band is allocated to the Amateur service on a secondary basis in ITU Regions 2 and 3. Amateur stations in this band in ITU Regions 2 and 3 must not cause harmful interference to stations authorized by other nations in the radiolocation service and are not protected from interference due to the operation of stations authorized by other nations in the radiolocation service. In ITU Region 1 the 430-440 MHz band is allocated to the Amateur service on a co-primary basis with the radiolocation service. As between these two services in this band in Region 1 the basic principle which applies is the equality of right to operate. Amateur stations authorized by the United States and radiolocation stations authorized by other nations in Region 1 must operate so as not to cause harmful interference to each other.

(11) In the 1240-1260 MHz band amateur stations must not cause harmful

interference to stations authorized by other nations in the radionavigation-satellite service and are not protected from interference due to the operation of stations authorized by other nations in the radionavigation-satellite service.

(12) In the United States, the 2300-2310 MHz band is allocated to the Amateur service on a co-secondary basis with the Government fixed and mobile services. In this band, the fixed and mobile services must not cause harmful interference to the Amateur service.

(13) In the 2300-2310 MHz and 2390-2450 MHz bands, the Amateur service is allocated on a secondary basis in all ITU Regions. In ITU Region 1, stations in the Amateur service must not cause harmful interference to stations authorized by other nations in the fixed service, and are not protected from interference due to the operation of stations authorized by other nations in the fixed service. In ITU Regions 2 and 3, stations in the Amateur service must not cause harmful interference to stations authorized by other nations in the fixed, mobile and radiolocation services, and are not protected from interference due to the operation of stations authorized by other nations in the fixed, mobile and radiolocation services.

(14) Amateur stations in the 2400-2450 MHz band are not protected from interference due to the operation of industrial, scientific and medical devices on 2450 MHz.

(15) Amateur stations in the 3.332-3.339 GHz, 3.3458-3.3525 GHz, 119.98-120.02 GHz, 144.68-144.98 GHz, 145.45-145.75 GHz, 146.82-147.12 GHz and 343-348 GHz bands must not cause harmful interference to stations in the radio astronomy service. Amateur stations in the 300-302 GHz, 324-326 GHz, 345-347 GHz, 363-365 GHz and 379-381 GHz bands must not cause harmful interference to stations in the space research service (passive) or Earth exploration-satellite service (passive).

(16) In both ITU Regions 2 and 3 the 3.3-3.5 GHz band is allocated to the Amateur service on a secondary basis. In the 3.3-3.4 GHz band amateur stations must not cause harmful interference to

stations authorized by other nations in the radiolocation service, and are not protected from interference due to the operation of stations authorized by other nations in the radiolocation service. In the 3.4-3.5 GHz band amateur stations must not cause harmful interference to stations authorized by other nations in the fixed and fixed-satellite services, and are not protected from interference due to the operation of stations authorized by other nations in the fixed and fixed-satellite services.

(17) In the United States the 3.3-3.5 GHz band is allocated to the amateur service on a co-secondary basis with the non-government radiolocation service.

(18) In the 5.650-5.725 GHz band, the Amateur service is allocated in all ITU regions on a co-secondary basis with the space research (deep space) service. In the 5.725-5.850 GHz band the Amateur service is allocated in all ITU regions on a secondary basis. In the 5.650-6.850 GHz band amateur stations must not cause harmful interference to stations authorized by other nations in the radiolocation service, and are not protected from interference due to the operation of stations authorized by other nations in the radiolocation service. In the 5.725-5.850 GHz band amateur stations must not cause harmful interference to stations authorized by other nations in the fixed-satellite service in ITU Region 1, and are not protected from interference due to the operation of stations authorized by other nations in the fixed-satellite service in ITU Region 1. In the 5.850-5.925 GHz band the Amateur service is allocated in ITU Region 2 on a co-secondary basis with the radiolocation service. In the 5.850-5.925 GHz band amateur stations must not cause harmful interference to stations authorized by other nations in the fixed, fixed-satellite and mobile services, and are not protected from interference due to the operation of stations authorized by other nations in the fixed, fixed-satellite and mobile services.

(19) In the United States, the 5.850-5.925 GHz band is allocated to the Amateur service on a secondary basis to the non-government fixed-satellite service. In the 5.850-5.925 GHz band amateur stations must not cause harmful interference to stations in the non-government fixed- satellite service and are not protected from interference due to the operation of stations in the non-government fixed-satellite service.

(20) Amateur stations in the 5.725-5.875 GHz band are not protected from interference due to the operation of industrial, scientific and medical devices on 5.8 GHz.

(21) Amateur stations in the 1900-2000 kHz, 10.45-10.50 GHz, 76-81 GHz, 144-149 GHz and 241-248 GHz bands must not cause harmful interference to stations in the non-government radiolocation service and are not protected from interference due to the operation of stations in the non- government radiolocation service.

(22) Amateur stations in the 1240-1300 MHz, 10.0-10.5 GHz, 24.05-24.25 GHz, 76-81 GHz, 144-149 GHz and 241-248 GHz bands must not cause harmful interference to stations authorized by other nations in the radiolocation service and are not protected from interference due to the operation of stations authorized by other nations in the radiolocation service.

(23) In the 10.00-10.45 GHz band in ITU Regions 1 and 3 amateur stations must not cause harmful interference to stations authorized by other nations in the fixed and mobile services, and are not protected from interference due to the operation of stations authorized by other nations in the fixed and mobile services.

(24) In the United States, the 24.05-24.25 GHz band is allocated to the Amateur service on a co-secondary basis with the non-government radiolocation and Government and non-government Earth exploration-satellite (active) services.

(25) The 119.98-120.02 GHz band is allocated to the Amateur service on a secondary basis. Amateur stations in this band must not cause harmful interference to stations operating in the fixed, inter-satellite and mobile services, and are not protected from interference caused by the operation of stations in the fixed, inter-satellite and mobile services.

(26) Amateur stations in the 24.00-24.25 GHz band are not protected

from interference due to the operation of industrial, scientific and medical devices on 24.125 GHz.

(27) Amateur stations in the 244-246 GHz band are not protected from interference due to the operation of industrial, scientific and medical devices on 245 GHz.

(28) Amateur stations in the 10100-10150 kHz band must not cause harmful interference to stations authorized by other nations in the fixed service. Amateur stations shall make all necessary adjustments (including termination of transmission) if harmful interference is caused.

(29) Until July 1, 1989, amateur stations in this band must not cause harmful interference to stations authorized by other nations in the fixed and mobile services. Amateur stations must make all necessary adjustments (including termination of transmission) if harmful interference is caused.

(30) Amateur stations in the 449.5-450 MHz band must not cause interference to and are not protected from interference due to the operation of stations in the space operation service, the space research service, or for space telecommand.

(31) In the United States, the 10.0-10.5 GHz band is allocated to the Amateur service on a co-secondary basis with the non-government radiolocation service.

(32) Amateur stations in these bands may be used for communications related to relief operations in connection with natural disasters. See Appendix 6 to this Part.

§97.9 Eligibility for new operator license.

Anyone except a representative of a foreign government is eligible for an amateur operator license.

§97.11 Application for operator license.

(a) An application (FCC Form 610) for a new operator license, including an application for change in operating privileges which will require an examination, shall be submitted in accordance with the provisions of §97.26.

(b) An application (FCC Form 610) for renewal and/or modification of license when no change in operating privileges is involved shall be submitted to the Commission's office at Gettysburg, Pennsylvania 17325.

§97.13 Renewal or modification of operator license.

(a) An amateur operator license may be renewed upon proper application.

(b) The applicant shall qualify for a new license by examination if the requirements of this section are not fulfilled.

(c) Application for renewal and/or modification of an amateur operator license shall be submitted on FCC Form 610 and shall be accompanied by the applicant's license or a photocopy thereof. Application for renewal of unexpired licenses must be made during the license term and should be filed within 90 days, but not later than 30 days, prior to the end of the license term. In any case in which the licensee has, in accordance with the provisions of this chapter, made timely and sufficient application for renewal of an unexpired license, no license with reference to any activity of a continuing nature shall expire until such application shall have been finally determined.

(d) If a license is allowed to expire, application for renewal may be made during a grace period of two years after the expiration date. During this grace period, an expired license is not valid. A license renewed during the grace period will be dated currently and will not be backdated to the date of its expiration. Application for renewal shall be submitted on FCC Form 610 and shall be accompanied by the applicant's expired license or a photocopy thereof.

OPERATOR LICENSE EXAMINATIONS

§97.19 When examination is required.

Examination is required for the issuance of a new amateur operator license, and for a change in class of operating privileges. Credit may be given, however, for certain elements of examination as provided in §97.25.

§97.21 Examination elements.

Examination for amateur operator privileges will comprise one or more of

132

the following examination elements:

(a) Element 1(A): Beginner's code test at five (5) words per minute;

(b) Element 1(B): General code test at thirteen (13) words per minute;

(c) Element 1(C): Expert's code test at twenty (20) words per minute;

(d) Element 2: Basic law comprising rules and regulations essential to beginners operation, including sufficient elementary radio theory for the understanding of those rules;

(e) Element 3: General amateur practice and regulations involving radio operation and apparatus and provisions of treaties, statutes, and rules affecting amateur stations and operators.

(f) Element 4(A): Intermediate amateur practice involving intermediate level radio theory and operation as applicable to modern amateur techniques, including, but not limited to, radiotelephony and radiotelegraphy;

(g) Element 4(B): Advanced amateur practice involving advanced radio theory and operation as applicable to modern amateur techniques, including, but not limited to, radiotelephony, radiotelegraphy, and transmissions of energy for measurements and observations applied to propagation, for the radio control of remote objects and for similar experimental purposes.

§97.23 Examination requirements.

Applicants for operator licenses will be required to pass the following examination elements:

(a) Amateur Extra Class: Elements 1(C), 2, 3, 4(A) and 4(B).

(b) Advanced Class: Elements 1(B), 2 3 and 4(A);

(c) General Class: Elements 1(B), 2 and 3;

(d) Technician Class: Elements 1(A), 2 and 3;

(e) Novice Class: Elements 1(A) and 2.

§97.25 Examination credit.

(a) An applicant for a higher class of amateur operator license who holds any valid amateur license will be required to pass only those elements of the higher class examination that are not included in the examination for the amateur license held.

(b) A certificate of successful completion of an examination will be issued to applicants who successfully complete an examination element. Upon presentation of this certificate for telegraphy examination elements 1(A), 1(B) or 1(C), examiners shall give the applicant for an amateur radio operator license examination credit for the code speed associated with the previously completed element. For purposes of examination credit, this certificate is valid for a period of one year from the date of its issuance.

(c) A person who applies for an amateur operator license will be given credit for any telegraphy element if that person holds a commercial radiotelegraph operator license or permit issued by the Federal Communications Commission, or has held one within 5 years of the Commission's receipt of that person's application for an amateur operator license.

(d) No examination credit, except as herein provided, shall be allowed on the basis of holding or having held any amateur or commercial operator license.

§97.26 Examination procedure.

(a) Each examination for an amateur operator license must be administered at a place and time chosen by the examiner(s). The number of candidates at any examination session may be limited. Public announcement must be made before all examinations for elements 1(B), 1(C), 3, 4(A) or 4(B).

(b) The examiner(s) must be present and observing the candidate throughout the entire examination.

(c) The examiner(s) will be responsible for the proper conduct and necessary supervision during each examination.

(d) Each candidate for an amateur radio license, which requires the applicant to pass one or more examination elements, must present the examiner(s) with a properly completed FCC Form 610 on or before the registration deadline date for those examination sessions for which registration is required; otherwise, applicants shall submit FCC Form 610 at the examination session before the start of the examination(s). In cases where a registration deadline is required, it shall be specified by the VEC that issues the examination papers to the examiner.

(e) The candidate shall comply with the instructions given by the examiner(s). The examiner(s) must immediately terminate the examination upon failure of the candidate to comply with the examiner(s)' instructions.

(f) At the completion of the examination, the candidate shall return all test papers to the examiner(s).

(g) A candidate whose physical disabilities require special procedures to allow participation in examination sessions shall attach a statement to his/her application. For examinations other than Novice Class the statement shall be retained in the files of the VEC that issues the test papers. The statement for Novice Class examinations shall be retained by the examiner for one year. The statement shall include:

(1) a physician's certification indicating the nature of the disability; AND

(2) the name(s) of the person(s) taking and transcribing the applicant's dictation of test questions and answers, if such a procedure is necessary.

(h) (reserved)

§97.27 Examination preparation.

(a) Element 1(A) shall be prepared by the examiner. The preparer must hold an Amateur Extra, Advanced, or General Class operator license. The test shall be such as to prove the applicant's ability to transmit correctly by hand key, straight key, or, if supplied by the applicant, any other type of hand operated key such as a semi-automatic or electronic key, but not a keyboard keyer, and to receive correctly by ear texts in the international Morse code at a rate of not less than five (5) words per minute. (Special procedures may be employed in cases of physical disability. See §97.26(g).) The applicant is responsible for knowing, and may be tested on, the twenty-six letters of the alphabet, the numerals 0-9, the period, the comma, the question mark, $\overline{AR}$, $\overline{SK}$, $\overline{BT}$ and $\overline{DN}$. See §97.29(c).)

(b) Elements 1(B) and 1(C) shall be prepared by the examiners or be obtained by the examiners from the VEC. The preparer must hold an Amateur Extra Class license. The test shall be such as to prove the applicant's ability to transmit correctly by hand key, straight key, or, if supplied by the applicant, any other type of hand operated key such as a semi-automatic or electronic key, but not a keyboard keyer, and to receive correctly by ear texts in the international Morse code at not less than the prescribed speed. (Special procedures may be employed in cases of physical disability. See §97.26(g).) The applicant is responsible for knowing, and may be tested on, the twenty-six letters of the alphabet, the numerals 0-9, the period, the comma, the question mark, $\overline{AR}$, $\overline{SK}$, $\overline{BT}$ and $\overline{DN}$. See §97.29(c).

(c) Element 2 shall be designed by the examiner from PR Bulletin 1035A (latest date of issue), entitled *Questions for the Element 2 Amateur Radio Operator License Examination.*

(d) Elements 3, 4(A) and 4(B) will be designed by the VEC. The VEC will select questions for each test from the appropriate list of questions approved by the Commission (either PR Bulletin 1035B, C, or D, latest date of issue). The VEC must select the appropriate number of questions from each category of the syllabus (PR Bulletin 1035) as specified in PR Bulletin 1035B, C, or D. These questions must be taken verbatim from the appropriate PR Bulletin in the form in which they have been approved by the Commission. Beginning January 1, 1987, volunteer examiners may also design Elements 3, 4(A), and 4(B) in accord with the provisions of this paragraph. Each VEC and each volunteer examiner is required to hold current examination designs in confidence.

(e) PR Bulletins 1035A, B, and C and D will be composed of questions originated by the FCC and questions submitted by amateur radio operators in accordance with the instructions in the Bulletin. Amateur radio operators holding Amateur Extra Class licenses may submit questions for any written examination element. Amateur radio operators holding Advanced Class licenses may only submit questions for Element 2 and 3. Amateur radio operators holding General Class or Technician Class licenses may only submit questions for Element 2.

§97.28 Examination administration.

(a) Unless otherwise prescribed by the Commission, each examination for an amateur radio operator license (except the Novice Class operator license) shall be administered by three accredited (see §97.515) volunteer examiners. An examiner administering telegraphy examination Element 1(A) or written examination Element 2 (in conjunction with an examination other than a Novice Class examination) or written examination Element 3 must hold an Amateur Extra Class or Advanced Class radio operator license. An examiner administering telegraphy examination Element 1(B) or 1(C) or written examination Element 4(A) or 4(B) must hold an Amateur Extra Class radio operator license.

(b) Unless otherwise prescribed by the Commission, each examination for the Novice Class operator license shall be administered by one volunteer examiner. The examiner does not have to be accredited. The volunteer examiner must hold a current General, Advanced or Amateur Extra Class operator license issued by the Commission.

(c) Upon completion of an examination element, the examiner(s) shall immediately grade the test papers.

(d) When the candidate does not score a passing grade on an examination element, the examiner(s) shall so inform the candidate by providing the percentage of questions answered correctly, and by returning the application (see §97.26) to the candidate. For examinations other than Novice Class examinations, the test papers, including answer sheets, shall be returned to the VEC that issued them. For Novice Class examinations, the test papers, including answer sheets, must be retained as part of the volunteer examiner's station records for one year from the date the examination is administered.

(e) When the candidate scores a passing grade on an examination element, the examiner(s) (except for examinations for the Novice Class operator license) must issue a certificate of successful completion of the examination. This certificate may be used for a period of one year for examination credit for telegraphy elements 1 (A), 1 (B) or 1 (C) (see §97.25 (b)).

(f) When the candidate scores a passing grade on all examination elements required for the operator license class sought (see §97.23), the examiners shall certify to the following information on the candidate's application form (see §97.26):

(1) Examiners' names and amateur radio station call signs;

(2) Examiners' qualifications to administer the examination; (see §97.31); *AND*

(3) Examiners' signed statements that the applicant has passed the required examination elements.

(g) Within ten days of the administration of a successful examination for the Novice Class operator license, the examiner shall submit the candidate's application to:

Federal Communications Commission
Gettysburg, Pennsylvania 17325

(h) Within ten days of the administration of a successful examination for the Technician, General, Advanced or Amateur Extra Class operator license, the examiners shall submit the successful candidates' applications and all test papers to the VEC that originally issued that test.

(i) The FCC reserves the right, without qualification, to:

(1) administer examinations itself; *OR*

(2) readminister examinations itself or under the supervision of an examiner designated by the FCC, to any person who obtained an operator license above the Novice Class through the volunteer examination process.

(j) If a licensee fails to appear for readministration of an examination pursuant to paragraph (i)(2) of this section, or does not successfully complete the examination element(s) which are readministered, the licensee's operator license is subject to cancellation; in an instance of such cancellation, the licensee will be issued an operator license consistent with the completed examination elements which have not been invalidated by not appearing for or failing readministration of an examination.

§97.29 Examination grading.

(a) Each examination element shall be graded separately by the examiners.

(b) An applicant passes a written examination if he/she answers at least 74 percent of the questions correctly.

(c) An applicant passes a code element examination if he/she proves his/her ability to transmit correctly by hand key (straight key, or, if supplied by the applicant, any other type of hand operated key such as a semi-automatic or electronic key, but not a keyboard keyer) and to receive correctly by ear texts in the international Morse code at not less than the prescribed speed during a five-minute test period. Each five characters shall be counted as one word. Each punctuation mark and numeral shall be counted as two characters.

§97.31 Volunteer examiner requirements.

(a) Each volunteer examiner administering an examination for an amateur radio operator license must:

    (i) be at least 18 years of age; *AND*

    (ii) not be related to the candidate.

(b) Any person who owns a significant interest in, or is an employee of, any company or other entity which is engaged in the manufacture or distribution of equipment used in connection with amateur radio transmissions, or in the preparation or distribution of any publication used in preparation for obtaining amateur station operator licenses, is ineligible to be a volunteer examiner for purposes of administering an amateur radio operator examination. However, a person who does not normally communicate with that part of an entity engaged in the manufacture or distribution of such equipment, or in the preparation or distribution of any publication used in preparation for obtaining amateur operator licenses, is eligible to be a volunteer examiner.

(c) Volunteer examiners may not be compensated for services. They may be reimbursed for out-of-pocket expenses, except for Novice class examinations (see §97.36).

(d) Each volunteer examiner administering an examination for the Technician, General, Advanced or Amateur Extra Class operator license must be accredited by the Volunteer-Examiner Coordinator (see Subpart I).

(e) The FCC will not accept the services of any person seeking to be a volunteer examiner if that person's amateur radio station license or amateur radio station operator's license has ever been revoked or suspended.

§97.33 Volunteer examiner conduct.

No volunteer examiner shall give or certify any examination by fraudulent means or for monetary or other consideration. Violation of this provision may result in the revocation of the amateur radio station license and the suspension of the amateur radio operator license of the volunteer examiner. This does not preclude a volunteer examiner from accepting reimbursement for out-of-pocket expenses under §97.36. Reimbursement in any amount in excess of that permitted may result in the sanctions specified herein.

§97.35 Temporary operating authority.

Unless the FCC otherwise prescribes, an applicant already licensed in the Amateur Radio Service, upon successfully completing the amateur radio examination(s) required for a higher class, may operate an amateur radio station consistent with the rights and privileges of the higher class for a period of one year from the date of the most recently completed examination for that operator class provided that the applicant retains the certificate(s) for successful completion of the examination(s) (see §97.28(e)) at the station location, provided that the applicant uses the identifier code of the new class of license for which the applicant has qualified (KT for Technician Class, AG for General Class, AA for Advanced Class and AE for Amateur Extra Class) as a suffix to the present call sign (see §97.84), and provided that the FCC has not yet acted upon the application for a higher class of license.

§97.36 Reimbursement for expenses.

(a) Each volunteer examiner coordinator and each volunteer examiner may be reimbursed by examinees for out-of-pocket expenses incurred in preparing, processing or administering examinations for amateur station operator licenses above the Novice class. The volunteer examiner coordinator or the volunteer examiners must collect the reimbursement fee, if any, from the examinees. No reimbursement may be accepted for preparing, processing or administering Novice class examination.

(b) The maximum amount of reimbursement is $4.00 for 1984 and will be adjusted annually each January 1 thereafter for changes in the Department of Labor Consumer Price Index. Changes in the maximum amount of reimbursement will be announced by the Commission in a Public Notice. The amount of such reimbursement fee from any examinee for any one examination at a particular session regardless of the number of examination elements taken must not exceed the published maximum.

(c) Each volunteer examiner coordinator and each volunteer examiner who accepts reimbursement must maintain records of out-of-pocket expenses and reimbursements for each examination session. They must certify on or before January 31 of each year to the Commission's office in Gettysburg, PA 17325 that all expenses for the period from January 1 to December 31 of the preceding year for which reimbursement was obtained were necessarily and prudently incurred.

(d) The expense and reimbursement records must be retained by each volunteer examiner coordinator and each volunteer examiner for 3 years and made available to the FCC upon request.

(e) Each volunteer examiner must forward on or before January 15 of each year the certification concerning expenses to the volunteer examiner coordinator who coordinated the efforts of the volunteer examiner and for which reimbursement was received. The volunteer examiner coordinator must forward all such certifications and its own certification concerning expenses to the FCC on or before January 31 of each year.

(f) The volunteer examiner coordinator must disaccredit any volunteer examiner who fails to provide the annual certification. The volunteer examiner coordinator must advise the FCC on January 31 of each year of the volunteer examiners that it has disaccredited for this reason.

STATION LICENSES

§97.37 General eligibility for station license.

(a) An Amateur Radio station license will be issued only to a licensed Amateur Radio operator, except that a military recreation station license may also be issued to an individual not licensed as an Amateur Radio operator (other than a representative of a foreign government), who is in charge of a proposed military recreation station not operated by the U.S. Government but which is to be located in approved public quarters.

(b) Only modification and/or renewal station licenses will be issued for club and military recreation stations. No new licenses will be issued for these types of stations.

§ 97.39 Eligibility of corporations or organizations to hold station license.

An amateur station will not be issued to a school, company, corporation, association, or other organization, except that in the case of a *bona fide* Amateur Radio organization or society meeting the criteria set forth in Section 97.3, a station license may be issued to a licensed amateur operator, other than the holder of a Novice class license, as trustee for such society.

§97.40 Station license required.

(a) No transmitting station shall be operated in the Amateur Radio Service without being licensed by the Federal Communications Commission, except that an Amateur Radio station licensed by the Government of Canada may, in accordance with Section 97.41, be operated in the United States without the prior approval of the Commission.

(b) Every Amateur Radio operator shall have one, but only one, primary Amateur Radio station license.

§97.41 Operation of Canadian amateur stations in the United States.

(a) An Amateur Radio station licensed by the Government of Canada may be operated in the United States without the prior approval of the Federal Communications Commission.

(b) Operation of a Canadian amateur station in the United States must comply with all of the following:

(1) The terms of the Convention between the United States and Canada (TIAS No. 2508) relating to the operation by citizens of either country of certain radio equipment or stations in the other country. (See Appendix 4 to Part 97.)

(2) The operating terms and conditions of the amateur station license issued by the Government of Canada.

(3) The provisions of subpart A through E of Part 97.

(4) Any further conditions the Commission may impose upon the privilege of operating in the United States.

(c) At any time the Commission may, in its discretion, modify, suspend, or cancel the privilege of any Canadian licensee operating an Amateur Radio station in the United States.

§97.42 Application for station license.

(a) Each application for a club or military recreation station license in the Amateur Radio Service shall be made on the FCC Form 610-B. Each application for any other Amateur Radio license shall be made on the FCC Form 610.

(b) One application and all papers incorporated therein and made a part thereof shall be submitted for each amateur station license. If the application is only for a station license, it shall be filed directly with the Commission's Gettysburg, Pennsylvania office. If the application also contains an application for any class of amateur operator license, it shall be filed in accordance with the provisions of §97.11.

(c) Each applicant in the Private Radio Services (1) for modification of a station license involving a site change or a substantial increase in tower height or (2) for a license for a new station must, before commencing construction, supply the environmental information, where required, and must follow the procedure prescribed by Subpart 1 of Part 1 of this chapter (§1.1301 through 1.1319) unless Commission action authorizing such construction would be a minor action within the meaning of Subpart 1 of Part 1.

(d) Protection for Federal Communications Commission Monitoring Stations:

(1) Applicants for an Amateur Radio station license to operate in the vicinity of an FCC monitoring station are advised to give consideration, prior to filing applications, to the possible need to protect the FCC stations from harmful interference. Geographical coordinates of the facilities which require protection are listed in Section 0.121(c) of the Commission's Rules. Applications for stations (except mobile stations) in the vicinity of monitoring stations may be reviewed by Commission staff on a case-by-case basis to determine the potential for harmful interference to the monitoring station. Depending on the theoretical field strength value and existing root-sum-square or other ambient radio field signal levels at the indicated coordinates, a clause protecting the monitoring station may be added to the station license.

(2) Advance consultation with the Commission is suggested prior to filing an initial application for station license if the proposed station will be located within one mile of any of the above-referenced monitoring station coordinates and is to be operated on frequencies below 1000 MHz. Such consultations are also suggested for proposed stations operating above 1000 MHz if they are to be located within one mile of any monitoring station designated in Section 0.121(c) as a satellite monitoring facility.

(3) Regardless of any coordination prior to filing initial applications, it is suggested that licensees within one mile of a monitoring station consult the Commission before initiating any changes in the station which would increase the field strength produced over the monitoring station.

(4) Applicants and licensees desiring such consultations should communicate with: Chief, Field Operations Bureau,

Federal Communications Commission, Washington, DC 20054, Telephone 202-632-6980.

(5) The Commission will not screen applications to determine whether advance consultation has taken place. However, applicants are advised that such consultation can avoid objections from the Federal Communications Commission or modification of any authorization which will cause harmful interference.

§97.43 Mailing address furnished by licensee.

Each application shall set forth and each licensee shall furnish the Commission with an address in the United States to be used by the Commission in serving documents or directing correspondence to that licensee. Unless any licensee advises the Commission to the contrary, the address contained in the licensee's most recent application will be used by the Commission for this purpose.

§97.44 Location of station.

Every amateur radio station shall have one land location, the address of which appears in the station license, and at least one control point.

§97.45 Limitations on antenna structures.

(a) Except as provided in paragraph (b) of this section, an antenna for a station in the Amateur Radio Service which exceeds the following height limitations may not be erected or used unless notice has been filed with both the FAA on FAA Form 7460-1 and with the Commission on Form 854 or on the license application form, and prior approval by the Commission has been obtained for:

(1) Any construction or alteration of more than 200 feet in height above ground level at its site (§17.7(a) of this chapter).

(2) Any construction or alteration of greater height than an imaginary surface extending outward and upward at one of the following slopes (§17.7(b) of this chapter):

(i) 100 to 1 for a horizontal distance of 20,000 feet from the nearest point of the nearest runway of each airport with at least one runway more than 3,200 feet in length, excluding heliports and seaplane bases without specified boundaries, if that airport is either listed in the Airport Directory of the current Airman's Information Manual or is operated by a Federal military agency.

(ii) 50 to 1 for a horizontal distance of 10,000 feet from the nearest point of the nearest runway of each airport with its longest runway no more than 3,200 feet in length, excluding heliports and seaplane bases without specified boundaries, if that airport is either listed in the Airport Directory or is operated by a Federal military agency.

(iii) 25 to 1 for a horizontal distance of 5,000 feet from the nearest point of the nearest landing and takeoff area of each heliport listed in the Airport Directory or operated by a Federal military agency.

(3) Any construction or alteration on an airport listed in the Airport Directory of the Airman's Information Manual (§17.7(c) of this chapter).

(b) A notification to the Federal Aviation Administration is not required for any of the following construction or alteration:

(1) Any object that would be shielded by existing structures of a permanent and substantial character or by natural terrain or topographic features of equal or greater height, and would be located in the congested area of a city, town, or settlement where it is evident beyond all reasonable doubt that the structure so shielded will not adversely affect safety in air navigation. Applicants claiming such exemption shall submit a statement with their application to the Commission explaining the basis in detail for their finding (§17.14(a) of this chapter).

(2) Any antenna structure of 20 feet or less in height except one that would increase the height of another antenna structure (§17.14(b) of this chapter).

(c) Further details as to whether an aeronautical study and/or obstruction marking and lighting may be required, and specifications for obstruction marking and lighting when required, may be obtained from Part 17 of this chapter, "Construction, Marking and Lighting of Antenna Structures." Information regarding the inspection and maintenance of antenna structures requiring obstruction marking and lighting is also contained in Part 17 of this chapter.

§97.47 Renewal and/or modification of amateur station license.

(a) Application for renewal and/or modification of an individual station license shall be submitted on FCC Form 610, and application for renewal and/or modification of an amateur club or military recreation station shall be submitted on FCC Form 610-B. In every case the application shall be accompanied by the applicant's license or photocopy thereof. Applications for renewal of unexpired licenses must be made during the license term and should be filed not later than 60 days prior to the end of the license term. In any case in which the licensee has in accordance with the provisions of this chapter, made timely and sufficient application for renewal of an unexpired license, no license with reference to any activity of a continuing nature shall expire until such application shall have been finally determined.

(b) If a license is allowed to expire, application for renewal may be made during a grace period of two years after the expiration date. During this grace period, an expired license is not valid. A license renewal during the grace period will be dated currently and will not be backdated to the date of its expiration. An application for an individual station license shall be submitted on FCC Form 610. An application for an amateur club or military recreation station license shall be submitted on FCC Form 610-B. In every case the application shall be accompanied by the applicant's expired license or a photocopy thereof.

§97.49 Commission modification of station license.

(a) Whenever the Commission shall determine that the public interest, convenience, and necessity would be served, or any treaty ratified by the United States will be more fully complied with, by the modification of any radio station license either for a limited time, or for the duration of the term thereof, it shall issue an order for such licensee to show cause why such license should not be modified.

(b) Such order to show cause shall contain a statement of the grounds and reasons for such proposed modification, and shall specify wherein the said license is required to be modified. It shall require the licensee against whom it is directed to appear at a place and time therein named, in no event to be less than 30 days from the date of receipt of the order, to show cause why the proposed modification should not be made and the order of modification issued.

(c) If the licensee against whom the order to show cause is directed does not appear at the time and place provided in said order, a final order of modification shall issue forthwith.

CALL SIGNS

§97.51 Assignment of call signs.

(a) The Commission shall assign the call sign of an amateur radio station on a systematic basis.

(b) The Commission shall not grant any request for a specific call sign.

(c) From time to time the Commission will issue public announcements detailing the policies and procedures governing the systematic assignment of call signs and any changes in those policies and procedures.

DUPLICATE LICENSES AND LICENSE TERM

§97.57 Duplicate license.

Any licensee requesting a duplicate license to replace an original which has been lost, mutilated, or destroyed, shall submit a statement setting forth the facts regarding the manner in which original license was lost, mutilated, or destroyed. If, subsequent to receipt by the licensee of the duplicate license, the original license is found, either the duplicate or the original license shall be returned immediately to the Commission.

§97.59 License term.

(a) Amateur operator licenses are normally valid for a period of ten years from the date of issuance of a new, modified or renewed license.

(b) Amateur station licenses are normally valid for a period of ten years from the date of issuance of a new, modified or renewed license. All amateur station licenses, regardless of when issued, will expire on the same date as the licensee's amateur operator license.

(c) A duplicate license shall bear the same expiration date as the license for which it is a duplicate.

Subpart C—Technical Standards

§97.61 Authorized emissions.

(a) <u>kilohertz</u>:

Frequency Band	Emissions	Limitations (see paragraph (d))
1800-2000	A1A, F1B, A3E, F3E, G3E, A3C, F3C, A3F, F3F, H3E, J3E, R3E	
3500-3750	A1A, F1B	1
3750-4000	A1A, A3E, F3E, G3E, A3C, A3F, F3C, F3F, H3E, J3E, R3E	
5167.5	J3E, R3E	
7000-7075	A1A, F1B	1
7075-7100	A1A, F1B	1, 2
7100-7150	A1A, F1B	1
7150-7300	A1A, A3E, F3E, G3E, A3C, F3C, A3F, F3F, H3E, J3E, R3E	
10100-10150	A1A, F1B	
14000-14150	A1A, F1B	
14150-14350	A1A, A3E, F3E, A3C, F3C, A3F, F3F, H3E, J3E, R3E	
21000-21200	A1A, F1B	1
21200-21450	A1A, A3E, F3E, A3C, F3C, A3F, F3F, H3E, J3E, R3E	
24890-24930	A1A, F1B	
24930-24990	A1A, A3E, F3E, G3E, A3C, F3C, A3F, F3F, H3E, J3E, R3E	
28000-28300	A1A, F1B	1
28300-29500	A1A, A3E, F3E, G3E, A3C, F3C, A3F, F3F, H3E, J3E, R3E	
29500-29700	A1A, A3E, F2A, F3E, G3E, A3C, F3C, A3F, F3F, H3E, J3E, R3E	

(b) <u>50-144.1 MHz</u>:

50.0-50.1	A1A	
50.1-51.0	A1A, A2A, A2B, A3E, A3C, A3F, F1B, F2A, F2B, F3E, G3E, F3C, F3F, H3E, J3E, R3E	
51.0-54.0	NØN, A1A, A2A, A2B, A3E, A3C, A3F, F1B, F2A, F2B, F3E, G3E, F3C, F3F, H3E, J3E, R3E	
144.0-144.1	A1A	

(c) <u>Above 144.1 MHz</u>: Amateur stations are authorized to transmit the following emissions on amateur frequencies above 144.1 MHz: NØN, A1A, A2A, A2B, A3E, A3C, A3F, F1B, F2B, F3E, G3E, F3C, F3F, H3E, J3E and R3E. PØN emissions (the emission letters "K, L, M, Q, V, W and X" may also be used in

place of the letter "P" for pulsed radars) may be transmitted at all amateur frequencies above 2300 MHz,* except in the 10.0-10.5 GHz band. In the 902-928 MHz band F8E emissions may also be used. Emission F2A may also be used in the following frequency subbands: 144.1-148.0, 220-225, 420-450, 902-928, 1215-1300, 2300-2310 and 2390-2450 MHz. Emission F2A may also be used on all Gigahertz frequencies.

(d) Limitations:

(1) Novice and Technician class radio operators may not use F1B emissions in this band.

(2) Amateur stations located in Regions 1 and 3, and amateur radio stations located within Region 2 which are west of 130 degrees West longitude or south of 20 degrees North latitude may also use A3E, F3E, G3E, H3E, J3E and R3E emissions.

§97.63 Selection and use of frequencies.

(a) An amateur station may transmit on any frequency within any authorized amateur frequency band.

(b) Sideband frequencies resulting from keying or modulating a carrier wave shall be confined within the authorized amateur band.

(c) The frequencies available for use by a control operator of an amateur station are dependent on the operator license classification of the control operator and are listed in §97.7.

§97.65 Emission limitations.

(a) Type NØN emission, where not specifically designated in the bands listed on §97.61, may be used for short periods of time when required for authorized remote control purposes or for experimental purposes. However, these limitations do not apply where type NØN emission is specifically designated.

(b) Whenever code practice, in accordance with §97.91(d), is conducted in

bands authorized for A3E emission tone modulation of the radiotelephone transmitter may be utilized when interspersed with appropriate voice instructions.

(c) On frequencies below 29.0 MHz, the bandwidth of an F3E or G3E emission (frequency or phase modulation) shall not exceed that of an A3E emission having the same audio characteristics.

(d) On frequencies below 50 MHz, the bandwidth of A3C, A3F, F3C and F3F emissions shall not exceed that of an J3E single-sideband emission.

(e) On frequencies between 50 MHz and 225 MHz:

(1) The bandwidth of A3C and A3F single-sideband emissions shall not exceed the bandwidth of a J3E single-sideband emission.

(2) The bandwidth of A3C and A3F double-sideband emissions shall not exceed the bandwidth of an A3E double-sideband emissions.

(3) F3C and F3F emissions shall utilize a peak carrier deviation no greater than 5 kHz and a maximum modulating frequency no greater than 3 kHz or, alternatively, shall occupy a bandwidth no greater than 20 kHz. (For this purpose the bandwidth is defined as the width of the frequency band, outside of which the mean power of any emission is attenuated by at least 26 decibels below the mean power level of the total emission. A 3 kHz sampling bandwidth is used by the FCC in making this determination.)

(f) Below 225 MHz, an A3C or A3F emission may be used simultaneously with an A3E emission on the same carrier frequency, provided that the total bandwidth does not exceed that of an A3E double-sideband emission.

§97.67 Maximum authorized transmitting power.

(a) Amateur stations may use no more than the maximum transmitter power specified in this Part. Additionally, within the constraints of this section, amateur stations must use no more than the minimum transmitter power necessary to carry out the desired communications.

(b) Unless otherwise provided in this section, each amateur transmitter may be

---

*Editor's Note: The Commission inadvertently removed pulse emission (PØN) from the 902-928 MHz band in PR Docket 85-23. ARRL has been informed by the Commission that it will be shortly issue an editorial revision allowing pulse emission again on that band.

operated with a transmitter power not exceeding 1500 watts.

(c) Reserved.

(d) The peak envelope power output (transmitter power) of each amateur radio transmitter shall not exceed 200 watts when transmitting in any of the following frequency bands:

(1) 3700-3750 kHz;

(2) 7050-7075 kHz when the terrestrial location of the station is within Regions 1 or 3;

(3) 7100-7150 kHz;

(4) 10100-10150 kHz;

(5) 21100-21200 kHz; or

(6) 28100-28200 kHz.

(e) Within the limitations of paragraph (a) of this section, the peak envelope power output of an amateur radio station in beacon operation shall not exceed 100 watts.

(f) An amateur radio station may transmit A3 emissions on or before June 1, 1990 with a transmitter power exceeding that authorized by paragraph (b) of this section, provided that the power input (both radio frequency and direct current) to the final amplifying stage supplying radio frequency power to the antenna feedline does not exceed 1000 watts, exclusive of power for heating the cathodes of vacuum tubes. Limitations of paragraphs (a), (c) and (d) of this section and limitations of §97.61 still apply.

(g) On 5167.5 kHz the transmitter power shall not exceed 150 watts.

(h) In the 420-450 MHz frequency band the transmitter power shall not exceed 50 watts in the following areas unless expressly authorized by the Federal Communications Commission after mutual agreement, on a case-by-case basis, between the Commission Engineer-in Charge at the appropriate District Office and the Military Area Frequency Coordinator at the appropriate military base:

(1) Those portions of Texas and New Mexico bounded on the south by latitude 31° 45 ′ N, on the east by longitude 104° 00 ′ W, on the north by latitude 34° 30 ′ N and on the west by longitude 107° 30 ′ W. (The Military Area Frequency Coordinator for this area is located at White Sands Missile Range, New Mexico.)

(2) The entire State of Florida including the Key West area and the areas enclosed within a 200 mile radius of Patrick Air Force Base, Florida (latitude 28° 21 ′ N, longitude 80° 43 ′ W), and within a 200-mile radius of Eglin Air Force Base, Florida (latitude 30° 30 ′ N, longitude 86° 30 ′ W).

(3) The entire State of Arizona.

(4) Those portions of California and Nevada south of latitude 37° 10 ′ N, and the area within a 200-mile radius of the Pacific Missile Test Center, Point Mugu, California (latitude 34° 09 ′ N, longitude 119° 11 ′ W).

(5) In the State of Massachusetts within a 160- kilometer (100 mile) radius around locations at Otis Air Force Base, Massachusetts (latitude 41° 45 ′ N, longitude 70° 32 ′ W).

(6) In the State of California within a 240-kilometer (150 mile) radius around locations at Beale Air Force Base, California (latitude 39° 09 ′ N, longitude 121° 26 ′ W).

(7) In the State of Alaska within a 160-kilometer (100 mile) radius of Clear, Alaska (latitude 64° 17 ′ N, longitude 149° 10 ′ W). (The Military Area Frequency Coordinator for this area is located at Elmendorf Air Force Base, Alaska.)

(8) In the State of North Dakota within a 160-kilometer (100 mile) radius of Concrete, North Dakota (latitude 48° 43 ′ N, longitude 97° 54 ′ W). (The Military Area Frequency Coordinator for this area can be contacted at: HQ SAC/SXOE, Offutt Air Force Base, Nebraska 68113.)

(9) In the States of Alabama, Florida, Georgia and South Carolina within a 200 kilometer (124 mile) radius of Warner Robins Air Force Base, Georgia (latitude 32° 38 ′ N, longitude 83° 35 ′ W).

(10) In the State of Texas within a 200 kilometer (124 mile) radius of Goodfellow Air Force Base, Texas (latitude 31° 25 ′ N, longitude 100° 24 ′ W).

(i) In the 902-928 MHz frequency band the transmitter power shall not exceed 50 watts outside of but within 150 miles of the following boundaries of the White Sands Missile Range, New Mexico: those portions of Texas and New Mexico bounded on the south by latitude 31° 41′ N, on the east by longitude 104° 11′ W, on the north by latitude 34° 30′ N, and on the west by longitude 107° 30′ W.

§97.69 Digital communications.

Subject to the special conditions contained in paragraphs (a), (b) and (c) below, an amateur radio communication may include digital codes which represent alphanumeric characters, analogue measurements or other information. These digital codes may be used for such communications as (but not limited to) radio teleprinter, voice, facsimile, television, communications to control amateur radio stations, models and other objects, transference of computer programs or direct computer-to-computer communications, and communications in various types of data networks (including so-called "packet switching" systems); provided that such digital codes are not intended to obscure the meaning of, but are only to facilitate, the communications, and further provided that such operation is carried out in accordance with other regulations set forth in this part. (For purposes of this section, the sending speed (signaling rate), in baud, is defined as the reciprocal of the shortest (signaling) time interval (in seconds) that occurs during a transmission, where each time interval is the period between changes of transmitter state (including changes in emission amplitude, frequency, phase, or combination of these, as authorized).)

(a) The use of the digital codes specified in paragraph (b) of this section is permitted on any amateur frequency where F1B emission is permitted, subject to the following requirements:

(1) The sending speed shall not exceed the following:

(i) 300 baud on frequencies below 28 MHz;

(ii) 1200 baud on frequencies between 28 and 50 MHz;

(iii) 19.6 kilobaud on frequencies between 50 and 220 MHz;

(iv) 56 kilobaud on frequencies above 220 MHz.

(2) When type A2B, F1B, F2B emissions are used on frequencies below 50 MHz, the radio or audio frequency shift (the difference between the frequency for the "mark" signal and that for the "space" signal), as appropriate, shall not exceed 1000 Hz. When these emissions are used on frequencies above 50 MHz, the frequency shift, in hertz, shall not exceed the sending speed, in baud, of the transmission, or 1000 Hz, whichever is greater.

(b) Except as provided for in paragraph (c) of this section, only the following digital codes, as specified, may be used:

(1) The International Telegraph Alphabet Number 2 (commonly known as Baudot); provided that transmission shall consist of a single channel, five unit (start-stop) teleprinter code conforming to the International Telegraph Alphabet Number 2 with respect to all letters and numerals (including the slant sign or fraction bar); however, in the "figures" positions not utilized for numerals, special signals may be employed for the remote control of receiving printers, or for other purposes indicated in this section.

(2) The American Standard Code for Information Interchange (commonly known as ASCII); provided that the code shall conform to the American Standard Code for Information Interchange as defined in American National Standards Institute (ANSI) Standard X3.4-1968.

(3) The International Radio Consultative Committee (CCIR) Recommendations 476-2 and 476-3 (commonly known as AMTOR); provided that the code, baud rate and emission timing shall conform to the specifications of CCIR 476-2 (1978) or CCIR 476-3 (1982), Mode A or Mode B.

(c) In addition to the above provisions, the use of any digital code is permitted on amateur frequencies above 50 MHz, except those on which only A1 emission is permitted, subject to the following requirements:

(1) Communications using such digital codes are authorized for domestic operation only (communications between points within areas where radio services

are regulated by the U.S. Federal Communications Commission), except when special arrangements have been made between the United States and the administration of any other country concerned.

(2) The bandwidth of an emission from a station using such digital codes shall not exceed the following (where for this purpose the bandwidth is defined as the width of the frequency band, outside of which the mean power of any emission is attenuated by at least 26 decibels below the mean power of the total emission; a 3 kHz sampling bandwidth being used by the FCC in making this determination):

(i) 20 kHz on frequencies between 50 and 220 MHz;

(ii) 100 kHz on frequencies between 220 and 902 MHz;

(iii) On frequencies above 902 MHz any bandwidth may be used provided that the emission is in accordance with §97.63(b) and §97.73(c).

(d) An amateur station may be under automatic control when transmitting digital communications on frequencies 50 MHz and above.

(3) (Reserved.)

(4) When deemed necessary by an Engineer-in-Charge of a Commission field facility to assure compliance with the rules of this part, a station licensee shall:

(i) Cease the transmission of digital codes authorized under this paragraph.

(ii) Restrict the transmission of digital codes authorized under this paragraph to the extent instructed.

(iii) Maintain a record, convertible to the original information (voice, text, image, etc.), of all coded communications transmitted under authority of this paragraph.

§97.71 Spread-spectrum communications.

(a) Subject to special conditions in paragraphs (b) through (i) of this section, amateur stations may employ spread-spectrum transmissions to convey information containing voice, teleprinter, facsimile, television, signals for remote control of objects, computer programs, data, and other communications including communication protocol elements.

Spread-spectrum transmissions must not be used for the purpose of obscuring the meaning of, but only to facilitate transmission.

(b) Spread-spectrum transmissions are authorized on amateur frequencies above 420 MHz.

(c) Stations employing spread-spectrum transmissions shall not cause harmful interference to stations of good engineering design employing other authorized emissions specified in the table. Stations employing spread spectrum must also accept all interference caused by stations of good engineering design employing other authorized emissions specified in the table. (For the purposes of this subparagraph, unintended triggering of carrier operated repeaters is not considered to be harmful interference. Nevertheless, spread spectrum users should take reasonable steps to avoid this situation from occurring.)

(d) Spread-spectrum transmissions are authorized for domestic radio communication only (communication between points within areas where radio services are regulated by the U.S. Federal Communications Commission), except where special arrangements have been made between the United States and the administration of any other country concerned.

(e) Only frequency hopping and direct sequence transmissions are authorized. Hybrid spread-spectrum transmissions (transmissions involving both spreading techniques) are prohibited.

(1) Frequency hopping. The carrier is modulated with unciphered information and changes at fixed intervals under the direction of a high-speed code sequence.

(2) Direct sequence. The information is modulo-2 added to a high-speed code sequence. The combined information and code are then used to modulate a RF carrier. The high-speed code sequence dominates the modulating function, and is the direct cause of the wide spreading of the transmitted signal.

(f) The only spreading sequences which are authorized must be from the output of one binary linear feedback shift register (which may be implemented in hardware or software).

(1) Only the following sets of connections may be used:

Number of stages in shift register	Taps used in feedback
7	[7,1]
13	[13,4,3,1]
19	[19,5,2,1]

(The numbers in brackets indicate which binary stages are combined with modulo-2 addition to form the input to the shift register in stage 1. The output is taken from the highest numbered stage.)

(2) The shift register must not be reset other than by its feedback during an individual transmission. The shift register must be used as follows.

(i) For frequency hopping transmissions using x frequencies, n consecutive bits from the shift register must be used to select the next frequency from a list of frequencies sorted in ascending order. Each consecutive frequency must be selected by a consecutive block of n bits. (Where n is the smallest integer greater than $log_2 x$.)

(ii) For a direct sequence transmissions using m-ary modulation, consecutive blocks of $log_2 m$ bits from the shift register must be used to select the transmitted signal during each interval.

(g) The station records shall document all spread-spectrum transmissions and shall be retained for a period of one year following the last entry. The station records must include sufficient information to enable the Commission, using the information contained therein, to demodulate all transmissions. The station records must contain at least the following:

(1) A technical description of the transmitted signal.

(2) Pertinent parameters describing the transmitted signal including the frequency or frequencies of operation, and, where applicable, the chip rate, the code, the code rate, the spreading function, the transmission protocol(s) including the method of achieving synchronization, and the modulation type;

(3) A general description of the type of information being conveyed, for example, voice, text, memory dump, facsimile, television, etc.;

(4) The method and, if applicable, the frequency or frequencies used for station identification.

(5) The date of beginning and the date of ending use of each type of transmitted signal.

(h) When deemed necessary by an Engineer-in-Charge of a Commission field facility to assure compliance with the rules of this part, a station licensee shall:

(1) Cease spread-spectrum transmissions authorized under this paragraph;

(2) Restrict spread-spectrum transmissions authorized under this paragraph to the extent instructed;

(3) Maintain a record, convertible to the original information (voice, text, image, etc.) of all spread-spectrum communications transmitted under the authority of this paragraph.

(i) The peak envelope power at the transmitter output shall not exceed 100 watts.

§97.73 Purity of emissions.

(a) Except for a transmitter or transceiver built before April 15, 1977 or first marketed before January 1, 1978, the mean power of any spurious emission or radiation from an amateur transmitter, transceiver, or external radio frequency power amplifier being operated with a carrier frequency below 30 MHz shall be at least 40 decibels below the mean power of the fundamental without exceeding the power of 50 milliwatts. For equipment of mean power less than five watts, the attenuation shall be at least 30 decibels.

(b) Except for a transmitter or transceiver built before April 15, 1977 or first marketed before January 1, 1978, the mean power of any spurious emission or radiation from an amateur transmitter, transceiver, or external radio frequency power amplifier being operated with a carrier frequency above 30 MHz but below 225 MHz shall be at least 60 decibels below the mean power of the fundamental. For a transmitter having a mean power of 25 watts or less, the mean power of any spurious radiation supplied to the antenna transmission line shall be at least 40 decibels below the mean power of the fundamental without exceeding the power of 25 microwatts, but need not be reduced below the power of 10 microwatts.

(c) Paragraphs (a) and (b) of this section notwithstanding, all spurious emissions or radiation from an amateur transmitter, transceiver, or external radio frequency power amplifier shall be reduced or eliminated in accordance with good engineering practice.

(d) If any spurious radiation, including chassis or power line radiation, causes harmful interference to the reception of another radio station, the licensee may be required to take steps to eliminate the interference in accordance with good engineering practice.

NOTE: For the purpose of this section, a spurious emission or radiation means any emission or radiation from a transmitter, transceiver, or external radio frequency power amplifier which is outside of the authorized Amateur Radio Service frequency band being used.

§97.74 (Reserved).

§97.75 Use of external radio frequency (RF) power amplifiers.

(a) Any external radio frequency (RF) power amplifier used or attached at any amateur radio station shall be type accepted in accordance with Subpart J of Part 2 of the FCC's Rules for operation in the Amateur Radio Service, unless one or more of the following conditions are met:

(1) The amplifier is not capable of operation on any frequency or frequencies below 144 MHz (the amplifier shall be considered incapable of operation below 144 MHz if the mean output power decreases, as frequency decreases from 144 MHz, to a point where 0 decibels or less gain is exhibited at 120 MHz and below and the amplifier is not capable of being easily modified to provide amplification below 120 MHz);

(2) The amplifier was originally purchased before April 28, 1978;

(3) The amplifier was—

(i) Constructed by the licensee, not from an external RF power amplifier kit, for use at his amateur radio station;

(ii) Purchased by the licensee as an external RF power amplifier kit before April 28, 1978 for use at his amateur radio station; or

(iii) Modified by the licensee for use at his amateur radio station in accordance with §2.1001 of the FCC's Rules;

(4) The amplifier was purchased by the licensee from another amateur radio operator who—

(i) Constructed the amplifier, but not from an external RF power amplifier kit;

(ii) Purchased the amplifier as an external RF power amplifier kit before April 28, 1978 for use at his amateur radio station; or

(iii) Modified the amplifier for use at his amateur radio station in accordance with §2.1001 of the FCC's Rules;

(5) The external RF power amplifier was purchased from a dealer who obtained it from an amateur radio operator who—

(i) Constructed the amplifier, but not from an external RF power amplifier kit;

(ii) Purchased the amplifier as an external RF power amplifier kit before April 28, 1978, for use at his amateur radio station; or

(iii) Modified the amplifier for use at his amateur radio station in accordance with §2.1001 of the FCC's Rules; or

(6) The amplifier was originally purchased after April 28, 1978 and has been issued a marketing waiver by the FCC.

(b) A list of type-accepted equipment may be inspected at FCC headquarters in Washington, DC or at any FCC field office. Any external RF power amplifier appearing on this list as type accepted for use in the Amateur Radio Service may be used in the Amateur Radio service.

NOTE: No more than one unit of one model of an external RF power amplifier shall be constructed or modified during any calendar year by an amateur radio operator for use in the Amateur Radio Service without a grant of type acceptance.

§97.76 Requirements for type acceptance of external radio frequency (RF) power amplifiers and external radio frequency power amplifier kits.

(a) Any external radio frequency (RF) power amplifier or external RF power amplifier kit marketed (as defined in §2.815), manufactured, imported or modified for use in the Amateur Radio Service shall be type accepted for use in the Amateur Radio Service in accordance with Subpart J of Part 2 of the FCC's Rules. This requirement does not apply if one or more of the following conditions are met:

(1) The amplifier is not capable of operation on any frequency or frequencies below 144 MHz. For the purpose of this part, an amplifier will be deemed to be incapable of operation below 144 MHz if the amplifier is not capable of being easily modified to increase its amplification characteristics below 120 MHz, and either;

(i) The mean output power of the amplifier decreases, as frequency decreases from 144 MHz, to a point where 0 decibels or less gain is exhibited at 120 MHz and below 120 MHz; or

(ii) The amplifier is not capable of even short periods of operation below 120 MHz without sustaining permanent damage to its amplification circuitry.

(2) The amplifier was originally purchased before April 28, 1978 by an amateur radio operator for use at his amateur radio station;

(3) The amplifier was constructed or modified by an amateur radio operator for use at his amateur radio station in accordance with §2.1001 of the FCC's Rules;

(4) The amplifier was constructed or modified by an amateur radio operator in accordance with §2.1001 of the FCC's Rules and sold to another amateur radio operator or to a dealer;

(5) The amplifier is purchased in used condition by an equipment dealer from a licensed amateur radio operator who constructed or modified the equipment in accordance with §2.1001 of the FCC's Rules and the amplifier is further sold to another amateur radio operator for use

at his/her licensed amateur radio station.

(6) The amplifier was manufactured before April 28, 1978 and has been issued a marketing waiver by the FCC.

(b) No more than one unit of one model of an external RF power amplifier shall be constructed or modified during any calendar year by an amateur radio operator for use in the Amateur Radio Service without a grant of type acceptance.

(c) A list of type-accepted equipment may be inspected at FCC headquarters in Washington, DC or at any FCC field office. Any external RF power amplifier appearing on this list as type-accepted for use in the Amateur Radio Service may be marketed for use in the Amateur Radio Service.

§97.77 Standards for type acceptance of external radio frequency (RF) power amplifiers and external radio frequency power amplifier kits.

(a) An external radio frequency (RF) power amplifier or external RF power amplifier kit will receive a grant of type acceptance under this Part only if a grant of type acceptance would serve the public interest, convenience or necessity.

(b) To receive a grant of type acceptance under this Part, an external RF power amplifier shall meet the emission limitations of §97.73 when the amplifier is—

(1) Operated at its full output power;

(2) Placed in the "standby" or "off" positions, but still connected to the transmitter; and

(3) Driven with at least 50 watts mean radio frequency input power (unless a higher drive level is specified).

(c) To receive a grant of type acceptance under this part, an external RF power amplifier shall not be capable of operation on any frequency or frequencies between 24.00 MHz and 35.00 MHz. The amplifier will be deemed incapable of operation between 24.00 MHz and 35.00 MHz if—

(1) The amplifier has no more than 6 decibels of gain between 24.00 MHz and 26.00 MHz and between 28.00 and 35.00 MHz. (This gain is determined by the ratio of the input RF driving signal (mean

power measurement) to the mean RF output power of the amplifier); and

(2) The amplifier exhibits no amplification (0 decibels of gain) between 26.00 MHz and 28.00 MHz.

(d) Type acceptance of external radio frequency power amplifiers or amplifier kits may be denied when denial serves the public interest, convenience or necessity by preventing the use of these amplifiers in services other than the Amateur Radio Service. Other uses of these amplifiers, such as in the Citizens Band Radio Service, are prohibited (Section 95.509). Examples of features which may result in dismissal or denial of an application for type acceptance of an external RF power amplifier include, but are not limited to, the following:

(1) Any accessible wiring which, when altered, would permit operation of the amplifier in a manner contrary to the FCC's Rules;

(2) Circuit boards or similar circuitry to facilitate the addition of components to change the amplifier's operating characteristics in a manner contrary to the FCC's Rules;

(3) Instructions for operation or modification of the amplifier in a manner contrary to the FCC's Rules;

(4) Any internal or external controls or adjustments to facilitate operation of the amplifier in a manner contrary to the FCC's Rules;

(5) Any internal radio frequency sensing circuitry or any external switch, the purpose of which is to place the amplifier in the transmit mode;

(6) The incorporation of more gain in the amplifier than is necessary to operate in the Amateur Radio Service. For purposes of this paragraph, an amplifier must meet the following requirements:

(i) No amplifier shall be capable of achieving designed output (or designed d.c. input) power when driven with less than 50 watts mean radio frequency input power;

(ii) No amplifier shall be capable of amplifying the input RF driving signal by more than 15 decibels. (This gain limitation is determined by the ratio of the input RF driving signal to the RF output power of the amplifier where both signals are expressed in peak envelope power or mean power.) If the amplifier has a designed peak envelope power output of less than 1,500 watts, the gain allowance is reduced accordingly. For example, an amplifier with a designed peak envelope output power of 500 watts shall not be capable of amplifying the input RF driving signal by more than 10 decibels.

(ii) The amplifier shall not exhibit more gain than permitted by paragraph (d)(6)(ii) of this section when driven by a radio frequency input signal of less than 50 watts mean power; and

(iv) The amplifier shall be capable of sustained operation at its designed power level.

(7) Any attenuation in the input of the amplifier which, when removed or modified, would permit the amplifier to function at its designed output power when driven by a radio frequency input signal of less than 50 watts mean power.

Subpart D—Operating Requirements and Procedures

§97.78 Practice to be observed by all licensees.

In all respects not specifically covered by these regulations each amateur station shall be operated in accordance with good engineering and good amateur practice.

§97.79 Control operator requirements.

(a) The licensee of an amateur station shall be responsible for its proper operation.

(b) Every amateur radio station, when transmitting, must have a control operator. The control operator must be present at the control point of the station, except when the station is transmitting under automatic control. The control operator must be a licensed amateur radio operator or permittee designated by the station licensee. The control operator and the station licensee are both responsible for the proper operation of the station. For purposes of enforcement of the rules of this part, the FCC will presume that the station licensee is the control operator of the station, unless documentation to the contrary exists.

§97.80 Operation under automatic control.

(a) When under automatic control, devices must be installed and procedures must be implemented which will ensure compliance with the rules when the control operator is not present at the control point of the amateur station.

*(b) No amateur station may be operated under automatic control while transmitting third-party traffic.

(c) Automatic control of an amateur station must cease upon notification by the Engineer-in-Charge of a Commission field office that the station is transmitting improperly or causing harmful interference to other stations. Automatic operation must not be resumed without

prior approval of the Engineer-in-Charge.

§97.81 Authorized apparatus.

(a) An amateur station license authorizes the use, under control of the licensee, of all transmitting apparatus at the fixed location specified in the station license which is operated on any frequency or frequencies allocated to the Amateur Radio Service, and, in addition, authorizes the use, under control of the licensee, of portable and mobile transmitting apparatus operated at other locations.

(b) The apparatus authorized for us by paragraph (a) of this section shall be available for inspection upon request by an authorized Commission representative.

§97.82 Availability of operator license.

Each amateur radio operator must have the original or photocopy of his or her operator license in his or her personal possession when serving as the control operator of an amateur radio station. The original license shall be available for inspection by any authorized government official upon request made by an authorized representative of the Commission, except when such license has been filed with application for modification or renewal thereof, or has been mutilated, lost or destroyed, and request has been made for a duplicate license in accordance with Section 97.57.

§97.83 Availability of station license.

The original license of each amateur station or a photocopy thereof shall be posted in a conspicuous place in the room occupied by the licensed operator while the station is being operated at a fixed location or shall be kept in his or her personal possession. When the station is operated at other than a fixed location, the original station license or a photocopy thereof shall be kept in the personal possession of the station licensee (or a

*Editor's Note: The Commission has temporarily waived §§97.80(b) and 97.114(b)(4).

licensed representative) who shall be present at the station while it is being operated as a portable or mobile station. The original station license shall be available for inspection by any authorized Government official at all times while the station is being operated and at other times upon request made by an authorized representative of the Commission, except when such license has been filed with application for modification or renewal thereof, or has been mutilated, lost, or destroyed, and request has been made for a duplicate license in accordance with §97.57.

§97.84 Station identification.

(a) Each amateur radio station shall give its call sign at the end of each communication, and every ten minutes or less during a communication.

(b) Under conditions when the control operator is other than the station licensee, the station identification shall be the assigned call sign for that station. However, when a station is operated within the privileges of the operator's class of license but which exceeds those of the station licensee, station identification shall be made by following the station call sign with the operator's primary station call sign (i.e., WN4XYZ/W4XX).

(c) An amateur radio station in repeater operation or a station in auxiliary operation used to relay automatically the signals of other stations in a system of stations shall be identified by radiotelephony or radiotelegraphy at a level of modulation sufficient to be intelligible through the repeated transmission at intervals not to exceed ten minutes.

(d) When an amateur radio station is in repeater, auxiliary or beacon operation, the following additional requirements shall apply:

(1) When identifying by radiotelephony, a station in repeater operation shall transmit the word "repeater" at the end of the station call sign. When identifying by radiotelegraphy, a station in repeater operation shall transmit the fraction bar $\overline{DN}$ followed by the letters "RPT" or "R" at the end of the station call sign.

(2) When identifying by radiotele-

phony, a station in auxiliary operation shall transmit the word "auxiliary" at the end of the station call sign. When identifying by radiotelegraphy, a station in auxiliary operation shall transmit the fraction bar $\overline{DN}$ followed by the letters "AUX" or "A" at the end of the station call sign.

(3) When identifying by radiotelephony, a station in beacon operation shall transmit the word "beacon" at the end of the station call sign. When identifying by radiotelegraphy, a station in beacon operation shall transmit the fraction bar $\overline{DN}$ followed by the letters "BCN" or "B" at the end of the station call sign. This station identification shall be made at intervals not to exceed one minute during any period of operation.

(e) A station in auxiliary operation may be identified by the call sign of its associated station.

(f) When operating under the temporary operating authority permitted by §97.35 with privileges which exceed the privileges for the class of operator license currently held by the licensee, a licensee must identify in the following manner:

(1) On radiotelephony, by the transmission of the station call sign, followed by the word "temporary," followed by the identifier code for the new class of license for which the licensee has qualified (see §97.35).

(2) On radiotelegraphy, by the transmission of the station call sign, followed by the fraction bar $\overline{DN}$, followed by the identifier code for the new class of license for which the licensee has qualified (see §97.35).

(g) The identification required by this section shall be given on each frequency being utilized for transmission and shall be made in one of the following manners:

(1) By telegraphy using the international Morse code (if this identification is made by an automatic device used only for identification, the code speed shall not exceed 20 words per minute);

(2) By telephony using the English language (the Commission encourages the use of a nationally or internationally recognized standard phonetic alphabet as an aid for correct telephone identification);

(3) By telegraphy using any code authorized by §97.69(b), when the particular code is used for transmission of all or part of the communication or when the communication is transmitted in any digital code on frequencies above 50 MHz; or

(4) By video using readily legible characters when A5 emissions are used, the monochrome portions of which conform, at a minimum, to the monochrome transmission standards of §73.682(a)(6) through §73.682(a)(13), inclusive (with the exception of §73.682(a)(9)(iii) and §73.682(a)(9)(iv)).

(5) When transmitting spread spectrum, by narrow band emission using the method described in (1) or (2) above, narrow band identification transmissions must be on only one frequency in each band being used. Alternatively, the station identification may be transmitted while in spread-spectrum operation by changing one or more parameters of the emission in a fashion such that CW or SSB or narrow band FM receivers can be used to identify the sending station.

(h) At the end of an exchange of third-party communications with a station located in a foreign country, each amateur radio station shall also give the call sign of the station with which third-party communications were exchanged.

§97.85 Repeater operation.

(a) Emissions from a station in repeater operation shall be discontinued within five seconds after cessation of radiocommunications by the user station. Provisions to limit automatically the access to a station in repeater operation may be incorporated but are not mandatory.

(b) Except for operation under automatic control, as provided in paragraph (e) of this section, the transmitting and receiving frequencies used by a station in repeater operation shall be continuously monitored by a control operator immediately before and during periods of operation.

(c) A station in repeater operation shall not concurrently retransmit amateur radio signals on more than one frequency in the same amateur frequency band, from the same location.

(d) A station in repeater operation shall be operated in a manner ensuring that it is not used for broadcasting (see §97.113).

(e) A station in repeater operation, either locally controlled or remotely controlled, may also be operated by automatic control when devices have been installed and procedures have been implemented to ensure compliance with the rules when a duty control operator is not present at a control point of the station. Upon notification by the Commission of improper operation of a station under automatic control, operation under automatic control shall be immediately discontinued until all deficiencies have been corrected.

(f) The licensee of an Amateur Radio station, before modifying an existing station in repeater operation in the National Radio Quiet Zone, or before placing his/her amateur station in repeater operation in the National Radio Quiet Zone, shall, after May 13, 1981, give written notification thereof to the Director, National Radio Astronomy Observatory, P.O. Box No. 2, Green Bank, West Virginia 24944. Station modification is any change in frequency, power, antenna height or directivity or the location of the station.

(1) The notification shall include the geographical coordinates of the antenna, antenna height, antenna directivity, if any, proposed frequency, type of emission and power.

(2) The National Radio Quiet Zone is the area bounded by 39° 15′ N. on the north, 78° 30′ W. on the east, 37° 30′ N. on the south and 80° 30′ W. on the west.

(3) If an objection to the proposed operation is received by the Commission from the National Radio Astronomy Observatory at Green Bank, Pocahontas County, West Virginia, for itself or on behalf of the Naval Research Laboratory at Sugar Grove, Pendleton County, West Virginia, within 20 days from the date of notification, the Commission will consider all aspects of the problem and take whatever action is deemed appropriate.

(g) Where an amateur radio station in

repeater or auxiliary operation causes harmful interference to the repeater or auxiliary operation of another amateur radio station, the two stations are equally and fully responsible for resolving the interference unless one station's operation is coordinated (see 97.3(k)) and the other's is not. In that case, the station engaged in the non-coordinated operation has primary responsibility to resolve the interference.

(1) The location of the station transmitting antenna marked upon a topographic map having contour intervals and having a scale of 1:250,000 (indexes and ordering information for suitable maps are available from the U.S. Geological Survey, Washington, D.C. 20242, or from the Federal Center, Denver, CO 80255);

(2) The effective radiated power in the horizontal plane for the main lobe of antenna pattern, calculated for the maximum transmitter output power which occurs during operation;

(4) The maximum transmitter output power which occurs during operation;

(5) The loss in the transmission line between the transmitter and the antenna (including devices such as duplexers, cavities or circulators), expressed in decibels; and

(6) The relative gain in the horizontal plane of the transmitting antenna.

(h) All amateur frequency bands above 29.5 MHz are available for repeater operation, except 50.0-52.0 MHz, 144.0-144.5 MHz, 145.5-146.0 MHz, 220.0-220.5 MHz, 431.0-433.0 MHz, and 435.0-438.0 MHz. Both the input (receiving) and output (transmitting) frequency of a station in repeater operation shall be frequencies available for repeater operation.

§97.86 Auxiliary operation.

(a) A station in auxiliary operation, either locally controlled or remotely controlled, may also be operated by automatic control when it is operated as part of a system of stations in repeater operation operated under automatic control.

(b) If a station in auxiliary operation is relaying signals of another amateur radio station(s) to a station in repeater operation, the station in auxiliary operation may use an input (receiving) frequency in frequency bands reserved for auxiliary operation, repeater operation, or both.

(c) A station in auxiliary operation shall be used only to communicate with stations shown in the system network diagram.

(d) All amateur frequency bands above 220.5 MHz, except 431-433 MHz and 435-438 MHz, are available for auxiliary operation.

§97.87 Beacon operation.

(a) A station in beacon operation shall not concurrently operate on more than one frequency in the same amateur frequency band, from the same location.

(b) A station in beacon operation, either locally controlled or remotely controlled, may also be operated by automatic control when devices have been installed and procedures have been implemented to ensure compliance with the rules when the duty control operator is not present at a control point of the station.

(c) Beacon operation shall cease upon notification by an Engineer-in-Charge of a Commission field facility that the station is operating improperly or causing undue interference to other operations. Beacon operation shall not resume without prior approval of the Engineer-in-Charge.

(d) The licensee of an amateur radio station, before modifying an existing station in automatically-controlled beacon operation in the National Radio Quiet Zone, or before placing his/her station in the National Radio Quiet Zone, shall give written notification thereof to the Director, National Radio Astronomy Observatory, P.O. Box 2, Green Bank, West Virginia 24944. Station modification is any change in frequency, power, antenna height or directivity, or the location of the station. In such cases, the rules of §97.85(f)(1) and (2) shall apply.

(e) The following amateur frequency bands and emissions are available for automatically-controlled beacon operation: 28.20-28.30 MHz, 50.06-50.08 MHz, 144.05-144.06 MHz, 220.05-220.06 MHz, 222.05-222.06 MHz, and

432.07-432.08 MHz using type NØN, A1A, F1B or J2A emissions (when type F1B or J2A emissions are employed in these bands, the radio or audio frequency shift, as appropriate, shall not exceed 1000 Hz). Additionally, all amateur frequency bands above 450 MHz are available for automatically-controlled beacon operation using emission types authorized under Section 97.61, provided that the licensee is authorized to operate on the frequency under Section 97.7.

§97.88 Operation of a station by remote control.

An amateur radio station may be operated by remote control only if there is compliance with the following:

(a) A photocopy of the license for the remotely controlled station shall be posted in a conspicuous place at the station location.

(b) The name, address, and telephone number of the remotely controlled station licensee and at least one control operator shall be posted in a conspicuous place at the remotely controlled transmitter location.

(c) Except for operation under automatic control, a control operator shall be on duty when the station is being remotely controlled. Immediately before and during the periods the remotely controlled station is in operation, the frequencies used for emission by the remotely controlled station shall be monitored by the control operator. The control operator shall terminate all transmissions upon any deviation from the rules.

(d) Provisions must be incorporated to limit transmission to a period of no more than 3 minutes in the event of malfunction in the control link.

(e) A station in repeater operation shall be operated by radio remote control only when the control link uses frequencies other than the input (receiving) frequencies of the station in repeater operation.

(f) The station records shall include during any period of operation:

(1) The names, addresses, and call signs of all persons authorized by the station licensee to be control operators; and

(2) A functional block diagram of the control link and a technical explanation sufficient to describe its operation.

(g) Each remotely controlled station shall be protected against unauthorized station operation, whether caused by activation of the control link, or otherwise.

§97.89 Point of Communications.

(a) Amateur stations may communicate with:

(1) Other amateur stations, excepting those prohibited by Appendix 2.

(2) Stations in other services licensed by the Commission and with the U.S. Government stations for civil defense purposes in accordance with Subpart F of this Part, in emergencies and, on a temporary basis, for test purposes.

(3) Any station which is authorized by the Commission to communicate with amateur stations.

(b) Amateur radio stations may transmit one-way signals to receiving apparatus while in beacon operation or radio control operation.

§97.90 System network diagram required.

When a station has one or more associated stations, that is, stations in repeater or auxiliary operation, a system network diagram (see §97.3(u)) shall be included in the station records during any period of operation.

§97.91 (reserved)

§97.92 Record of operations.

When deemed necessary by the Engineer-in-Charge (EIC) of a Commission field facility to assure compliance with the rules of this Part, a station licensee shall maintain a record of station operations containing such items of information as the EIC may require under Section 0.314(x).

§97.93 Modulation of carrier.

Except for brief tests or adjustments, an amateur radiotelephone station shall not emit a carrier wave on frequencies below 51 megahertz unless modulated for the purpose of communication. Single audio frequency tones may be transmitted for test purposes of short duration for the development and perfection of amateur radio telephone equipment.

STATION OPERATION AWAY FROM AUTHORIZED LOCATION

§97.95 Operation away from the authorized fixed station location.

(a) Operation within the United States, its territories or possessions is permitted as follows:

(1) When there is no change in the authorized fixed operation station location, an amateur radio station, other than a military recreation station, may be operated portable or mobile under its station license anywhere in the United States, its territories or possessions, subject to §97.61.

(2) When the authorized fixed station location is changed, the licensee shall submit an application for modification of the station license in accordance with §97.47.

(b) When outside the continental limits of the United States, its territories, or possessions, an amateur radio station may be operated as portable or mobile only under the following conditions:

(1) Operation may not be conducted within the jurisdiction of a foreign government except pursuant to, and in accordance with express authority granted to the licensee by such foreign government. When a foreign government permits Commission licensees to operate within its territory, the amateur frequency bands which may be used shall be as prescribed or limited by that government (See Appendix 4 of this Part for the text of treaties or agreements between the United States and foreign governments relative to reciprocal amateur radio operation.)

(2) (Reserved.)

(3) (Reserved.)

(4) Except as otherwise provided, amateur operation conducted outside the jurisdiction of a foreign government shall comply with all requirements of Part 97 of this chapter.

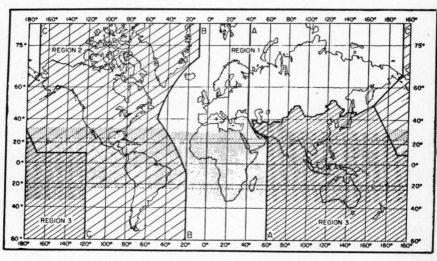

Note: Region 2 is defined as follows: On the east, a line (B) extending from the North Pole along meridian 10° of Greenwich to its intersection with parallel 72°; thence by Great Circle Arc to the intersection of meridian 50° W and parallel 40° N; thence by Great Circle Arc to the intersection of meridian 20° W and parallel 10° S; thence along meridian 20 degrees west to the South Pole. On the west, a line (C) extending from the North Pole by Great Circle Arc to the intersection of parallel 65°, 30′ N with the international boundary in Bering Strait; thence by Great Circle Arc to the intersection of meridian 165° East of Greenwich and parallel 50° N; thence by Great Circle Arc to the intersection of meridian 170° West and parallel 10° N; thence along parallel 10° N to its intersection with meridian 120° West thence along meridian 12° West to the South Pole.

SPECIAL PROVISIONS

§97.99 Stations used only for radio control of remote model craft and vehicles.

An amateur radio station in radio control operation with a mean output power not exceeding one watt may, when used for the control of a remote model craft or vehicle, be operated under the special provisions of this section, provided that a writing indicating the station call sign and the licensee's name and address is affixed to the transmitter.

(a) Station identification is not required for transmission directed only to a remote model craft or vehicle.

(b) Transmissions containing only control signals directed only to a remote model craft or vehicle are not considered to be codes or ciphers in the context of the meaning of §97.117.

§97.101 Mobile stations aboard ships or aircraft.

In addition to complying with all other applicable rules, an amateur mobile station operated on board a ship or aircraft must comply with all of the following special conditions: (a) The installation and operation of the amateur mobile station shall be approved by the master of the ship or captain of the aircraft; (b) The amateur mobile station shall be separate from and independent of all other radio equipment, if any, installed on board the same ship or aircraft; (c) The electrical installation of the amateur mobile station shall be in accord with the rules applicable to ships or aircraft as promulgated by the appropriate government agency; (d) The operation of the amateur mobile station shall not interfere with the efficient operation of any other radio equipment installed on board the same ship or aircraft; and (e) The amateur mobile station and its associated equipment, either in itself or in its method of operation, shall not constitute a hazard to the safety of life or property.

EMERGENCY OPERATIONS

§97.107 Operation in emergencies.

In the event of an emergency disrupting normally available communication facilities in any widespread area or areas, the Commission, in its discretion, may declare that a general state of communications emergency exists, designate the area or areas concerned, and specify the amateur frequency bands, or segments of such bands, for use only by amateurs participating in emergency communication within or with such affected area or areas. Amateurs desiring to request the declaration of such a state of emergency should communicate with the Commission's Engineer-in-Charge of the area concerned. Whenever such declaration has been made, operation of and with amateur stations in the area concerned shall be only in accordance with the requirements set forth in this section, but such requirements shall in nowise affect other normal amateur communication in the affected areas when conducted on frequencies not designated for emergency operation.

(a) All transmissions within all designated amateur communications bands[1] other than communications relating directly to relief work, emergency service or the establishment and maintenance of efficient Amateur Radio networks for the handling of such communications shall be suspended. Incidental calling, answering, testing or working (including casual conversations, remarks or messages) not pertinent to constructive handling of the emergency situation shall be prohibited within these bands.

(b) The Commission may designate certain amateur stations to assist in the promulgation of information relating to the declaration of a general state of communications emergency, to monitor

---

[1]The frequency 5167.5 kHz may be used by any station authorized under this part to communicate with any other station in the State of Alaska for emergency communications. No airborne operations will be permitted on this frequency. All stations operating on this frequency must be located in or within 50 nautical miles of the State of Alaska. The frequency 5167.5 kHz may be used by licensees in the Alaska-private fixed service for calling and listening, but only for establishing communication before switching to another frequency.

the designated amateur emergency communications bands, and to warn non-complying stations observed to be operating in those bands. Such station, when so designated, may transmit for that purpose on any frequency or frequencies authorized to be used by that station, provided such transmissions do not interfere with essential emergency communications in progress; however, such transmissions shall preferably be made on authorized frequencies immediately adjacent to those segments of the amateur bands being cleared for the emergency. Individual transmissions for the purpose of advising other stations of the existence of the communications emergency shall refer to this section by number (§97.107) and shall specify, briefly and concisely, the date of the Commission's declaration, the area and nature of the emergency, and the amateur frequency bands or segments of such bands which constitute the amateur emergency communications bands at the time. The designated stations shall not enter into discussions with other stations beyond furnishing essential facts relative to the emergency, or acting as advisors to stations desiring to assist in the emergency, and the operators of such designated stations shall report fully to the Commission the identity of any stations failing to comply, after notice, with any of the pertinent provisions of this section.

(c) The special conditions imposed under the provisions of this section shall cease to apply only after the Commission or its authorized representative, shall have declared such general state of communications emergency to be terminated; however, nothing in this paragraph shall be deemed to prevent the Commission from modifying the terms of its declaration from time to time as may be necessary during the period of a communications emergency, or from removing those conditions with respect to any amateur frequency band or segment of such band which no longer appears essential to the conduct of the emergency communications.

Subpart E—Prohibited Practices and Administrative Sanctions

PROHIBITED TRANSMISSIONS AND PRACTICES

§97.110 Business communications prohibited.

The transmission of business communications by an amateur radio station is prohibited except for emergency communications (see §97.3(w)).

§97.111 Limitations on international communications.

Transmissions between amateur radio stations of different countries, when permitted, must be limited to messages of a technical nature relating to tests, and, to remarks of a personal character for which, by reason of their unimportance, recourse to the public telecommunications service is not justified.

§97.112 No remuneration for use of station.

(a) An amateur station shall not be used to transmit or receive messages for hire, nor for communication for material compensation, direct or indirect, paid or promised.

(b) Control operators of a club station may be compensated when the club station is operated primarily for the purpose of conducting amateur radiocommunication to provide telegraphy practice transmissions intended for persons learning or improving proficiency in the international Morse code, or to disseminate information bulletins consisting solely of subject matter having direct interest to the Amateur Radio Service provided:

(1) The station conducts telegraphy practice and bulletin transmission for at least 40 hours per week.

(2) The station schedules operations on at least six (6) allocated medium and high frequency amateur bands using reasonable measures to maximize coverage.

(3) The schedule of normal operating times and frequencies is published at least 30 days in advance of the actual transmissions.

Control operators may accept compensation only for such periods of time during which the station is transmitting telegraphy practice or bulletins. A control operator shall not accept any direct or indirect compensation for periods during which the station is transmitting material other than telegraphy practice or bulletins.

§97.113 Broadcasting and broadcast related activities prohibited.

(a) An amateur station shall not be used to engage in any form of broadcasting, that is, the dissemination of radio communications intended to be received by the public directly or by intermediary relay stations.

(b) An amateur station may not be used for any activity directly related to program production or newsgathering for broadcast purposes.

(c) An amateur station shall not retransmit programs or signals emanating from any class of radio station other than amateur, except for emergency communications (see §97.3(w)).

(d) The following one-way amateur transmissions are not considered broadcasting:

(1) Beacon or radio control operation;

(2) Information bulletins consisting solely of subject matter relating to amateur radio;

(3) Transmissions intended for persons learning or improving proficiency in the international Morse code; and

(4) Emergency communications (see §97.3(w)).

(e) Round table discussions or net operations where more than two amateur stations are in communication with one another are not considered broadcasting.

§97.114 Limitations on third-party traffic.

(a) Subject to the limitations specified in paragraphs (b) and (c) of this section, an amateur radio station may transmit third-party traffic.

(b) The transmission or delivery of the following third-party traffic is prohibited:

(1) International third-party traffic except with countries which have assented thereto;

(2) Third-party traffic involving material compensation, either tangible or intangible, direct or indirect, to a third party, a station licensee, a control operator or any other person;

(3) Except for emergency communications as defined in this part, third-party traffic consisting of business communications on behalf of any party.

(4) Third-party traffic from an amateur station under automatic control.

(c) The licensee of an amateur radio station may not permit any person to participate in traffic from that station as a third party if:

(1) The control operator is not present at the control point and is not continuously monitoring and supervising the third-party participation to ensure compliance with the rules;

(2) The third party is a prior amateur radio licensee whose license was revoked; suspended for less than the balance of the license term and the suspension is still in effect; suspended for the balance of the license term and relicensing has not taken place; surrendered for cancellation following notice of revocation, suspension or monetary forfeiture proceedings; or who is the subject of a cease and desist order which relates to amateur operation and which is still in effect.

§97.115 Music prohibited.

The transmission of music by an amateur station is forbidden.

§97.116 Amateur radiocommunication for unlawful purposes prohibited.

The transmission of radio communication or messages by an amateur radio station for any purpose, or in connection with any activity, which is contrary to Federal, State or local law is prohibited.

§97.117 Codes and ciphers prohibited

The transmission by radio of messages in codes or ciphers in domestic and international communications to or between amateur stations is prohibited. All communications regardless of type of emission employed shall be in plain language except that generally recognized abbreviations established by regulation or custom and usage are permissible as are any other abbreviations or signals where the intent is not to obscure the meaning but only to facilitate communications.

§97.119 Obscenity, indecency, profanity.

No licensed radio operator or other person shall transmit communications containing obscene, indecent, or profane words, language, or meaning.

§97.121 False Signals.

An amateur radio station must not transmit:

(a) False or deceptive signals or communications by radio; *NOR*

(b) For purposes of identifying the station, any call sign which has not been assigned to it. Notwithstanding the foregoing, when a station is operated within the privileges of the operator's class of license but which exceed those of the station licensee, station identification must be made by following the station call sign of the station being operated with the operator's primary station call sign in accordance with Section 97.84(b).

§97.123 Unidentified communications.

No licensed radio operator shall transmit unidentified radio communications or signals.

§97.125 Interference.

No licensed radio operator shall willfully or maliciously interfere with or cause interference to any radio communication or signal.

§97.126 Retransmitting radio signals.

(a) An amateur radio station, except a station in repeater operation or auxiliary operation, shall not automatically retransmit the radio signals of other amateur radio stations.

(b) A remotely controlled station,

other than a remotely controlled station in repeater operation or auxiliary operation, shall automatically retransmit only the radio signals of stations in auxiliary operation shown on the remotely controlled station's system network diagram.

§97.127 Damage to apparatus.

No licensed radio operator shall willfully damage, or cause or permit to be damaged, any radio apparatus or installation in any licensed radio station.

§97.129 Fraudulent licenses.

No licensed radio operator or other person shall obtain or attempt to obtain, or assist another to obtain or attempt to obtain, an operator license by fraudulent means.

ADMINISTRATIVE SANCTIONS

§97.131 Restricted operation.

(a) If the operation of an amateur station causes general interference to the reception of transmissions from stations operating in the domestic broadcast service when receivers of good engineering design including adequate selectivity characteristics are used to receive such transmission and this fact is made known to the amateur station licensee, the amateur station shall not be operated during the hours from 8 p.m. to 10:30 p.m., local time, and on Sunday for the additional period from 10:30 a.m. until 1 p.m., local time, upon the frequency or frequencies used when the interference is created.

(b) In general, such steps as may be necessary to minimize interference to stations operating in other services may be required after investigation by the Commission.

§97.133 Second notice of same violation.

In every case where an amateur station licensee is cited within a period of 12 consecutive months for the second violation of the provisions of §§97.61, 97.63, 97.65, or 97.73, the station licensee, if directed to do so by the Commission, shall not operate the station and shall not permit it to be operated from 6 p.m. to 10:30 p.m., local time, until written notice has

been received authorizing the resumption of full-time operation. This notice will not be issued until the licensee has reported on the results of tests which he/she has conducted with at least two other amateur stations at hours other than 6 p.m. to 10:30 p.m., local time. Such tests are to be made for the specific purpose of aiding the licensee in determining whether the emissions of the station are in accordance with the Commission's rules. The licensee shall report to the Commission the observations made by the cooperating amateur licensee in relation to reported violations. This report shall include a statement as to the corrective measures taken to insure compliance with the rules.

§97.135 Third notice of same violation.

In every case where an amateur station licensee is cited within a period of 12 consecutive months for the third violation of §§97.61, 97.63, 97.65, or 97.73, the station licensee, if directed by the Commission, shall not operate the station and shall not permit it to be operated from 8 a.m. to 12 midnight, local time, except for the purpose of transmitting a prearranged test to be observed by a monitoring station of the Commission to be designated in each particular case. The station shall not be permitted to resume operation during these hours until the licensee is authorized by the Commission following the test, to resume full-time operation. The results of the test and the licensee's record shall be considered in determining the advisability of suspending the operator license or revoking the station license, or both.

§97.137 Answers to notices of violation.

Any licensee receiving official notice of a violation of the terms of the Communications of 1934, as amended, any legislative act, Executive order, treaty to which the United States is a party, or the rules of the Federal Communications Commission, shall, within 10 days from such receipt, send a written answer direct to the office of the Commission originating the official notice: Provided, however, that if an answer cannot be sent or an acknowledgment made within such 10-day period by reason of illness or other unavoidable circumstances, acknowledgment and answer shall be made at the earliest practicable date with a satisfactory explanation of the delay. The answer to each notice shall be complete in itself and shall not be abbreviated by reference to other communications or answers to other notices. If the notice relates to some violation that may be due to the physical or electrical characteristics of transmitting apparatus, the answer shall state fully what steps, if any, are taken to prevent future violations, and if any new apparatus is to be installed, the date such apparatus was ordered, the name of the manufacturer, and promised date of delivery. If the notice of violation related to some lack of attention to or improper operation of the transmitter, the name of the operator in charge shall be given.

Subpart F—Radio Amateur Civil Emergency Services (RACES)

GENERAL

§97.161 Basis and purpose.

The Radio Amateur Civil Emergency Service provides for amateur radio operation for civil defense communications purposes only, during periods of local, regional or national civil emergencies, including any emergency which may necessitate invoking of the President's War Emergency Powers under the provisions of section 606 of the Communications Act of 1934, as amended.

§97.163 Definitions.

For the purposes of this Subpart, the following definitions are applicable:

(a) Radio Amateur Civil Emergency Service. A radio communication service conducted by volunteer licensed amateur radio operators, for providing emergency radiocommunications to local, regional, or state civil defense organizations.

(b) RACES station. An amateur radio station licensed to a civil defense organization, at a specific land location, for the purpose of providing the facilities for amateur radio operators to conduct amateur radiocommunications in the Radio Amateur Civil Emergency Service.

§97.165 Applicability of rules.

In all cases not specifically covered by the provisions contained in this Subpart, amateur radio stations and RACES stations shall be governed by the provisions of the rules governing amateur radio stations and operators (Subpart A through E of this part).

STATION AUTHORIZATIONS

§97.169 Station license required.

No transmitting station shall be operated in the Radio Amateur Civil Emergency Service unless:

(a) The station is licensed as a RACES station by the Federal Communications Commission, or

(b) The station is an amateur station licensed by the Federal Communications Commission, and is certified by the responsible civil defense organization as registered with that organization.

§97.171 Eligibility for RACES station license.

(a) A RACES station will only be licensed to a local, regional, or state civil defense organization.

(b) Only modification and/or renewal station licenses will be issued for RACES stations. No new licenses will be issued for RACES stations.

§97.173 Application for RACES station license.

(a) Each application for a RACES station license shall be made on the FCC Form 610-B.

(b) The application shall be signed by the civil defense official responsible for the coordination of all civil defense activities in the area concerned.

(c) The application shall be countersigned by the responsible official for the governmental entity served by the civil defense organization.

(d) If the application is for a RACES station to be in any special manner covered by §97.42, those showings specified for non-RACES stations shall also be submitted.

§97.175 Amateur radio station registration in civil defense organization.

No amateur radio station shall be operated in the Radio Amateur Civil Emergency Service unless it is certified as registered in a civil defense organization by that organization.

OPERATING REQUIREMENTS

§97.177 Operator requirements.

No person shall be the control operator of a RACES station, or shall be the control operator of an amateur radio station conducting communications in the Radio Amateur Civil Emergency Service unless that person holds a valid amateur radio operator license and is certified as enrolled in a civil defense organization by that organization.

§97.179 Operator privileges.

Operator privileges in the Radio Amateur Civil Emergency Service are dependent upon, and identical to, those for the class of operator license held in the Amateur Radio Service.

§97.181 Availability of RACES station license and operator licenses.

(a) The original license of each RACES station, or a photocopy thereof, shall be attached to each transmitter of such station, and at each control point of such station. Whenever a photocopy of the RACES station license is utilized in compliance with this requirement, the original station license shall be available for inspection by any authorized Government official at all times when the station is being operated and at other times upon request made by an authorized representative of the Commission, except when such license has been filed with application for modification or renewal thereof, or has been mutilated, lost, or destroyed, and request has been made for a duplicate license in accordance with §97.57.

(b) In addition to the operator license availability requirements of §97.82, a photocopy of the control operator's amateur radio operator license shall be posted at a conspicuous place at the control point for the RACES station.

TECHNICAL REQUIREMENTS

§97.185 Frequencies available.

(a) All of the authorized frequencies and emissions allocated to the Amateur Radio Service are also available to the Radio Amateur Civil Emergency Service on a shared basis.

(b) In the event of an emergency which necessitates the invoking of the Presi-

dent's War Emergency Powers under the provisions of §606 of the Communications Act of 1934, as amended, unless otherwise modified or directed, RACES stations and amateur radio stations participating in RACES will be limited in operation to the following frequencies and frequency bands unless otherwise directed by the President of the United States, by a person or persons designated by the President of the United States or by the FCC on behalf of the President of the United States:

Frequency or Frequency Bands

kHz	Limitations	MHz	Limitations
1800-1825		28.55-28.75	
1975-2000		29.237-29.273	
3500-3550		29.45-29.65	
3930-3980		50.35-50.75	
3984-4000		52-54	
3997	2	53.30	2
7079-7125		53.35-53.75	
7245-7255		144.50-145.71	
10100-10150	1	146-148	
14047-14053		220-225	4
14220-14230		420-450	3, 5
14331-14350		1240-1300	3
21047-21053		2390-2450	3
21228-21267			

(c) Limitations:

(1) This band is allocated to the fixed service on a primary basis outside the United States and its possessions. Transmissions of stations in the Amateur Radio Service in this band are secondary to foreign fixed service use in this band.

(2) For use in emergency areas when required to make initial contact with a military unit; also, for communications with military stations on matters requiring coordination.

(3) Those stations operating in the bands 420-450, 1240-1300 and 2390-2450 MHz shall not cause harmful interference to, and must tolerate any interference from, the Government Radiolocation Service; and also the Aeronautical Radionavigation Service in the case of the 1240-1300 MHz band.

(4) Those stations operating in the band 220-225 MHz shall not cause harmful interference to, and must tolerate any interference from, the Government

Radiolocation Service until January 1, 1990. Additionally, the Fixed and Mobile Services shall have equal right of operation.

(5) No station shall operate north of Line A (see §97.3(i)) in the 420-430 MHz band.

(6) (Reserved.)

§97.189 Point of communications.

(a) RACES stations may only be used to communicate with:

(1) Other RACES stations;

(2) Amateur radio stations certified as being registered with a civil defense organization, by that organization;

(3) Stations in the Disaster Communications Service;

(4) Stations of the United States Government authorized by the responsible agency to exchange communications with RACES stations;

(5) Any other station in any other service regulated by the Federal Communications Commission, whenever such station is authorized by the Commission, to exchange communications with stations in the Radio Amateur Civil Emergency Service.

(b) Amateur radio stations registered with a civil defense organization may only be used to communicate with:

(1) RACES stations licensed to the civil defense organization with which the amateur radio station is registered:

(2) Any of the following stations upon authorization of the responsible civil defense official for the organization in which the amateur radio station is registered:

(i) Any RACES station licensed to other civil defense organizations;

(ii) Amateur radio stations registered with the same or another civil defense organization;

(iii) Stations in the Disaster Communications Service;

(iv) Stations of the United States Government authorized by the responsible agency to exchange communications with RACES stations;

(v) Any other station in any other service regulated by the Federal Communications Commission, whenever such station is authorized by the Commission to exchange communications with stations in the Radio Amateur Civil Emergency Service.

§97.191 Permissible communications.

All communications in the Radio Amateur Civil Emergency Service must be specifically authorized by the civil defense organization for the area served. Stations in this service may transmit only civil defense communications of the following types:

(a) Communications concerning impending or actual conditions jeopardizing the public safety, or affecting the national defense or security during periods of local, regional, or national civil emergencies:

(1) Communications directly concerning the immediate safety of life or individuals, the immediate protection of property, maintenance of law and order, alleviation of human suffering and need, and the combating of armed attack or sabotage;

(2) Communications directly concerning the accumulation and dissemination of public information or instructions to the civilian population essential to the activities of the civil defense organization or other authorized governmental or relief agencies.

(b) Communications for training drills and tests necessary to ensure the establishment and maintenance of orderly and efficient operation of the Radio Amateur Civil Emergency Service as ordered by the responsible civil defense organization served. Such tests and drills may not exceed a total time of one hour per week.

(c) Brief one way transmissions for the testing and adjustment of equipment.

§97.193 Limitations on the use of RACES stations.

(a) No station in the Radio Amateur Civil Emergency Service shall be used to transmit or to receive messages for hire, nor for communications for material compensation, direct or indirect, paid or promised.

(b) All messages which are transmitted in connection with drills or tests shall be clearly identified as such by use of the words "drill" or "test", as appropriate, in the body of the messages.

Subpart G—Operation of Amateur Radio Stations in the United States by Aliens Pursuant to Reciprocal Agreements

§97.301 Basis, purpose, and scope.

(a) The rules in this subpart are based on, and are applicable solely to, alien amateur operations pursuant to section 303(1)(3) and 310(a) of the Communications Act of 1934, as amended. (See Pub. L 93-505, 88 Stat. 1576.)

(b) The purpose of this subpart is to implement Public Law 88-383 by prescribing the rules under which an alien, who holds an amateur operator and station license issued by his government (referred to in this subpart as an alien amateur), may operate an amateur radio station in the United States, in its possessions, and the Commonwealth of Puerto Rico (referred to in this subpart only as the United States).

§97.303 Permit required.

Before he may operate an amateur radio station in the United States, under the provisions of sections 303(1)(3) and 310(c) of the Communications Act of 1934, as amended, an alien amateur licensee must obtain a permit for such operation from the Federal Communications Commission. A permit for such operation shall be issued only to an alien holding a valid amateur operator and station authorization from his government, and only when there is in effect a bilateral agreement between the United States and that government for such operation on a reciprocal basis by United States amateur radio operators.

§97.305 Application for permit.

(a) Application for a permit shall be made on FCC Form 610-A. Form 610-A may be obtained from the Commission's Washington, DC, office, from any of the Commission's field offices and, in some instances, from United States missions abroad.

(b) The application form shall be completed in full in English and signed by the applicant. A photocopy of the applicant's amateur operator and station license issued by his government shall be filed with the application. The Commission may require the applicant to furnish additional information. The application must be filed by mail or in person with the Federal Communications Commission, Gettysburg, PA 17325, USA. To allow sufficient time for processing, the application should be filed at least 60 days before the date on which the applicant desires to commence operation.

§97.307 Issuance of permit.

(a) The Commission may issue a permit to an alien amateur under such terms and conditions as it deems appropriate. If a change in the terms of a permit is desired, an application for modification of the permit is required. If operation beyond the expiration date of a permit is desired, an application for renewal of the permit is required. In any case in which the permittee has, in accordance with the provisions of this subpart, made a timely and sufficient application for renewal of an unexpired permit, such permit shall not expire until the application has been finally determined. Applications for modification or for renewal of a permit shall be filed on FCC Form 610-A.

(b) The Commission, in its discretion, may deny any application for a permit under this subpart. If an application is denied, the applicant will be notified by letter. The applicant may, within 90 days of the mailing of such letter, request the Commission to reconsider its action.

(c) Normally, a permit will be issued to expire 1 year after issuance but in no event after the expiration of the license issued to the alien amateur by his government.

§97.309 Modification, suspension, or cancellation of permit.

At any time the Commission may, in its discretion, modify, suspend, or cancel any permit issued under this subpart. In this event, the permittee will be notified of the Commission's action by letter mailed to his mailing address in the United States and the permittee shall comply immediately. A permittee may, within 90 days of the mailing of such letter, request the Commission to reconsider its action. The filing of a request for reconsideration shall not stay the effectiveness of the action, but the Commission may stay its action on its own motion.

§97.311 Operating conditions.

(a) The alien amateur may not under any circumstances begin operation until he has received a permit issued by the Commission.

(b) Operation of an amateur station by an alien amateur under a permit issued by the Commission must comply with all of the following:

(1) The terms of the bilateral agreement between ιe alien amateur's government and the government of the United States;

(2) The provisions of this subpart and of Subparts A through E of this part;

(3) The operating terms and conditions of the license issued to the alien amateur by his government; and

(4) Any further conditions specified on the permit issued by the Commission.

§97.313 Station identification.

(a) The alien amateur shall identify his station as follows:

(1) Radio telegraph operation: The amateur shall transmit the call sign issued to him by the licensing country followed by a slant (/) sign and the United States amateur call sign prefix letter(s) and number appropriate to the location of his station.

(2) Radiotelephone operation: The amateur shall transmit the call sign issued to him by the licensing country followed by the words "fixed", "portable" or "mobile", as appropriate, and the United States amateur call sign prefix letter(s) and number appropriate to the location of his station. The identification shall be made in the English language.

(b) At least once during each contact with another amateur station, the alien amateur shall indicate, in English, the geographical location of his station as nearly as possible by city and state, commonwealth or possession.

Subpart H—Amateur-Satellite Service

GENERAL

§97.401 Purposes.

The Amateur-Satellite Service is a radiocommunication service using stations on earth satellites for the same purpose as those of the Amateur Radio Service.

§97.403 Definitions.

(a) *Space operation.* Space-to-earth, and space-to-space, Amateur Radio communication from a station which is beyond, is intended to go beyond, or has been beyond the major portion of the earth's atmosphere.

(b) *Earth operation.* Earth-to-space-to-earth amateur radiocommunication by means of radio signals automatically retransmitted by stations in space operation.

(c) *Telecommand operation.* Earth-to-space Amateur Radio communication to initiate, modify, or terminate functions of a station in space operation.

(d) *Telemetry.* Space-to-earth transmissions, by a station in space operation, of results of measurements made in the station, including those relating to the function of the station.

§97.405 Applicability of rules.

The rules contained in this Subpart apply to radio stations in the Amateur-Satellite Service. All cases not specifically covered by the provisions of this Subpart shall be governed by the provisions of the rules governing Amateur Radio stations and operators (Subpart A through E of this Part).

§97.407 Eligibility for space operation.

Amateur Radio stations licensed to Amateur Extra Class operators are eligible for space operation (see §97.403(a)). The station licensee may permit any Amateur Radio operator to be the control operator, subject to the privileges of the control operator's class of license (see §97.7).

§97.409 Eligibility for earth operation.

Any Amateur Radio station is eligible for earth operation (see §97.403(b)), subject to the privileges of the control operator's class of license (see §97.7).

§97.411 Eligibility for telecommand operation.

Any Amateur Radio station designated by the licensee of a station in space operation is eligible to conduct telecommand operation with the station in space operation, subject to the privileges of the control operator's class of license (see §97.7).

§97.413 Space operations requirements.

An Amateur Radio station may be in space operation where:

(a) The station has not been ordered by the Commission to cease radio transmissions.

(b) The station is capable of effecting a cessation of radio transmissions by commands transmitted by station(s) in telecommand operation whenever such cessation is ordered by the Commission.

(c) There are, in place, sufficient Amateur Radio stations licensed by the Commission capable of telecommand operation to effect cessation of space operation, whenever such is ordered by the Commission.

TECHNICAL REQUIREMENTS

§97.415 Frequencies available.

(a) The frequency bands in the following table are available for space operation, Earth operation and telecommand operation. Unless otherwise specified in this Subpart the rules for authorized emission modes (§97.61 and 97.65) and authorized transmitting power (§97.67) are applicable for each of the listed frequency bands.

Frequency band *kilohertz*	Limitations (see paragraph (b))
7000-7100	
14000-14250	
21000-21450	
24890-24990	
28000-29700	
megahertz	
144-146	1
435-438	1, 4
1260-1270	1
2400-2450	
gigahertz	
3.40-3.41	1, 2
5.65-5.67	1, 4
5.83-5.85	1, 3
10.45-10.50	5
24.00-24.05	
47.0-47.2	
75.5-81.0	
142-149	
241-250	

(b) <u>Limitations</u>:

(1) Stations in the Amateur-Satellite Service must not cause harmful interference to other authorized stations operating in accordance with the Table of Frequency Allocations in this band, except radiolocation systems authorized in accordance with Footnote US217.

(2) This frequency band is not available in ITU Region 1.

(3) Stations in the Amateur-Satellite Service in this band are limited to Earth-to-space transmissions and are not protected from interference caused by fixed-satellite stations in Region 1, radiolocation stations, or industrial, scientific and medical equipment operating in this band.

(4) Stations in the Amateur-Satellite Service in this band are limited to Earth-to-space transmissions.

(5) Stations in the Amateur-Satellite Service in this band must not cause harmful interference to and are not protected from interference caused by stations in the Government radiolocation service.

SPECIAL PROVISIONS

§97.417 Space operation.

(a) Stations in space operation are exempt from the station identification requirements of §97.84 on each frequency band when in use.

(b) Stations in space operation may automatically retransmit the radio signals of other stations in earth operation, and space operation.

(c) Stations in space operation are exempt from the control operator requirements of §97.79 and from the provisions of §97.88 pertaining to the operation of a station by remote control.

§97.419 Telemetry.

(a) Telemetry transmission by stations in space operation may consist of specially coded messages intended to facilitate communications.

(b) Telemetry transmissions by stations in space operation are permissible one-way communications.

§97.421 Telecommand operation.

(a) Stations in telecommand operation may transmit special codes intended to obscure the meaning of command messages to the station in space operation.

(b) Stations in telecommand operation are exempt from the station identification requirements of §97.84.

(c) Stations in telecommand operation may transmit from within the military areas designated in §97.61(b)(7) in the frequency band 435-438 MHz with a maximum of 611 watts effective radiated power (1000 watts equivalent isotropically radiated power). The transmitting-antenna elevation angle between the lower half-power (-3 decibels relative to the peak or antenna bore sight) point and horizon must always be greater than 10°.

§97.422 Earth operation.

Stations in earth operation may transmit from within the military areas designated in §97.61(b)(7) in the frequency band 435-438 MHz with a maximum of 611 watts effective radiated power (1000 watts equivalent isotropically radiated power). The transmitting-antenna elevation angle between the lower half-power (-3 decibels relative to the peak or antenna bore sight) point and the horizon must always be greater than 10°.

§97.423 Notification required.

(a) The licensee of every station in space operation shall give written notifications to the Private Radio Bureau, Federal Communications Commission, Washington, DC 20554.

(b) *Pre-space operation notification.*

(1) Three notifications are required prior to initiating space operation. They are:

First notification. Required no less than twenty-seven months prior to initiating space operation.

Second notification. Required no less than fifteen months prior to initiating space operation.

Third notification. Required no less than three months prior to initiating space operation.

(2) The pre-space operation notification shall consist of:

Space operation date. A statement of the expected date space operations will be initiated, and a prediction of the duration of the operation.

Identity of satellite. The name by which the satellite will be known.

Service area. A description of the geographic area on the Earth's surface which is capable of being served by the station in space operation. Specify for both the transmitting and receiving antennas of this station.

Orbital parameters. A description of the anticipated orbital parameters as follows:

Non-geostationary satellite
1) Angle of inclination
2) Period
3) Apogee (kilometers)
4) Perigee (kilometers)
5) Number of satellites having the same orbital characteristics

Geostationary satellite
1) Nominal geographical longitude
2) Longitudinal tolerance
3) Inclination tolerance
4) Geographical longitudes marking the extremities of the orbital arc over which the satellite is visible at a minimum angle of elevation of 10° at points within the associated service area.

5) Geographical longitudes marking the extremities of the orbital arc within which the satellite must be located to provide communications to the specified service area.

6) Reason when the orbital arc of (5) is less than that of (4)

Technical Parameters. A description of the proposed technical parameters for:

(1) the station in space operation; and

(2) a station in earth operation suitable for use with the station in space operation; and

(3) a station in telecommand operation suitable for use with the station in space operation. The description shall include:

(1) Carrier frequencies if known; otherwise give frequency range where carrier frequencies will be located.

(2) Necessary bandwidth.

(3) Class of emission.

(4) Total peak power.

(5) Maximum power density (watts/Hz)

(6) Antenna radiation pattern[1]

(7) Antenna gain (main beam)[1]

(8) Antenna pointing accuracy (geostationary satellites only)[1]

(9) Receiving system noise temperature[2]

(10) Lowest equivalent satellite link noise temperature[3]

---

[1]These antenna characteristics shall be provided for both transmitting and receiving antennas.

[2]For a station in space operation.

[3]The total noise temperature at the input of a typical amateur radio station receiver shall include the antenna noise (generated by external sources (ground, sky, etc.) peripheral to the receiving antenna and noise re-radiated by the satellite), plus noise generated internally to the receiver. The additional receiver noise is above thermal noise, kT_oB. Referred to the antenna input terminals, the total system noise temperature is given by
$$T_s = T_a + (L - 1)T_o = LT_r$$
where:

T_a: antenna noise temperature

L: line losses between antenna output terminals and receiver input terminals

T_o: ambient temperature, usually given as 290° K

T_r: receiver noise temperature; this is also given as $(NF - 1)T_o$, where NF is receiver noise figure.

(c) In-space operation notification. Notification is required after space operation has been initiated. The notification shall update the information contained in the pre-space notification. In-space operation notification is required no later than seven days following initiation of space operation.

(d) Post-space operation notification. Notification of termination of space operation is required no later than three months after termination is complete. If the termination is ordered by the Commission, notification is required no later than twenty-four hours after termination is complete.

Subpart I—Volunteer-Examiner Coordinators

§97.501 Purpose.

The rules in this subpart are designed to provide for the establishment of volunteer-examiner coordinators to coordinate the efforts of volunteer examiners in preparing and administering examinations for amateur radio operator licenses.

§ 97.503 Definitions.

For the purpose of this subpart, the following definitions are applicable:

(a) Volunteer-examiner coordinator (VEC). An organization which has entered into an agreement with the Federal Communications Commission to coordinate the efforts of volunteer examiners in preparing and administering examination for amateur radio operator licenses.

(b) Volunteer examiner. An amateur radio operator who prepares or administers examinations to applicants for amateur radio operator licenses.

§97.505 Applicability of rules.

These rules apply to each organization that serves as a volunteer-examiner coordinator.

§97.507 VEC Qualifications.

In order to be a VEC, an organization must:

(a) Be organized at least partially for the purpose of furthering amateur radio;

(b) Be at least regional in scope, serving one or more of the following regions:

(1) Connecticut, Maine, Massachusetts, New Hampshire, Rhode Island and Vermont;

(2) New Jersey and New York;

(3) Delaware, the District of Columbia, Maryland and Pennsylvania;

(4) Alabama, Florida, Georgia, Kentucky, North Carolina, South Carolina, Tennessee and Virginia;

(5) Arkansas, Louisiana, Mississippi, New Mexico, Oklahoma and Texas;

(6) California;

(7) Arizona, Idaho, Montana, Nevada, Oregon, Utah, Washington, and Wyoming;

(8) Michigan, Ohio and West Virginia;

(9) Illinois, Indiana and Wisconsin;

(10) Colorado, Iowa, Kansas, Minnesota, Missouri, Nebraska, North Dakota and South Dakota;

(11) Alaska;

(12) Caribbean Insular areas: Commonwealth of Puerto Rico, United States Virgin Islands (50 islets and cays) and Navassa Island; *AND*

(13) Pacific Insular areas: Hawaii, American Samoa (seven islands), Baker Island, Commonwealth of Northern Mariannas Islands, Guam Island, Howland Island, Jarvis Island, Johnston Island (Islets East, Johnston, North and Sand), Kingman Reef, Midway Island (Islets Eastern and Sand), Palmyra Island (more than 50 islets) and Wake Island (Islets Peale, Wake and Wilkes).

(c) Be capable of acting as a VEC in one or more of the regions listed in paragraph (b);

(d) Agree to coordinate all amateur radio operator examination elements for all amateur radio operator license classes except Novice Class;

(e) Agree not to accept any compensation from any source for its services as a VEC, except reimbursement for out-of-pocket expenses permitted by §97.36; and

(f) Agree to assure that for any examination every candidate qualified under these rules is registered without regard to race, sex, religion, national origin or membership (or lack thereof) in any amateur radio organization.

§97.509 Conflicts of interest.

An organization engaged in the manufacture or distribution of equipment used in connection with amateur radio transmissions, or in the preparation or distribution of any publication used in preparation for obtaining amateur radio station operator licenses, may be a VEC only upon a persuasive showing to the Commission that preventive measures have been taken to preclude any possible conflict of interest.

VOLUNTEER-EXAMINER COORDINATOR FUNCTIONS

§97.511 Agreement required.

No organization may serve as a VEC until that organization has entered into a written agreement with the Federal Communications Commission to do so. The VEC must abide by the terms of the agreement.

§97.513 Scheduling of examinations.

A VEC will coordinate the dates and times for scheduling examinations (see §97.26) throughout the region(s) it serves. Any VEC may also coordinate the scheduling of testing opportunities outside of the regions listed in Section 97.507(b).

§97.515 Coordinating Volunteer examiners.

A VEC will accredit amateur radio operators, licensed by the Federal Communications Commission, as volunteer examiners (see §97.30). A VEC will seek to recruit a broad representation of amateur radio operators to be volunteer examiners. A VEC may not discriminate in accrediting volunteer examiners on the basis of race, sex, religion or national origin. A VEC may not refuse to accredit a volunteer on the basis of membership (or lack thereof) in an amateur radio organization. A VEC may not discriminate in accrediting volunteer examiners based upon their accepting or declining to accept reimbursement. A VEC must not accredit an amateur radio operator volunteering to be an examiner if:

(a) the volunteer examiner does not meet minimum statutory qualifications or minimum qualifications as prescribed by the rules;

(b) the FCC refuses to accept the voluntary and uncompensated services of the volunteer examiner;

(c) the VEC determines that the volunteer is not competent to perform the function for which he/she volunteered; OR

(d) the VEC determines that questions of the volunteer's integrity or honesty could compromise the examination(s).

§97.517 Examinations.

A VEC will design (see §97.27(d), assemble, print and distribute written examination Elements 3, 4(A) and 4(B). A VEC may design, assemble, print and distribute examination Elements 1(B) and 1(C). A VEC is required to hold examination designs in confidence.

§97.519 Examination procedures.

At the completion of each examination, a VEC will collect the candidates' application forms, answer sheets and test results from the volunteer examiners (see §97.28(h)). A VEC will:

(a) Make a record of the date and place of the test; the names of the volunteer examiners and their qualifications; the names of the candidates; the test results; and, related information.

(b) Screen the application for completeness and authenticity.

(c) Forward the application within ten days of its receipt from the examiners to: Federal Communications Commission, Licensing Division, Private Radio Bureau, Gettysburg, PA 17325.

(d) Make available to any authorized FCC representative any requested examination records.

§97.521 Evaluation of questions.

A VEC will be expected to evaluate the clarity and accuracy of examination questions on the basis of experience, and to bring ambiguous or inaccurate questions to the attention of the Commission, with a recommendation on whether to revise the question or to delete the question from the Commission's list of examination questions.

§97.523 Reserved.

APPENDICES

APPENDIX 1
Reserved

APPENDIX 2

Extracts from the International Telecommunications Convention (Malaga-Torremolinos, 1973), as revised by the World Administrative Radio Conference, Geneva, 1979.

Article 1—Terms and Definitions

Section III. Radio Services

§3.34 *Amateur Service:*

A *radiocommunication service* for the purpose of self-training, intercommunication and technical investigations carried out by amateurs, that is, by duly authorized persons interested in radio technique solely with a personal aim and without pecuniary interest.

§3.35 *Amateur-Satellite Service:*

A *radiocommunications* service using *space stations* on earth *satellites* for the same purposes as those of the *amateur service.*

Article 32—Amateur Service and Amateur-Satellite Service

Section I. Amateur Service

§1. Radiocommunications between amateur stations of different countries[1] shall be forbidden if the administration of one of the countries concerned has notified that it objects to such radiocommunications.

§2. (1) When transmissions between amateur stations of different countries are permitted, they shall be made in plain language and shall be limited to messages of a technical nature relating to tests and to remarks of a personal character for which, by reason of their unimportance, recourse to the public telecommunications service is not justified.

[1] As may appear in public notices issued by the Commission

(2) It is absolutely forbidden for amateur stations to be used for transmitting international communications on behalf of third parties.

(3) The preceding provisions may be modified by special arrangements between the administrations of the countries concerned.

§3. (1) Any person seeking a license to operate the apparatus of an amateur station shall prove that he is able to send correctly by hand and to receive correctly by ear texts in Morse code signals. The administrations concerned may, however, waive this requirement in the case of stations making use exclusively of frequencies above 30 MHz.

(2) Administrations shall take such measures as they judge necessary to verify the operational and technical qualifications of any person wishing to operate the apparatus of an amateur station.

§4. The maximum power of amateur stations shall be fixed by the administrations concerned, having regard to the technical qualifications of the operators and to the conditions under which these stations are to operate.

§5. (1) All the general rules of the Convention and of these Regulations shall apply to amateur stations. In particular, the emitted frequency shall be as stable and as free from spurious emissions as the state of technical development for such stations permits.

(2) During the course of their transmissions, amateur stations shall transmit their call sign at short intervals.

Section II. Amateur-Satellite Service

§6. The provisions of Section I of this Article shall apply equally, as appropriate, to the Amateur-Satellite Service.

§7. Space stations in the Amateur-Satellite Service operating in bands shared with other services shall be fitted with appropriate devices for controlling emissions in the event that harmful interference is reported in accordance with the procedure laid down in Article 22. Administrations authorizing such space stations shall inform the IFRB and shall ensure that sufficient earth command stations are established before launch to guarantee that any harmful interference which might be reported can be terminated by the authorizing administration.

RESOLUTION No. 641

Relating to the Use of the Frequency Band 7000-7100 kHz

The World Administrative Radio Conference, Geneva, 1979.

considering

a) that the sharing of frequency bands by amateur and broadcasting services is undesirable and should be avoided;

b) that it is desirable to have worldwide exclusive allocations for these services in Band 7;

c) that the band 7000-7100 kHz is allocated on a worldwide basis exclusively to the amateur service; resolves the the broadcasting service shall be prohibited from the band 7000-7100 kHz and that the broadcasting stations operating on frequencies in this band shall cease such operation.

APPENDIX

Classification of Emissions

For convenient reference, the tabulation below is extracted from the classification of typical emissions in Part 2 of the Commission's Rules and Regulations. It includes only those general classifications which appear most applicable to the Amateur Radio Service.

Type of modulation	Type of transmission	Symbol
Amplitude	With no modulation	NØN
	Telegraphy without the use of modulating audio frequency (by on-off keying)	A1A
	Telegraphy by the on-off keying of an amplitude modulating audio frequency or audio frequencies or by the on-off keying of the modulated emission (special case: an unkeyed emission amplitude modulated).	A2A, A2B
	Telephony Double sideband	A3E
	Single Sideband Suppressed Carrier	J3E
	Reduced Carrier	R3E
	Full Carrier	H3E
	Facsimile	A3C
	Television	A3F
Frequency (or phase)	Telegraphy by frequency shift keying without the use of a modulating audio frequency.	F1B (G1B)
	Telegraphy by the on-off keying of a frequency modulating audio frequency or by the on-off keying of frequency modulated emission (special case; an unkeyed emission frequency modulated).	F2B (G2B)
	Telephony	F3E (G3E)
	Facsimile	F3C (G3C)
	Television	F3F (G3F)
Pulse		PØN1

APPENDIX 4

Convention Between Canada and the United States of America, Relating to the operation by Citizens of Either Country of Certain Radio Equipment or Stations in the Other Country (Effective May 15, 1952)

Article III

It is agreed that persons holding

1The letters "K, L, M, Q, V, W and X" may also be used in place of the letter"P" for pulse radar.

appropriate amateur licenses issued by either country may operate their amateur stations in the territory of the other country under the following conditions:

(a) Each visiting amateur may be required to register and receive a permit before operating any amateur station licensed by his government.

(b) The visiting amateur will identify his station by:

(1) Radiotelegraph operation. The amateur call sign issued to him/her by the licensing country followed by a slant (/) sign and the amateur call sign prefix and call area number of the country he is visiting.

(2) Radiotelephone operation. The amateur call sign in English issued to him by the licensing country followed by the words, "fixed" "portable" or "mobile," as appropriate, and the amateur call sign prefix and call area number of the country he is visiting.

(c) Each amateur station shall indicate at least once during each contact with another station its geographical location as nearly as possible by city and state or city and province.

(d) In other respects the amateur station shall be operated in accordance with the laws and regulations of the country in which the station is temporarily located.

APPENDIX 5

Reserved

APPENDIX 6

Extracts from the International Telecommunications Convention (Malaga-Torremolinos, 1973), as revised by the World Administrative Radio Conference, Geneva, 1979.

Resolution No. 640

Relating to the International Use of Radiocommunications, in the Event of Natural Disasters, in Frequency Bands Allocated to the Amateur Service.

Considering

a) that in the event of natural disaster normal communication systems are frequently overloaded, damaged, or completely disrupted.

b) that rapid establishment of communications is essential to facilitate worldwide relief actions.

c) that the amateur bands are not bound by international plans or notification procedures, and are therefore well adapted for short-term use in emergency cases.

d) that international disaster communications would be facilitated by temporary use of certain frequency bands allocated to the amateur service.

e) that under those circumstances the stations of the amateur service because of their widespread distribution and their demonstrated capacity in such cases, can assist in meeting essential communication needs.

f) that existence of national and regional amateur emergency networks using frequencies throughout the bands allocated to the amateur service.

g) that in the event of a natural disaster, direct communications between amateur stations and other stations might enable vital communications to be carried out until normal communications are restored.

Recognizing

that the rights and responsibilities for communications in the event of a natural disaster rest with the administrations involved.

Resolves

1. that the bands allocated to the amateur service which are specified in No. 510 may be used by administrations to meet the needs of international disaster communications.

2. that such use of these bands shall be only for communications in relation to relief operations in connection with natural disasters.

3. that the use of specified bands allocated to the amateur service by non-amateur stations for disaster communications shall be limited to the duration of the emergency and to the specific geographical areas as defined by the responsible authority of the affected country.

4. that disaster communications shall take place within the disaster area and between the disaster area and the permanent headquarters of the organization providing relief.

5. that such communications shall be carried out only with the consent of the administration of the country in which the disaster has occurred.

6. that relief communications provided from outside the country in which the disaster has occurred shall not replace existing national or international amateur emergency networks.

7. that close cooperation is desirable between amateur stations and the stations of other radio services which may find it necessary to use amateur frequencies in disaster communications.

8. that such international relief communications shall avoid, as far as practicable, interference to the amateur service networks.

Invites Administrations

1. to provide for the needs of international disaster communications.

2. to provide for the needs of emergency communications with their national regulations.

APPENDIX 7

Extracts from the International Telecommunications Convention (Malaga-Torremolinos, 1973), as revised by the World Administrative Radio Conference, Geneva, 1979.

Resolution No. 641

Relating to the use of the Frequency Band 7000-7100 kHz

Considering

a) that the sharing of frequency bands by amateur and broadcasting services is undesirable and should be avoided.

b) that it is desirable to have worldwide exclusive allocations for these services in Band 7.

c) that the band 7000-7100 kHz is allocated on a worldwide basis exclusively to the amateur service.

Resolves

that the broadcasting service shall be prohibited from the band 7000-7100 kHz and that the broadcasting stations operating on frequencies in this band shall cease such operation.

APPENDIX 8

Extracts from the International Telecommunications Convention (Malaga-Torremolinos, 1973), as revised by the World Administrative Radio Conference, Geneva, 1979.

Resolution No. 642

Relating to the Bringing into Use of Earth Stations in the Amateur-Satellite Service.

Recognizing

that the procedures of Articles 11 and 13 are applicable to the Amateur-Satellite Service.

Recognizing Further

a) that the characteristics of each station in the Amateur-Satellite Service vary widely.

b) that space stations in the Amateur-Satellite Service are intended for multiple access by amateur earth stations in all countries.

c) that coordination among stations in the amateur and Amateur Satellite Services is accomplished without the need for formal procedures.

d) that the burden of terminating any harmful interference is placed upon the administration authorizing a space station in the Amateur-Satellite Service pursuant to the provisions of No. 2741 of the Radio Regulations.

Notes

that certain information specified in Appendices 3 and 4 cannot reasonably be provided for earth stations in the Amateur-Satellite Service.

Resolves

1. that when an administration (or one acting on behalf of a group of named administrations) intends to establish a satellite system in the Amateur-Satellite Service and wishes to publish information with respect to earth stations in the system it may:

1.1 communicate to the IFRB all or part of the information listed in Appendix 3; the IFRB shall publish such information in a special section of its weekly circular requesting comments to be communicated within a period of four months after the date of publication.

1.2 notify under Nos. 1488 to 1491 all or part of the information listed in Appendix 3; the IFRB shall record it in a special list.

2. that this information shall include at least the characteristics of a typical amateur earth station in the Amateur-Satellite Service having the facility to transmit signals of the space station to initiate, modify, or terminate the functions of the space station.

Memorandum Opinion and Order in PRB-1

Here's the full text of FCC's Memorandum Opinion and Order in PRB-1 (see page 3-11). If you require an "official" copy of PRB-1 for use in a legal proceeding, you may cite the *Federal Register:* 50 FR 38813.

Before the
Federal Communications Commission   FCC 85-506
Washington, DC 20554   36149

In the Matter of	)	
	)	
Federal preemption of state and	)	PRB-1
local regulations pertaining	)	
to Amateur radio facilities.	)	

MEMORANDUM OPINION AND ORDER

Adopted: September 16, 1985   ;   Released: September 19, 1985

By the Commission: Commissioner Rivera not participating.

Background

1. On July 16, 1984, the American Radio Relay League, Inc. (ARRL) filed a Request for Issuance of a Declaratory Ruling asking us to delineate the limitations of local zoning and other local and state regulatory authority over Federally-licensed radio facilities. Specifically, the ARRL wanted an explicit statement that would preempt all local ordinances which provably preclude or significantly inhibit effective reliable amateur radio communications. The ARRL acknowledges that local authorities can regulate amateur installations to insure the safety and health of persons in the community, but believes that those regulations cannot be so restrictive that they preclude effective amateur communications.

2. Interested parties were advised that they could file comments in the matter.[1] With extension, comments were due on or before December 26, 1984,[2] with reply comments due on or before January 25, 1985[3] Over sixteen hundred comments were filed.

Local Ordinances

3. Conflicts between amateur operators regarding radio antennas and local authorities regarding restrictive ordinances are common. The amateur operator is governed by the regulations contained in Part 97 of our rules. Those rules do not limit the height of an amateur antenna but they require, for aviation safety reasons, that certain FAA notification and FCC approval procedures must be followed for antennas which exceed 200 feet in height above ground level or antennas which are to be erected near airports. Thus, under FCC rules some amateur antenna support structures require obstruction marking and lighting. On the other hand, local municipalities or governing bodies frequently enact regulations limiting antennas and their support structures in height and location, e.g. to side or rear yards, for health, safety or aesthetic considerations. These limiting regulations can result in conflict because the effectiveness of the communications that emanate from an amateur radio station are directly dependent upon the location and the height of the antenna. Amateur operators maintain that they are precluded from operating in certain bands allocated for their use if the height of their antennas is limited by a local ordinance.

4. Examples of restrictive local ordinances were submitted by several amateur operators in this proceeding. Stanley J. Cichy, San Diego, California, noted that in

San Diego amateur radio antennas come under a structures ruling which limits building heights to 30 feet. Thus, antennas there are also limited to 30 feet. Alexander Vrenios, Mundelein, Illinois wrote that an ordinance of the Village of Mundelein provides that an antenna must be a distance from the property line that is equal to one and one-half times its height. In his case, he is limited to an antenna tower for his amateur station just over 53 feet in height.

5. John C. Chapman, an amateur living in Bloomington, Minnesota, commented that he was not able to obtain a building permit to install an amateur radio antenna exceeding 35 feet in height because the Bloomington city ordinance restricted "structures" heights to 35 feet. Mr. Chapman said that the ordinance, when written, undoubtedly applied to buildings but was now being applied to antennas in the absence of a specific ordinance regulating them. There were two options open to him if he wanted to engage in amateur communications. He could request a variance to the ordinance by way of a hearing before the City Council, or he could obtain affidavits from his neighbors swearing that they had no objection to the proposed antenna installation. He got the building permit after obtaining the cooperation of his neighbors. His concern, however, is that he had to get permission from several people before he could effectively engage in radio communications for which he had a valid FCC amateur license.

6. In addition to height restrictions, other limits are enacted by local jurisdictions—anti-climb devices on towers or fences around them; minimum distances from high voltage power lines; minimum distances of towers from property lines; and regulations pertaining to the structural soundness of the antenna installation. By and large, amateurs do not find these safety precautions objectionable. What they do object to are the sometimes prohibitive, non-refundable application filing fees to obtain a permit to erect an antenna installation and those provisions in ordinances which regulate antennas for purely aesthetic reasons. The amateurs contend, almost universally, that "beauty is in the eye of the beholder." They assert that an antenna installation is not more aesthetically displeasing than other objects that people keep on their property, e.g. motor homes, trailers, pick-up trucks, solar collectors and gardening equipment.

Restrictive Convenants

7. Amateur operators also oppose restrictions on their amateur operations which are contained in the deeds for their homes or in their apartment leases. Since these restrictive covenants are contractual agreements between private parties, they are not generally a matter of concern to the Commission. However, since some amateurs who commented in this proceeding provided us with examples of restrictive covenants, they are included for information. Mr. Eugene O. Thomas of Hollister, California included in his comments an extract of the Declaration of Covenants and Restrictions for Ridgemark Estates, County of San Benito, State of California. It provides:

No antenna for transmission or reception of radio signals shall be erected outdoors for use by any dwelling unit except upon approval of the Directors. No radio or television signals or any other form of electromagnetic radiation shall be permitted to originate from any lot which may unreasonably interfere with the reception of television or radio signals upon any other lot.

Marshall Wilson, Jr. provided a copy of the restrictive covenant contained in deeds for the Bell Martin Addition #2, Irving, Texas. It is binding upon all of the owners or purchasers of the lots in the said addition, his or their heirs, executors, administrators or assigns. It reads:

No antenna or tower shall be erected upon any lot for the purposes of radio operations.

William J. Hamilton resides in an apartment building in Gladstone, Missouri. He cites a clause in his lease prohibiting the erection of an antenna. He states that he has been forced to give up operating amateur radio equipment except a hand-held 2 meter (144-148 MHz) radio transceiver. He maintains that he should not be penalized just because he lives in an apartment.

Other restrictive covenants are less global in scope than those cited above. For example, Robert Webb purchased a home in Houston, Texas. His deed restriction prohibited "transmitting or receiving antennas extending above the roof line."

8. Amateur operators generally oppose restrictive covenants for several reasons. They maintain that such restrictions limit the places that they can reside if they want to pursue their hobby of amateur radio. Some state that they impinge on First Amendment rights of free speech. Others believe that a constitutional right is being abridged because, in their view, everyone has a right to access the airwaves regardless of where they live.

9. The contrary belief held by housing subdivision communities and condominium or homeowner's associations is that amateur radio installations constitute safety hazards, cause interference to other electronic equipment which may be operated in the home (television, radio, stereos) or are eyesores that detract from the aesthetic and tasteful appearance of the housing development or apartment complex. To counteract these negative consequences, the subdivisions and associations include in their deeds, leases or by-laws, restrictions and limitations on the location and height of antennas or, in some cases, prohibit them altogether. The restrictive covenants are contained in the contractual agreement entered into at the time of the sale or lease of the property. Purchasers or lessees are free to choose whether they wish to reside where such restrictions on amateur antennas are in effect or settle elsewhere.

Supporting Comments

10. The Department of Defense (DOD) supported the ARRL and emphasized in its comments that continued success of existing national security and emergency preparedness telecommunications plans involving amateur stations would be severely diminished if state and local ordinances were allowed to prohibit the construction and usage of effective amateur transmission facilities. DOD utilizes volunteers in the Military Affiliate Radio Service (MARS),[4] Civil Air Patrol (CAP) and the Radio Amateur Civil Emergency Service (RACES). It points out that these volunteer communicators are operating radio equipment installed in their homes and that undue restrictions on antennas by local authorities adversely affect their efforts. DOD states that the responsiveness of these volunteer systems would be impaired if local ordinances interfere with the effectiveness of these important national telecommunication resources. DOD favors the issuance of a ruling that would set limits for local and state regulatory bodies when they are dealing with amateur stations.

11. Various chapters of the American Red Cross also came forward to support the ARRL's request for a preemptive ruling. The Red Cross works closely with amateur radio volunteers. It believes that without amateurs' dedicated support, disaster relief operations would significantly suffer and that its ability to serve disaster victims would be hampered. It feels that antenna height limitations that might be imposed by local bodies will negatively affect the service now rendered by the volunteers.

12. Cities and counties from various parts of the United States filed comments in support of the ARRL's request for a Federal preemption ruling. The comments from the Director of Civil Defense, Port Arthur, Texas are representative:

> The Amateur Radio Service plays a vital role with our Civil Defense program here in Port Arthur and the design of these antennas and towers lends greatly to our ability to communicate during times of disaster.

We do not believe there should be any restrictions on the antennas and towers except for reasonable safety precautions. Tropical storms, hurricanes and tornadoes are a way of life here on the Texas Gulf Coast and good communications are absolutely essential when preparing for a hurricane and even more so during recovery operations after the hurricane has past.

13. The Quarter Century Wireless Association took a strong stand in favor of the Issuance of a declaratory ruling. It believes that Federal preemption is necessary so that there will be uniformity for all Amateur Radio installations on private property throughout the United States.

14. In its comments, the ARRL argued that the Commission has the jurisdiction to preempt certain local land use regulations which frustrate or prohibit amateur radio communications. It said that the appropriate standard in preemption cases is not the extent of state and local interest in a given regulation, but rather the impact of that regulation on Federal goals. Its position is that Federal preemption is warranted whenever local governmental regulations relate adversely to the operational aspects of amateur communication. The ARRL maintains that localities routinely employ a variety of land use devices to preclude the installation of effective amateur antennas, including height restrictions, conditional use permits, building setbacks and dimensional limitations on antennas. It sees a declaratory ruling of Federal preemption as necessary to cause municipalities to accommodate amateur operator needs in land use planning efforts.

15. James C. O'Connell, an attorney who has represented several amateurs before local zoning authorities, said that requiring amateurs to seek variances or special use approval to erect reasonable antennas unduly restricts the operation of amateur stations. He suggested that the Commission preempt zoning ordinances which impose antenna height limits of less than 65 feet. He said that this height would represent a reasonable accommodation of the communication needs of most amateurs and the legitimate concerns of local zoning authorities.

Opposing Comments

16. The City of La Mesa, California has a zoning regulation which controls amateur antennas. Its comments reflected an attempt to reach a balanced view.

This regulation has neither the intent, nor the effect, of precluding or inhibiting effective and reliable communications. Such antennas may be built as long as their construction does not unreasonably block views or constitute eyesores. The reasonable assumption is that there are always alternatives at a given site for different placement, and/or methods for aesthetic treatment. Thus, both public objectives of controlling land use for the public health, safety, and convenience, and providing an effective communications network, can be satisfied.

A blanket ruling to completely set aside local control, or a ruling which recognizes control only for the purpose of safety of antenna construction, would be contrary to. . . legitimate local control.

17. Comments from the County of San Diego state:

While we are aware of the benefits provided by amateur operators, we oppose the issuance of a preemption ruling which would elevate 'antenna effectiveness' to a position above all other considerations. We must, however, argue that the local government must have the ability to place reasonable limitations upon the placement and configuration of amateur radio transmitting and receiving antennas. Such ability is necessary to assure that the local decision-makers have the authority to protect the public health, safety and welfare of all citizens.

In conclusion, I would like to emphasize an important difference between your regulatory powers and that of local governments. Your Commission's approval of the preemptive requests would establish a "national policy." However, any regulation adopted by a local jurisdiction could be overturned by your Commission or a court if such regulation was determined to be unreasonable.

18. The City of Anderson, Indiana, summarized some of the problems that face local communities:

> I am sympathetic to the concerns of these antenna owners and I understand that to gain the maximum reception from their devices, optimal location is necessary. However, the preservation of residential zoning districts as "liveable" neighborhoods is jeopardized by placing these antennas in front yards of homes. Major problems of public safety have been encountered, particularly vision blockage for auto and pedestrian access. In addition, all communities are faced with various building lot sizes. Many building lots are so small that established setback requirements (in order to preserve adequate air and light) are vulnerable to the unregulated placement of antennas.
>
> ...the exercise of preemptive authority by the FCC in granting this request would not be in the best interest of the general public.

19. The National Association of Counties (NACO), the American Planning Association (APA) and the National League of Cities (NCL) all opposed the issuance of an antenna preemption ruling. NACO emphasized that federal and state power must be viewed in harmony and warns that Federal intrusion into local concerns of health, safety and welfare could weaken the traditional police power exercised by the state and unduly interfere with the legitimate activities of the states. NLC believed that both Federal and local interests can be accommodated without preempting local authority to regulate the installation of amateur radio antennas. The APA said that the FCC should continue to leave the issue of regulating amateur antennas with the local government and with the state and Federal courts.

Discussion

20. When considering preemption, we must begin with two constitutional provisions. The tenth amendment provides that any powers which the constitution either does not delegate to the United States or does not prohibit the states from exercising are reserved to the states. These are the police powers of the states. The Supremacy Clause, however, provides that the constitution and the laws of the United States shall supersede any state law to the contrary. Article III, Section 2. Given these basic premises, state laws may be preempted in three ways: First, Congress may expressly preempt the state law. See *Jones v. Rath Packing Co.,* 430 U.S. 519, 525 (1977). Or, Congress may indicate its intent to completely occupy a given field so that any state law encompassed within that field would implicitly be preempted. Such intent to preempt could be found in a congressional regulatory scheme that was so pervasive that it would be reasonable to assume that Congress did not intend to permit the states to supplement it. See *Fidelity Federal Savings & Loan Ass'n v. de la Cuesta,* 458 U.S. 141, 153 (1982). Finally, preemption may be warranted when state law conflicts with federal law. Such conflicts may occur when "compliance with both Federal and state regulations is a physical impossibility," *Florida Lime & Avocado Growers, Inc. v. Paul,* 373 U.S. 132, 142, 143 (1963), or when state law "stands as an obstacle to the accomplishment and execution of the full purposes and objectives of Congress," *Hines v. Davidowitz,* 312 U.S. 52, 67 (1941). Furthermore, federal regulations have the same preemptive effect as federal statues, *Fidelity Federal Savings & Loan Association v. de la Cuesta,* supra.

21. The situation before us requires us to determine the extent to which state and local zoning regulations may conflict with federal policies concerning amateur radio operators.

22. Few matters coming before us present such a clear dichotomy of view point as does the instant issue. The cities, countries, local communities and housing associations see an obligation to all of their citizens and try to address their concerns. This is accomplished through regulations, ordinances or covenants oriented toward the health, safety and general welfare of those they regulate. At the opposite pole

are the individual amateur operators and their support groups who are troubled by local regulations which may inhibit the use of amateur stations or, in some instances, totally preclude amateur communications. Aligned with the operators are such entities as the Department of Defense, the American Red Cross and local civil defense and emergency organizations who have found in Amateur Radio a pool of skilled radio operators and a readily available backup network. In this situation, we believe it is appropriate to strike a balance between the federal interest in promoting amateur operations and the legitimate interests of local governments in regulating local zoning matters. The cornerstone on which we will predicate our decision is that a reasonable accommodation may be made between the two sides.

23. Preemption is primarily a function of the extent of the conflict between federal and state and local regulation. Thus, in considering whether our regulations or policies can tolerate a state regulation, we may consider such factors as the severity of the conflict and the reasons underlying the state's regulations. In this regard, we have previously recognized the legitimate and important state interests reflected in local zoning regulations. For example, in *Earth Satellite Communications, Inc.,* 95 FCC 2d 1223 (1983), we recognized that

> ...countervailing state interests inhere in the present situation... For example, we do not wish to preclude a state or locality from exercising jurisdiction over certain elements of an SMATV operation that properly may fall within its authority, such as zoning or public safety and health, provided the regulation in question is not undertaken as a pretext for the actual purpose of frustrating achievement of the preeminent federal objective and so long as the non-federal regulation is applied in a nondiscriminatory manner.

24. Similarly, we recognize here that there are certain general state and local interests which may, in their even-handed application, legitimately affect amateur radio facilities. Nonetheless, there is also a strong federal interest in promoting amateur communications. Evidence of this interest may be found in the comprehensive set of rules that the Commission has adopted to regulate the amateur service.[5] Those rules set forth procedures for the licensing of stations and operators, frequency allocations, technical standards which amateur radio equipment must meet and operating practices which amateur operators must follow. We recognize the amateur radio service as a voluntary, noncommercial communication service, particularly with respect to providing emergency communications. Moreover, the amateur radio service provides a reservoir of trained operators, technicians and electronic experts who can be called on in times of national or local emergencies. By its nature, the Amateur Radio Service also provides the opportunity for individual operators to further international goodwill. Upon weighing these interests, we believe a limited preemption policy is warranted. State and local regulations that operate to preclude amateur communications in their communities are in direct conflict with federal objectives and must be preempted.

25. Because amateur station communications are only as effective as the antennas employed, antenna height restrictions directly affect the effectiveness of amateur communications. Some amateur antenna configurations require more substantial installations than others if they are to provide the amateur operator with the communications that he/she desires to engage in. For example, an antenna array for international amateur communications will differ from an antenna used to contact other amateur operators at shorter distances. We will not, however, specify any particular height limitation below which a local government may not regulate, nor will we suggest the precise language that must be contained in local ordinances, such as mechanisms for special exceptions, variances, or conditional use permits. Nevertheless, local regulations which involve placement, screening, or height of antennas based on health, safety, or aesthetic considerations must be crafted to accommodate reasonably amateur communications, and to represent the minimum practicable

regulation to accomplish the local authority's legitimate purpose.[6]

26. Obviously, we do not have the staff or financial resources to review all state and local laws that affect amateur operations. We are confident, however, that state and local governments will endeavor to legislate in a manner that affords appropriate recognition to the important federal interest at stake here and thereby avoid unnecessary conflicts with federal policy, as well as time-consuming and expensive litigation in this area. Amateur operators who believe that local or state governments have been overreaching and thereby have precluded accomplishment of their legitimate communications goals, may, in addition, use this document to bring our policies to the attention of local tribunals and forums.

27. Accordingly, the Request for Declaratory Ruling filed July 16, 1984, by the American Radio Relay League, Inc., IS GRANTED to the extent indicated herein and, in all other respects, IS DENIED.

FEDERAL COMMUNICATIONS COMMISSION
William J. Tricarico
Secretary

FOOTNOTES

[1] Public Notice, August 30, 1984, Mimeo. No. 6299, 49 F.R. 36113, September 14, 1984.
[2] Public Notice, December 19, 1984, Mimeo No. 1498.
[3] Order, November 8, 1984, Mimeo. No. 770.
[4] MARS is solely under the auspices of the military which recruits volunteer amateur operators to render assistance to it. The Commission is not involved in the MARS program.
[5] 47 CFR Part 97.
[6] We reiterate that our ruling herein does not reach restrictive covenants in private contractual agreements. Such agreements are voluntarily entered into by the buyer or tenant when the agreement is executed and do not usually concern this Commission

INDEX

187

Please use this form to give us your comments on this book. Tell us what you liked best about the book, and what improvements you would like to see us make in future editions.

Name

————————————————————————————— Call sign —————————

Daytime Phone (   ) ————————————————— Age —————————

Address ————————————————————————————————————

City, State, Zip ———————————————————————————————

How long have you been licensed? ——————————————————————

From ———————————————————

———————————————————

———————————————————

Editor, FCC Rule Book, Sixth Edition
American Radio Relay League
225 Main Street
Newington, CT USA 06111

•••••••••••••••••••••••••••••• please fold and tape ••••••••••••••••••••••••••••••